WHY ASIANS ARE
LESS CREATIVE
THAN WESTERNERS

WHY ASIANS ARE LESS CREATIVE THAN WESTERNERS

Ng Aik Kwang

Prentice
Hall

Singapore London New York Toronto Sydney Tokyo Madrid
Mexico City Munich Paris Capetown Hong Kong Montreal

Published in 2001 by
Prentice Hall
Pearson Education Asia Pte Ltd
23/25 First Lok Yang Road, Jurong
Singapore 629733

Pearson Education offices in Asia: *Bangkok, Beijing, Hong Kong, Jakarta, Kuala Lumpur, Manila, New Delhi, Seoul, Singapore, Taipei, Tokyo*

Cover illustration by Jay Belmore/The Image Bank/Getty Images
Cover design by Teri Tan
Interior illustrations by Edwin Ng

Printed in Singapore

5   4   3
05   04

ISBN 0-13-040475-6

Contents

Acknowledgements and Dedication

Writing a book of this nature is not the task of a solitary individual, and along the way, many people have assisted me. I would like to take this opportunity to thank them. First and foremost, I would like to express my eternal gratitude to my family, who provided me with the opportunity to do my PhD research on creativity in Australia. I would also like to express my heartfelt thanks to my principal supervisor, Dr Mark Griffin. The ideas in this book took shape during my tutelage under him, and he has served as a wonderful "mid-wife" in the birth of these ideas. I would also like to thank my associate supervisor, Professor Tian Oei, for his fatherly coaching and advice. I will always take his counsel to heart. Other people who have assisted me include Ian Smith, Katherine Yip and Kia Pei: they provided me with invaluable feedback on earlier drafts of the manuscript. My good friend Kok Keong was a constant source of encouragement to me as I struggled to develop the ideas in this book. Many thanks must also go to the staff at Prentice Hall, including Chiang Yew Kee, Irene Yeow and Pauline Chua, for their professionalism in the production of this book. Although the contents of this book took shape under the counsel and feedback of many individuals, I must stress that I as the author bear sole responsibility for my ideas. Finally, I wish to dedicate this book to my aunt, Ng Ah Chwee (1952–1998). She had longed for a last meeting with her nephew, but alas, it was not to be! She will be remembered in death as well as in life as an ordinary and benign, yet courageous and stoic lady, who faced her fate unflinchingly. May she rest in peace.

Foreword

Creativity is a hot topic these days. It is often discussed in the popular literature, as well as the social and behavioural sciences. This is because creativity has such value for both individual health and societal productivity. In fact, it also has value for individual productivity and societal health!

The present volume contributes to the social and behavioural sciences in several ways. Most obvious is, of course, the useful perspective on the relevance of culture to creativity. Culture is a surprisingly sparse focus of research, at least within creative studies. This is surprising because culture is omnipresent. Granted, "omnipresent" is a powerful term, but in the case of culture, it fits. Consider in this regard that, years ago, psychologists realised that it is impossible to develop culture-free tests of intelligence, for these would require that thinking and behaviour were entirely independent of culture. There can be no such thing as a culture-free test. (Efforts are still made for culture-fair tests of intelligence.) Perhaps the paucity of research on culture and creativity reflects the fact that culture *is* omnipresent.

What studies of culture and creativity do exist tend to focus entirely on contextual factors. They recognise ethnic, geographic and situational influences. One strength of the present volume is Kwang's inclusion of "the self" in the creativity equation. His discussion of context is quite thorough, but he recognises that there is an interaction between the individual and the situation, and between the self and the culture. This interaction probably occurs on many levels, in many ways. Kwang's discussion is provocative, reasonable and thorough. Apparently there are very significant differences between Eastern and Western perspectives on the self. These are reflected in the different assumptions about control, where the Eastern view traditionally emphasises control by the environment (and the individual adapts) and the Western view emphasises the individual (the individual changes the environment). Kwang ties this distinction specifically to aesthetics and artwork.

A second very realistic aspect of this volume is its recognition of the complexity of creativity. Creativity is so complex that it includes not just socially-desirable characteristics, but also those which can make life difficult for the creator himself. Life can be challenging for those who live and work with creative persons as well. Creativity is valuable but not always comfortable.

Kwang's discussion of the interaction of the self and culture is wonderfully precise. Unlike some simplistic works on culture, Kwang relates

culture to values and then in turn relates values and culture to "the challenge of being a person". In his view, this challenge is different in the East
and the West. This discussion is thought-provoking and relates directly
to cultural differences in relationships, marriages, families and both formal and informal education.

This volume captures what may be the key idea in cross-cultural studies, namely, that cultures differ but cannot and should not be directly
compared. Any such comparison is unfair, much like the common expression (in the West) about comparing apples and oranges. Just to name
one example, the West might seem to have an advantage for fulfilling
creative potentials in that it allows the individual more liberty. Individuality is encouraged, rewarded, expected. There is probably more autonomy
in the West, less pressure for conformity and harmony. On the other hand,
human emotions are treated in different ways in the East and the West,
with the East typically more in control of emotions. This is especially
significant when it comes to creativity because emotions have such weight
in creative work.

There are obvious practical implications of the ideas presented herein.
Most general is the likelihood of an increased appreciation for alternative
perspectives, especially those resulting from cultural differences. Though
general, this is an important implication, not the least because it, too,
relates directly to creativity. Simply put, creative insights are often a result of shifts in perspective, or they result from the use of, and recognition of, multiple perspectives. It might be called open-mindedness or flexibility, but whatever the description, the benefit involves multiple perspectives. This volume also contains ideas which could be applied in various organisations; Kwang discusses conflict resolution, for example, and
various approaches to education. Chapter 9 may strike most readers as
the most practical, for it focuses on nurturing creative individuals and a
more "creative society of Asians". This chapter contains numerous ideas
about parenting and strengthening a child's self-esteem and confidence.

Intriguingly, Kwang suggests that Confucian ideas can be used specifically within the family to create what he calls the "playground of life".
He suggests that families do "nothing without joy", and he explains how
this will help children to gain the confidence and the responsibility which
will allow them to be strong and creative. Kwang relates these ideas to
the individual's "voice of judgment", which is a tendency which can, if
not monitored, undermine creative thinking. Kwang also relates it to a
playful attitude towards life, and in turn relates this to the actions of famous creators, including Nobel laureate Richard Feynman.

Kwang talks a fair bit about education in this volume, and in Chapter 9, is very concrete in his suggestions about improving the educational
institution by aligning it specifically with creative potentials. He would
have us strengthen the confidence of students and rid them of *kiasi* (a
kind of fear). Here again it is easy to relate this directly to creativity re-

search, since it has long been recognised that creative thinking sometimes requires a tolerance of risk and a willingness to persist.

This volume will open the eyes of many readers. It is one of the most comprehensive and realistic works available on creativity and culture. In addition to culture *per se*, it covers marriage, children, education, values, and morality. Kwang discusses various countries in the East, including Japan, China, Taiwan, Korea, Hong Kong and Singapore. Kwang nicely ties his ideas to the existing research but also introduces a number of concepts which have never before been used to explain culture and creativity. This makes for excellent reading.

Professor Mark A. Runco
Chief Editor
Creativity Research Journal
California State University, Fullerton

A Word to the Reader

In recent years, there has been a heightened interest in the topic of creativity. This interest is not merely restricted to researchers in academic institutions like myself. Indeed, ordinary individuals from all walks of life are keen to know more about creativity. Much of this interest is fuelled by the personal desire to lead a more creative and fulfilling life. We will not all end up as Einsteins or Picassos, but it is hoped that we can be a little bit more imaginative and creative, in the way we think, feel and act as a person in society. The challenge of being creative is intricately connected to the type of society that we live in. More specifically, Asians are *less* creative than Westerners.[†] In making this rather controversial statement which many people will no doubt disagree with, I do not mean that Asians cannot be creative. Indeed, there are many creative Asians around, past and present, whose creative accomplishments in various domains of life have been internationally recognised.

For example, the dissident Chinese writer Gao Xingjian – whose books are banned in China – has just been awarded this year's Nobel Prize for Literature "for an oeuvre of universal validity, bitter insight and linguistic ingenuity, which has opened new paths for the Chinese novel and drama" although his win has not pleased the Beijing authorities one bit (they accused the Nobel Award Committee of "playing politics"). Less controversial but no less significant was the Hollywood Oscar for lifetime achievement, which was awarded in 1990 to Akira Kurosawa, the late Japanese movie director, for his creative contributions to the movie-making industry. In the hyper-paced electronics industry, Sim Wong Hoo, the chairman and founder of Creative Technology, a billion-dollar multimedia computer company in Singapore which produces the highly-popular Soundblaster software program, is often compared to Bill Gates, the chairman and founder of Microsoft Corporation in America; while Jerry Yang, the creative mind behind Yahoo!, a famous Internet company which is based in Silicon Valley, the Mecca of the technological world, hails from Taiwan.

Instead, in asserting that Asians are *less* creative than Westerners, I mean that generally speaking, it is much harder for Asians to think, feel and act in a creative manner, compared to Westerners. In this book, I will

---

† In this book, the term *Asians* refers to people who live in Confucian-heritage societies e.g., the Chinese, Japanese and Koreans. The term *Westerners* refers to people who live in liberal individualistic societies e.g., the Americans, Australians and Anglo-Saxons.

A WORD TO THE READER

explain why this is so, by looking at how Asians and Westerners typically behave in their respective societies. Note that my emphasis in this book is on *explanation*, i.e., I want to explain to you – the reader – why in general Asians are *less* creative than Westerners. So I can make the promise that after reading this book, you will become more knowledgeable, especially in relation to the question of why Asians find it so much harder to behave in a creative manner within their society, compared to their counterparts in the West. However, I cannot make the promise that you will become more creative. This is because being a creative person is not simply an intellectual challenge, but an emotional one as well. However, you should not feel despair over what I have just said. Approached in the right spirit and discipline, this "tell-me-why" book can be an intellectual device to liberate you from those obsolete and uncreative patterns of behaviour which you have become habituated to. To assist you in realising this goal, I have provided ten comprehensive guidelines which explain how you can become a creative Asian (see pages 208–212).

Having stated my objective in writing this book, I will now describe its contents. In Chapter One, I will look at what creativity is. In Chapter Two, I will examine the differences between Asian and Western society. In Chapter Three, I will describe the psychological make-up of the Asian and Westerner. Then in Chapters Four and Five, I will look at how culture influences creative behaviour. With this intimate understanding of the relationship between culture and creativity, I will focus my intellectual spotlight on how Asian and Western students strive for success in Chapter Six. Then I will look at how Asians and Westerners deal with conflict in Chapter Seven. In each case, I will give real examples of creative and uncreative behaviour among Asians and Westerners, which you as the reader can identify with. In this way, I hope to reinforce your understanding of why Asians are less creative than Westerners. In Chapter Eight, I observe that uncreative societies in the East have totally disintegrated in the past, and pose this provocative question: can the East survive the West in the future? Finally, in Chapter Nine, I look at the practical question of how we can nurture a more creative society of Asians.

Three special features characterise this book. First, while it is based on the scientific research which I conducted as a doctorate candidate in the Department of Psychology at the University of Queensland, Australia, I have written this book, not for the specialised academic, but for the general public. As such, I have pruned this book of technical jargon wherever possible in an attempt to make it accessible to a broad spectrum of readers. But it is inevitable that psychological concepts do find their way into this book from page to page e.g., *openness to experience* as a basic dimension of the human personality which is closely related to creativity. In each instance, I explain the meaning of the psychological concept in simple terms which a layperson can understand. So you do not need a degree in psychology in order to read this book.

Second, I have sought to include real examples from different societies in the East and West e.g., the Chinese system of relationships, the "afraid to lose" syndrome of the Singaporean, the Japanese concern with group living, the American emphasis on individual rights and freedoms, and the laid-back and relaxed attitude of the Australians (they like to end a social conversation with the phrase "no worries", as I observed during my stay in this so-called Lucky Country), and so on and so forth. Readers will be able to develop a better understanding of the workings of these societies by reading this book.

Third, I have inserted many boxed articles throughout the book. These boxed articles provide a more in-depth look at certain issues which are not covered in the main text. For example, in Chapter One, there is a boxed article which looks at the making of a famous creator like Albert Einstein. In Chapter Four, there is a boxed article which makes this interesting assertion: by imagining that you are a butterfly dreaming that you are a human being, you can become more creative. In Chapter Six, there is a boxed article which looks at how you can increase your creativity by taking calculated risks. Finally in Chapter Nine, there is a boxed article which looks at how you can *play* your way to a Nobel Prize!

In addition to these three special features, I have decided to donate half of my royalties from this book to charitable organisations in society. I think it is right for me to do so, for two reasons. First, in this book, I actually encourage my readers to lead a creative and meaningful life by helping the less fortunate in society (for further details, see page 89). So naturally I must practise what I preach. Otherwise how can I be convincing to my readers? The second reason is this: the basic inspiration for writing this book comes from living in human society, so part of my earnings should go back to it. I am keeping the other half of my royalties because a good workman deserves his wages for the hard work he has put in!

To conclude, I hope that you will enjoy reading this book. In doing so, you will be killing two birds with one stone, as the saying goes, i.e., you will not only learn how to be a creative person in society; in addition, you will also assist the poor and needy of this world. Now that's what I call a creative and meaningful act indeed!

Ng Aik Kwang
November 2000

All the World's a Stage
And We're All Butterflies
Dreaming That We're Human Beings

chapter 1

The Paradoxical World
of the Creator

The Paradox of Creativity

Since the dawn of human history, our lives on this lonely planet have been greatly influenced by the creative contributions of people living in different cultures across the world. These creative contributions range from the cupboard-sized refrigerator, which enables us to store our food overnight, to the desktop computer, which allows us to edit our documents with ease. These inventions have vastly improved our lives. Unfortunately, at the same time they have opened up many potential areas of human conflict. For example, the discovery of nuclear fusion paves the way for our world to meet its energy needs indefinitely, at the same time that it threatens us all with a nuclear holocaust. Because creativity has a great impact on our lives – for better or for worse – scientists have long been interested in it. By storing up our scientific knowledge on creativity, two things can be achieved. First, we can make better and more efficient use of this precious human resource. Second, we can guard ourselves against its more negative and destructive impulses. However, our scientific research into creativity is hampered by a lack of agreement on what exactly creativity is. As Mumford and Gustafson have commented, an extensive review of the scholarly literature on this topic leaves one feeling like Lewis Caroll's Alice in Wonderland, who, upon reading *Jabberwocky*, remarks, "Somehow it seems to fill my head with ideas – only I don't exactly know what they are."[1]

Creativity As a Way of Solving Problems

A common understanding of what creativity is has been slow to emerge, because creativity is a *multidimensional concept*, which is understood by researchers in different ways.[2] In other words, what you mean by the term "creativity" will depend on which approach you are using to study it. There are at least four theoretical approaches to the study of creativity.

They include the **cognitive, personality, social psychological** and **systems** approaches to creativity. Each of these four approaches will be outlined in turn.

From the *cognitive* perspective, when we say that a person behaves in a creative way, we mean that he has come up with a novel, innovative and practical solution to a certain problem. The creator's solution meets a felt need in the situation. For example, a clever scientist develops a new scientific theory to explain a certain aspect of nature which has puzzled the rest of the scientific community. Or a humorous individual in a sluggish workgroup cracks a joke to liven up the group atmosphere. Or an imaginative artist paints an evocative image which stirs up a powerful feeling in everyone who looks at it.[3] This process of coming up with a novel and innovative solution to a certain problem is known as *creative problem-solving*. Creative problem-solving makes certain demands on the creator, which is not found in ordinary problem-solving. One of them is the ability of the creator to adapt to an *ill-defined situation*. In such a situation, it is not immediately clear at the outset what the exact nature of the problem is, i.e., what are we trying to achieve in this situation? What can we do to reach our goals? What information do we need to gather in order to solve this problem? To deal with this ill-defined situation, the creator engages in problem-*finding*, i.e., he defines the problem to be solved, how he should go about solving it, as well as what information he should gather, instead of dealing with the problem in a routine and conventional way.[4]

Let me give you an example of an ill-defined situation which requires problem-finding: raising money for charity during the Asian economic crisis. The conventional solution to this problem is to make an emotional appeal to the public through donation cards. However, this method may not be so effective in an economic crisis, as people will be keeping a tight watch on their pockets. In order to raise funds successfully, our creative fund-raiser will need to ask himself the following question: what can motivate a group of people to part with their money when times are bad? He will also need to dabble in a little bit of *divergent thinking*. Divergent thinking is different from *convergent thinking*. In convergent thinking, there is a standard solution to the problem at hand. In contrast, in divergent thinking there is no standard solution to the problem at hand. Instead, our creative fund-raiser proposes an unconventional solution to the problem. This solution requires him to think in a fluent, flexible and original manner. After coming up with this unconventional solution, he still needs to modify it, so that it can fit into the practical demands of the situation. An example of creative problem-solving can be seen in the following boxed article, which reports a novel and innovative way of raising funds for charity in Singapore during the Asian economic crisis.

Raising Funds for Charity, Singapore Style

Singapore is a clean, green and "fine" city, infamous all over the world for its harsh rules and regulations, as well as its fines for minor offences, like not flushing the toilet after you've used it. It also has the best workforce in the world, according to Business Environment Risk Intelligence (BERI),[5] but its people are generally not regarded as creative. However, a short article which appeared in *The Straits Times*, the local English newspaper, shows just how creative Singaporeans can be in raising funds for charity in an economic crisis.[6] According to this article, for S$120, which would go to charity, people could walk underwater with a television star, using a specially-designed helmet called the Seawalker. Although it weighed a hefty 37 kilograms, the Seawalker, which looked like a large gold fish bowl but was actually a helmet connected by a flexible hose to an air source, felt comfortable underwater, according to Ms Chang Ai-Lien, a journalist who gamely donned the Seawalker and took the plunge in the gigantic reef tank of Underwater World Singapore. In the words of this intrepid reporter, "… it was almost effortless walking around the tank. I came face to face with myriad fish and sea creatures, some of them friendly and curious, and almost rubbed noses with a giant bat fish that was hoping to get fed." Ms Chang was a solitary walker among the fish, but for S$120, members of the public could have a sea walk with a star for half an hour. Eight local television stars were roped in to play the role of underwater tourist guides. Via this innovative fund-raising programme, Underwater World hoped to raise at least S$10,000 for its Bone Marrow Donor Programme. According to Dr Frederic Chua, the curator of Underwater World, "this is the first time people will be able to take a walk among the fishes in an aquarium. The water will be clear and the fish, used to people. And bad weather won't be a problem."

The Creative Personality

We have seen that in the process of creative problem-solving, the creator will engage in problem-finding; he will think of an unconventional solution to the ill-defined problem, and then modify it in order to meet the practical demands of the situation. What are the psychological attributes of the creator? Researchers who look at creativity from the *personality* perspective have identified a number of attributes. First, the creator displays a genuine passion for what he is doing. Second, because of his passion, the creator is willing to expend a lot of time and energy to realise his goals. Third, he has a high tolerance of ambiguity, i.e., he can live with a lot of uncertainties during the whole creative problem-solving process. Fourth, he is willing to take calculated risks in the task. Fifth, the creator is attracted to deep and complex ideas, and has broad rather than narrow interests in life. Sixth, he is an open person, i.e., he is willing to seek out and undergo different experiences. Finally, the creator is very confident in what he is doing, and behaves with a lot of independence and autonomy as a person.[7]

Listen to me!

Mumford and Gustafson account for this set of creative attributes in the following way: being open to his experience in this world, having broad interests in life and being attracted to deep and complex ideas enable the creator to develop and make use of complex mental models to solve problems in the real world. However, as far as creative work is concerned, these complex mental models are not sufficient by themselves. This is because in every creative undertaking, an abstract and untested idea must eventually be translated into concrete action. In the process, the creator will encounter a lot of obstacles to the unconventional solution which he proposes. To overcome these obstacles, the creator needs to be passionate and committed to his work, to take calculated risks, as well as to persevere in the face of severe obstacles. The going will get especially tough when the creator faces the social resistance of his community, which is fearful of change. In such a situation, the creator needs to display great autonomy, independence and confidence in what he is doing; otherwise he will succumb to the pressure to conform to his community.[8]

In the case of our creative fund-raiser, contributing to charity by walking among the fish is a new and untested idea, and will meet with a lot of resistance in the community. For example, certain members of the public may not know how to swim, or may be scared of various sea creatures moving around them, or may find such an idea to be crazy. Our creative fund-raiser will have to deal with these obstacles in order to realise his altruistic objective. Using popular television stars helps him to achieve two goals. First, it will increase the social acceptability of his crazy idea. Second, getting popular television stars to act as underwater tourist guides will help to dispel the fears of those members of the public who are willing to give his crazy idea a go. This decision to use television stars will in turn require him to persevere in the face of rejections and turn-downs e.g., by the busy stars themselves.

The Creative Environment

In contrast to the cognitive and personality perspectives on creativity, the *social psychological* perspective deals with the question of how the social environment affects creative behaviour. The social psychologist T. M. Amabile has conducted a lot of research in this area which she described in her book *Creativity in Context*. In her research, Amabile defines creativity using the *consensual assessment technique*, which states that a product or response is creative to the extent that appropriate observers independently agree that it is creative. Appropriate observers are those experts who are familiar with the domain in which the product is created, e.g., artists in a painting competition, architects in a design competition and writers in an essay competition. Using this technique for assessing creativity, Amabile and her associates have conducted many empirical studies which highlight the importance of *intrinsic motivation*, i.e., enjoying what you are doing, in creative behaviour.[9]

Here is an example. Two groups of naïve subjects were taught how to compose *haiku*, a Japanese poem. When they have learned how to do so, they were told to evaluate various reasons for writing poems. The first group evaluated extrinsic reasons e.g., "I enjoy public recognition and financial rewards for my poem"; the second group evaluated intrinsic reasons e.g., "I like to play with words". After this experimental manipulation, both groups were told to compose their own *haikus*. Their poems were assessed by appropriate judges who were experts in composing *haiku*. It was found that the second group who evaluated intrinsic reasons performed better in the task, compared to the first group who evaluated extrinsic reasons. Through this and other similar studies, Amabile and her associates have concluded that intrinsic motivation is conducive to creativity. In contrast, extrinsic motivators like contracted-for rewards, competition, deadlines, surveillance and restricted choice have a detrimental effect on creativity by undermining intrinsic motivation in the task. This undermining of a person's intrinsic motivation by extrinsic rewards is known as the *overjustification effect*. The overjustification effect occurs because the extrinsic motivator has induced a psychological shift in the attribution of the activity from internal to external, from "I am doing this task because I enjoy doing it" to "I am doing this task because I am rewarded for it". Once this psychological shift in attribution occurs, it will be difficult to motivate the person in the activity without the use of extrinsic rewards.[10]

The crucial role of intrinsic motivation in the social psychology of creativity is spelled out by Amabile in her *componential model of creativity,* which highlights three major components of creativity. They include the **domain-relevant skills**, the **creativity-relevant skills** and **intrinsic motivation**. *Domain-relevant skills* refer to the knowledge, skills and abilities which pertain to the particular domain in which a person wishes to be creative. For example, a violinist will need an understanding of musical notations, as well as finger dexterity. *Creativity-relevant skills* refer to cognitive abilities like divergent thinking, as well as personality traits like openness to experience, a penchant for taking risk and a great tolerance for ambiguity, which we have already touched on. Finally, *intrinsic motivation* refers to the passion of the person to perform the task in question. Without this passion for what he is doing, he will find it very difficult to stay the course, especially with so many obstacles in his path e.g., extrinsic rewards which take his mind off the task. The boxed article which follows looks at how you can increase your creativity by protecting yourself from such rewards.

Increase Your Creativity By Protecting Yourself from Rewards

The componential model of creativity maintains that the relationship between intrinsic and extrinsic motivation is a *hydraulic* one, i.e., as extrinsic motivation increases, intrinsic motivation (and creativity) must decrease, and vice versa. However, it seems clear from anecdotal evidence in the real world that extrinsic motivators such as reward and competition need not necessarily undermine creativity. In fact, for some people, there seems to be an *additive* relationship: not only does their intrinsic motivation remain high, but their creativity may actually be enhanced in the face of extrinsic motivators.

For example, the Hollywood filmmaker Woody Allen maintains a high level of intrinsic motivation and creativity in the extremely competitive movie industry, ignoring the awards and critics, while continuing to innovate with new styles and themes. The American scientists Watson and Crick felt strong competitive pressure in their race to discover the structure of DNA. Yet, in those times that they made their most significant breakthroughs, they were so single-mindedly focused on the puzzle before them that they temporarily forgot not only about their competitors and the Nobel Prize awaiting the victor, but also about the time of day and their need for food.

Inspired by these examples from real life, Amabile and her associates set out to determine if it would be possible to inoculate people against the negative effects of extrinsic motivators on creativity. They trained them to think of these motivators as important, but still secondary to intrinsic motivation, in performing the creative task. Via this type of training, they hope to simulate the manner in which Woody Allen, as well as Watson and Crick, inoculated themselves from the temptation of fame and fortune in their creative work.

In one study, a videotape was made, in which two attractive children answered an adult's questions about their work. The script was written so as to portray these children as models of intrinsic motivation e.g., they spoke excitedly about different aspects of their schoolwork, and while acknowledging the importance of good grades and parental praise, they firmly stated that "those are not what's really important". Amabile and her associates then had one group of children (the trained group) watch this videotape, while another group of children (the control group) watch a tape which was based on a totally different topic. In a later testing session, it was found that the trained group of children scored higher on a measure of intrinsic motivation, compared to the control group of children. In addition, it was found that children in the control group exhibited lower creativity when offered a reward, while children in the trained group not only showed no such decrement, but actually produced higher levels of creativity under the contracted-for reward – a clearly additive effect.[11]

This experiment provides empirical evidence that extrinsic motivators are not always the bane of creativity. Instead, people can be trained to inoculate themselves against their negative effects. This is done by encouraging the person to treat these extrinsic motivators as important but still secondary to the passion for the activity itself. These motivators can then even enhance the creativity of the person. This conclusion will come as good news to harried officials and administrators who are trying to nurture more creativity in competitive schools and organisations.

I ORDER you to be creative!

Where Is Creativity?

The three approaches to creativity which I have described thus far highlight one key aspect of creativity: it does not occur in a social vacuum. Instead, there is an intimate connection between the creator and the social world in which he performs the creative act. This key aspect of creativity is explored more comprehensively by the *systems* perspective on creativity. Unlike the other approaches to creativity, which attempt to understand *what* creativity is, the systems perspective attempts to understand *where* creativity is. According to Csikszentmihalyi (roughly pronounced as *chick-sent-me-high*), the only sensible answer is that creativity is to be found in a system made up of three interlocking parts, which is shown in the figure below.

The Systems Perspective on Creativity

The first part is the *domain*, which consists of a set of symbolic rules and procedures e.g., architecture or mathematics. The second part is the *field*, which includes all the individuals who act as *gatekeepers* in this domain of creative work, and whose principal task is to decide whether a new idea or product should be included in the domain. In the arts, the gatekeepers will include art professors, patrons, collectors and critics. The third part is the *person*, who passionately restructures the conventional elements within the domain he is working in, and persuades the field of the importance of his creative transformation of the domain.[12]

In focusing on the dynamic relationship between the creator and the social world, the systems perspective on creativity allows for the often mysterious fluctuations in the social attribution of "creative genius" over time. For example, the reputation of Raphael as a painter has waxed and waned several times since his heyday at the court of Pope Julius II. The conventional explanation for the fluctuating fame of Raphael is that the person was creative; only his reputation changed with the vagaries of social recognition. However, the systems perspective, in stressing that creative work does not occur in a social vacuum, but is instead embedded within a cultural context, argues that it makes perfect sense to say that Raphael was creative in the 16th and 19th centuries, when the art community (field) was moved by his masterpieces in the domain, but not in between or afterward, when it found them to be routine and mannered. In other words, creativity is not merely the creator's *magnum opus* or masterpiece, as many of us are wont to believe. Instead, it is made possible by the interlocking parts of domain, field and person in time, and it can be socially constructed, deconstructed and reconstructed several times over the course of history, as the case may be.[13]

We Can All Be Creative, But Few of Us Can Be an Einstein

The creative genius who comes up with an innovative transformation of the domain which is accepted by the gatekeepers in the field will be hailed as an eminent creator by the rest of the world. People who fall into this category of *eminent creativity* are household names e.g., the Jewish scientist Albert Einstein, who transformed our understanding of the intricate relationship between space and time with his special theory of relativity; the English poet T. S. Eliot, whose famous poem *The Wasteland* sensitises us to the destructive impulses of our modern age; as well as the Indian freedom-fighter Mahatma Gandhi, who brought the rule of the British in India to an end with his creative method of opposing the mighty British empire. (Basically, he dared the British authority to arrest him on charges of breaking an unjust law in a peaceful and non-violent manner.)

Eminent creativity, which few of us will ever attain in our lifetime, is to be differentiated from *everyday creativity*, which most of us will engage in some of the time e.g., using a coin to loosen a screw, creating a new recipe for lunch or finding a novel way to entertain a group of guests at a birthday party.[14] Being an everyday creator will not bring us international renown. However, it will allow us to live in a way which is meaningful, healthy and balanced. It will also enable us to adapt ourselves to the fast-changing environment of the modern world. For example, the person who works smart at his job (modifies the way he does things in an innovative manner to improve efficiency and productivity) will feel invigorated and be given more challenging assignments to do in the future, while his counterpart who merely works hard at his job (sticks to the tried and tested way of performing a task) will feel like a cog in the machine, and be retrenched at the shortest notice.

What Does It Take to Be an Einstein?

At this juncture, a question may arise in the reader's mind: given the large gap between everyday and eminent creativity, what does it take for us to become an eminent creator like Einstein, who dazzles our world with his intellectual feats? K. Anders Ericsson gives us an idea of what it takes to become a talented individual who engages in exceptional performance in a certain field e.g., chess, mathematics or music. Ericsson begins with the observation that "in nearly every field of human endeavour, the performance of the best practitioners is so ... superior even to the performance of other highly experienced individuals in the field, that most people believe a unique, qualitative attribute, commonly called innate talent, must be invoked to account for this highest level of perform-ance".[15] This view – of the creative genius being born, not made – is evi-dent in many domains of expertise, like chess, music, science and the visual arts, where millions of individuals are active, but only a very small number reach the highest levels of performance.

Despite its popularity, there is little evidence to support this talent view of exceptional performance. For example, it has been established that the superior memory of the expert chess player over the novice, for brief presentations of chess positions on a chessboard, is eliminated when the chess pieces are presented in a random format. Ericsson has termed this phenomenon the *domain specificity* of expert performance. He argued – with much empirical evidence – that experts have acquired their supe-rior performance in a particular domain, not because they are born with a set of good genes, but because they have engaged in *deliberate practice*.

Deliberate practice is an individualised training programme selected by a qualified teacher, which is aimed at the goal of improving the prac-titioner's performance in that particular domain in question, be it in play-ing chess, composing music, solving a scientific puzzle, or pitching a base-ball. Unlike play, deliberate practice is not inherently motivating, and unlike work, it does not lead to immediate social and monetary rewards. As an example of deliberate practice, advanced chess players spend as many as four hours a day studying published games between interna-tional chess masters. The effective component in this study is predicting the chess master's next move without looking ahead. If the prediction is wrong, the advanced player examines the chess position more deeply to identify the reasons for the chess master's move. This extended evalua-tion of chess games improves the ability of the advanced player to inter-nally represent chess positions of played games.

How much time must a person spend on deliberate practice before he or she can become an expert performer? In a comprehensive review of studies comparing starting ages and amount of weekly practice for inter-national, national and regional-level performers in many different do-mains, Ericsson and his associates have found that performers who reached higher levels tended to start practising as many as from two to five years earlier than did their less accomplished counterparts. Perform-ers who attained higher levels of performance spent more time on delib-erate practice than did less accomplished performers, even when there was no difference in the total time both groups spent on domain-related activities. By the time performers approached their middle to late teens and were applying for scholarships and admission to the studios of mas-ter teachers and the best training environments, large differences in past practice and acquired expertise were already present. For example, by age 20, top-level violinists had practised an average of more than 10,000 hours, approximately 2,500 hours more than the next most accomplished group of expert violinists, and 5,000 hours more than the group who per-formed at the lowest level.[16] Deliberate practice in these domains was not inherently enjoyable, yet many individuals still engaged in it. The question is: how did they end up in this torturous regime?

From many interviews, Bloom has found that international-level performers started out as children by engaging in playful activities in the domain.[17] After a period of playful and enjoyable experience they revealed "talent" or "promise", at which point parents typically encouraged their children to engage in limited amounts of deliberate practice, as well as to take lessons from a teacher. The next phase was an extended period of preparation – as long as ten years or more – and this phase ended with the individual's commitment to pursue (or not to pursue) activities in the domain on a full-time basis. During this period, the daily amounts of deliberate practice were increased, and advanced teachers and training facilities were sought out. Occasionally parents even moved to a different region of the country to provide their children with the best possible training environment. In addition, Bloom also found that nearly all of the individuals who ultimately reached an international level of performance worked with master mentors who either had reached that level or had previously trained other individuals to that level.

This finding on the role of mentors in exceptional performance is in accord with a study on the importance of role modelling in science by Zuckerman, who studied American scientists who won the Nobel Prize between 1901 and 1972. Zuckerman found that more than half of the 94 Nobel laureates had themselves worked under or with other laureates, either as graduate students, postdoctoral fellows or collaborators. In interviews the laureates indicated that their mentors had served as role models from whom they had learned scientific techniques, standards for their work, ways of thinking about problems, taste for what constitutes an important problem, and how the community of scientists operates. The laureates were also more likely to have worked with their award-winning mentors before their mentors won the Nobel Prize rather than after.[18]

With regard to the question of how long it takes for "genius to hatch", Hayes has conducted studies of musical composers, painters and poets.[19] He found that a period of knowledge acquisition lasting approximately ten years is needed before creative masterworks are produced. This finding is evident across creators with diverse artistic orientations, from the 17th to 20th century. For example, 76 composers from Harold Schonberg's *The Lives of the Great Composers* were studied. The date on which each composer began studying music, and the dates of notable creative works (pieces recorded five or more times), were obtained. Out of more than 500 works, only three were composed before year ten of the composers' careers, and these three

works were composed in years eight and nine. Averaged over the whole group, the pattern of career productivity involved one decade of silence before the Big Bang. This is known as the *ten-year rule of creativity* in the research literature. That is, it takes approximately ten years of hard work for the person to master the accumulated wisdom in a particular domain of knowledge before he can produce a unique contribution which is recognised by the entire field.

In summary, if you intend to become a talented individual who engages in exceptional performance in a certain field, you need not have the best genes in the world. However, you must receive enough assistance from the people who are closest to you during your formative years. In addition, you must be prepared to slog away for ten or more years on a strict and pleasureless regime of deliberate practice. This will enable you to accumulate those abilities, skills, techniques, knowledge, concepts and theories which pertain to the particular domain in which you are developing your expertise. In this torturous process of deliberate practice, you will be supervised by increasingly demanding master mentors who know what it takes for you to reach the pinnacle of your profession. Only then will you stand a chance of achieving international fame and recognition for your hard work and dedication.

Creators Are Made, Not Born

Ericsson's research – which shows that genes are not the major determining factor in exceptional performance – challenges a major myth of creativity, which many individuals, including the creators themselves, like to propagate. This myth states that *creators are born, not made*, i.e., only certain individuals in this world can be creative, because they are born with the appropriate talent. Ericsson's contrary assertion, i.e., *creators are made, not born*, is in accord with the *threshold theory of intelligence*, which asserts that there is a positive and moderate correlation between intelligence and creativity up to an IQ of 120.[20] Beyond this IQ level, other factors are more important than intelligence in predicting creativity. In other words, being intelligent will assist the person in being creative, but the most intelligent person is not necessarily the most creative one as well. Other factors come into play.

Charles Darwin, one of the intellectual giants of our modern world, who scandalised the Christian Church with his theory of evolution which asserts that we evolved from the apes instead of being made in the image of God, gave us an insight into what these "other factors" might be. In a letter which he wrote to the psychologist Francis Galton, author of the influential *Hereditary Genius: An Inquiry into Its Laws and Consequences*, Darwin said, "You have made a convert of an opponent in one sense, for I have always maintained that excepting fools, we did not differ much in intellect, only in zeal and hard work; I still think this is an eminently important difference."[21] In a similar vein, the great Austrian composer Wolfgang Amadeus Mozart made this remark in a conversation with his conductor Kucharz, who was leading the rehearsal for *Don Giovanni*, a musical masterpiece which Mozart had written: "I have spared neither care nor labour to produce something excellent for Prague. Moreover, it is a mistake to think that the practice of my art has become easy to me. I assure you, dear friend, no one has given so much care to the study of composition as I. There is scarcely a famous master in music whose works I have not frequently and diligently studied."[22]

The experiences of other famous inventors testify to the importance of hard work and perseverance in creative work.[23] A good example is the American inventor Thomas Edison, who discovered 1,800 ways of how *not* to make a light bulb before he found that tungsten worked as a filament. Another good example is the German scientist Werner von Braun, who was developing a rocket which Germany would use to bomb London during World War II. His superiors, concerned that he had already failed over 65,000 times in developing such a rocket, asked him how much longer it would take. Werner von Braun replied that he would need to fail another few thousand times. But in the end, his perseverance paid off, in the form of a ballistic missile which Germany used to attack her enemies. In conclusion, it is not whether you have the talent, but whether you are psychologically prepared to make the necessary sacrifice, which will determine whether you can become an eminent creator.[24]

Chapter Summary

In this chapter, I began by observing that creativity is a multidimensional concept, and there are at least four major ways of studying it. They include the cognitive, personality, social psychological and systems perspectives. The cognitive perspective looks at creativity as a special form of problem-solving, while the personality perspective looks at the attributes of the creator. The social psychological perspective examines how the social environment influences creative behaviour via intrinsic motivation, while the systems perspective asserts that creativity is an interconnected system consisting of the person, field and domain. Following this review of theoretical approaches in the study of creativity, I made a distinction between eminent and everyday creativity, i.e., all of us can be everyday creators, but few of us will ever become an eminent creator like Albert Einstein. I then looked at what it takes for us to become such an eminent creator. The answer does not lie in our genes, but rather in whether we are willing to work extremely hard to develop our expertise in a certain domain. In other words, creators are made, not born. The following boxed article takes a closer look at the making of an eminent creator like Einstein; it argues provocatively that it does not pay for us to be such an eminent creator.

The Making of the Creator

We have seen that talented individuals with an exceptional flair in a certain domain has undergone an extremely torturous regime of deliberate practice to dazzle the world with their feats, be it in the area of chess-playing, musical composition or mathematical problem-solving. Such talented individuals can be broken down further into two groups: the expert performer and the creative genius. The expert performer is a highly *dedicated* individual who faithfully reenacts programmes or instructions approved by society, and who best brings again to life the work of somebody else e.g., a piece of painting by a master artist or a violin concerto by a master composer. In contrast, the creative genius is a highly *challenged* individual who brings about an innovative transformation of the domain he is working in, which is subsequently accepted by the rest of the field. A flawless imitation of a Rembrandt painting is an example of the work produced by the expert performer who is dedicated to his art, while the twisted, distorted and geometrical characters of Pablo Picasso, the Cubist artist, is an example of the work produced by the creative genius.

Why does the creative genius possess a challenged personality, rather than merely a dedicated one? According to Therivel, this is because he has experienced untold hardships and crises in his formative years.[25] Examples of these hardships and crises include the devastation and uprootedness of all-consuming war e.g., the radical philosopher of existentialism Jean-Paul Sartre fought in the French Resistance during World War II; a physical deformity which prevents the person from pursuing a normal course of life e.g., the brilliant astrophysicist Stephen Hawking was diagnosed with amyotrophic lateral sclerosis, a disease of the motor neurons which prevents him from eating, sleeping and walking in the normal way; and the loss of one's parents in early childhood e.g., Mahatma Gandhi lost his often absent, old and ailing father at the age of 16. One study estimated that the percentage of eminent creators who experienced early parental death is 28 percent, compared to the average of eight percent in the general population.[26]

These negative experiences in the formative years of the creative genius disrupt the conventional acquisition of cultural scripts. The lack of conventional scripts forces the precocious youth to build up his own scripts, by reading unconventional books, magazines and the like. Often, he discovers that things are not as people say they are. Thus there grows, day by day in him, what Therivel termed as an attitude of *de omnibus dubitandum* (doubt everything). Such a skeptical attitude eventually leads the challenged creator to adopt a vision of the world which is radically different from that of ordinary people. At the same time, the early misfortune of the creative genius has made him into a highly alert, hypersensitive and emotionally tense youth. This psychological intensity, coupled with his paucity of socially-prescribed scripts on the one hand, and the skeptical stance which he takes towards the ordinary world on the other, transforms him into a powerful divergent thinker who is capable of rapidly and brilliantly connecting a first idea with a dozen others without feeling that he is infringing on deeply ingrained taboos.

As an example, we might believe that True Love exists in this world, and give red roses to our loved ones on Valentine's Day, while the challenged creator might argue, much to our consternation, that "True Love is just a clumsy term to describe a complicated phenomenon which is unique to our human world, where people who inhabit an absurd and meaningless universe infuse their personal lives with meaning, in an attempt to ward off the nothingness which constantly stabs them from behind with the thought of annihilation". Or he might alternatively proclaim that "God is like Mickey Mouse, a fictitious character which we have invented to keep us company while we are living on this earth." That is, it is not God who have created us; it is we who have created God.

Misfortunes in the formative years may give birth to important new ways of looking at the world, but they are not enough by themselves to produce great works of art, music, poetry or philosophy. For as Therivel has noted, any youth must first survive and grow into a social being. Then, to profit from the hardships and crises of his earlier life, he needs much assistance: all kinds of friendly help from parents or parent substitutes, relatives, friends and teachers. Other forms of assistance come from a good job, a medium to high cultural and socioeconomic status, medical care, education and free time to pursue personal interests in life. In this respect, Therivel's theory of the challenged creator is closely aligned with the findings of other researchers, who have underscored the importance of the mentor in the life of the creative genius.

Examples of creative geniuses who have received assistance in their lives include the following: Mahatma Gandhi, who lost his father at a young age, came from a rich family, which enabled him to go out on long solitary walks, even though he was married at the age of 13. Amadeus Mozart, who had a musically-talented but failed father who never made it to the level of *Kapellmeister* or orchestra conductor, nevertheless benefited immensely from the musical training which he received from Papa Mozart, who hoped to redeem his unfulfilled career through his gifted son. Charles Dickens only spent five months of manual labour in a paste-blacking factory before he was plucked from its dark clutches by the timely death of his grandmother, who left enough money for his father to pay his business debts, leave prison, return to work and free his son from the soot and pollution of industrial Europe. In a similar vein, Einstein, whose father failed in business repeatedly and plunged the whole family into straitened circumstances, nevertheless had a stream of caring relatives and friends who instructed him in physics, mathematics and philosophy during his early formative years.

We have seen that the creative genius is characterised by a high level of crisis and assistance in life, i.e., he possesses a challenged personality. One additional point to note about the creative genius is this: he invariably creates in a fighting spirit. As Picasso has stated, concerning his aim as an artist, "I want to draw the mind in a direction it's not used to and wake it up. I want to help the viewer discover something he wouldn't have discovered without me. That's why I stress the dissimilarity, for example, between the left eye and the right eye ... So my purpose is to set things in movement, to provoke this movement by contradictory tensions, opposing forces." Or even more blatantly, he said, "Painting is not made to decorate apartments. It is an instrument of war, for attack and defence against the enemy."[27]

Why does the creative genius behave in such an iconoclastic manner? According to Sigmund Freud, the psychoanalytic genius, the reason is this: only then can he numb the dulling and indelible pain which resides in the deepest reaches of his psyche. From this psychoanalytic perspective, the creative genius is no different from the humble oyster which resides in the ocean: when foreign particles such as sand accidentally enter its shell, it secretes a nacre coating to make them less dangerous to its soft tissues. Eventually, the nacre coatings transform the irritant into a pearl of great beauty.

In a similar vein, the creative genius transforms the pain and torment which he experiences in his formative years into an invaluable and creative product which enriches our conventional world e.g., a mathematical theorem which explains the functioning of the universe, a melancholic piece of music which moves the listener to tears, or a complex novel which consumes the waking hours of the reader.[28] In other words, every time you treat yourself to a great piece of art, or lose yourself in a moving piece of music, you are able to do so only because its creator has suffered terribly, as can be gleaned in this remark by T. S. Eliot, who was an eminent and tormented creator himself: "The more perfect the artist, the more completely separate in him will be the man who suffers and the mind who creates."[29]

In my opinion, nothing illustrates this pain-soaked creative process better than the life of Viktor Frankl, a Jewish psychiatrist who founded logotherapy, a branch of psychiatry which deals with our existential search for meaning. Frankl developed his perspective on the human psyche while he was imprisoned in Auschwitz, a notorious concentration camp in Nazi Germany which did all it could to dehumanise certain groups of human beings (especially Jews). Frankl lost his entire family and friends in Auschwitz, but he survived the brutal and inhuman conditions there. But not only did Frankl survive, he also emerged with a resilient faith in the ability of the human spirit to resist and surmount the worst conditions of life, and he shared this indomitable faith with his readers in his highly-acclaimed book *Man's Search for Meaning*.[30]

By now, it should be clear to the reader why it does not pay for him or her to be a creative genius like Einstein: so much time, sacrifice, hard work, discipline, pain and torment are involved! It would be better for one to stick to being an everyday creator. We may not become famous like our eminent counterpart, but we can at least still pursue the simpler pleasures in life, like sipping coffee with bosom friends at a cafe, watching a movie on a romantic date, and stretching ourselves lazily on a sun-kissed beach, instead of giving all these activities away for a stab at stardom in the painful and disciplined world of the eminent creator.

There is another reason why it does not pay for us to be a creative genius: we will end up being maladjusted to life in some ways, especially in our relationship with our loved ones. The explanation is as follows: the creator of the highest rank is seized by a powerful desire to mould the world according to his own image. He is so caught up in the pursuit of this personal mission in life that he is willing to sacrifice many things, including the possibility of a rounded personal existence on earth. This phenomenon has been nicknamed the creator's *Faustian bargain* by Howard Gardner in his book *Creating Minds*, which is an in-depth study of the lives of seven eminent creators – Sigmund Freud, Albert Einstein, Pablo Picasso, Igor Stravinsky, T. S. Eliot, Martha Graham and Mahatma Gandhi.[31] Faust is an infamous figure in the literature of the West, who sold his soul to the Devil in exchange for knowledge and power. In Gardner's view, the creator's Faustian bargain is reflective of the widely-held belief that in lieu of his special talent or gift, the creative genius must of necessity pay some kind of price or adhere to some sort of social arrangement, in order to sustain this special talent or gift. The nature of this price or social arrangement differs, as can be gleaned in the personal lives of the two greatest scientists in the history of our world, Isaac Newton and Albert Einstein.

Isaac Newton, the renowned Enlightenment scientist who formulated the mechanical view of the universe with his famous laws of gravity, was born prematurely on Christmas Day in 1642, which was also the day when the great Renaissance scientist Galileo Galilei died. Newton's father had died three months before his birth, so that during this very early period of his existence, Newton had his mother's undivided attention. However, this idyll was rudely shattered by his mother's remarriage and removal to another house just after the boy's third birthday. Newton was left in the care of his maternal grandmother. Although his mother's new home was near enough for him to have been able to see her frequently, Newton passionately resented what he felt as a betrayal. In a confessional list of sins, recorded when he was 20, he blamed himself for having haboured the wish to burn the house of his mother and stepfather.[32]

Newton grew up to be an extremely cold and suspicious bachelor who seldom laughed. His reluctance to become involved with other people was so extreme that he sometimes failed to make due acknowledgements to his predecessors in his work, as if he felt that his own revelation must be uniquely personal and uncontaminated. This reluctance was also manifested in his unwillingness to face publicity, as he feared that it would lead to him being harassed by personal relationships. Even when he arrived at the solution to the greatest problem that astronomy has ever had to face, i.e., the law of universal gravitation, which explains the planetary movements in our solar system, he said nothing about it to anybody. Only the persuasion of the British astronomer and mathematician Edmund Halley moved him to write it down for posterity in his *Philosophiae Naturalis Principia Mathematica*.

Newton's achievement in cracking this "mother of all puzzles" led him to become knighted and to be elected as the president of the prestigious Royal Society in London, a post which he held for the rest of his life. As a powerful public figure, Sir Isaac Newton displayed an unsavoury side to his character, which led a modern-day biographer to paint him as a man "who is given to violent rages and unnecessarily rancorous disputes with his contemporaries, which makes him appear to modern eyes an unsympathetic figure".[33] For example, in an attempt to perfect his lunar theory, Newton made use of his position as president to force John Flamsteed, the Astronomer Royal, to publish his astronomical observations. He conducted the resulting conflict with Flamsteed in an insensitive and tyrannical manner.

Newton also engaged in a violent dispute with Leibniz over priority in the invention of the calculus. Again he made use of his position as president to have a committee of that body investigate the matter. He himself secretly wrote the committee's report, which charged Leibniz with deliberate plagiarism. He also compiled the book of evidence that the society subsequently published.[34] Newton had also been made the Master of the Mint. In this role, his task was to stamp out forgery. It was reported that Newton pursued and prosecuted coiners and counterfeiters with a fierce relish characteristic of paranoid men who attain power.[35] This paranoid side to his character is seen in the many letters which he wrote to his erstwhile friends, accusing them of a wide variety of "crimes", ranging from being atheists or Catholics to embroiling him with women.

Following on the heels of Isaac Newton was Albert Einstein, the most famous scientist of our modern era, who formulated a relativistic view of the universe with his special theory of relativity, which explained how matter and energy curve the geometry of space-time to create the phenomenon known as gravity. This friendly and affable "world citizen", who was welcomed with open arms wherever he went, adopted a rather bossy and callous attitude in his relationship with his loved ones, according to Dr Schulmann, the Director of the Einstein Papers Project, which is a massive effort to publish all the 43,000 or so documents which Einstein left behind at Princeton's Institute of Advanced Study when he died in 1955.[36]

Here is what the archives have unearthed. Albert Einstein was born in 1879 in Germany, and spent his youth in Munich, where his father owned a small shop that manufactured electric machinery. He was not what we would call a "promising lad", for he learned how to speak only when he was three. As a quiet and dreamy boy, he often cut classes, much to the chagrin of his teachers. He relied on the lecture notes of his friends to pass his exams; eventually he dropped out of school because he could not stand its regimented ways. He made his way to the Swiss National Polytechnic in Zurich, where he broke his mother's heart by falling in love with Mileva Maric, an older foreign woman, fathering an illegitimate child with her, and eventually marrying her. His professors refused to recommend him to a teaching position when he graduated from the university in Zurich, as they considered him to be dull and boring. So he was forced to work as a minor patent officer in a small office in Switzerland to feed his growing family.

While scrutinising the inventions of other people, Einstein moonlighted at science. In 1905, this part-time scientist published a series of stunning papers which challenged the Newtonian view of the universe. A series of scientific experiments on solar eclipses, which was conducted by scientific experts from the prestigious Royal Society in London, validated the special theory of relativity of Einstein. This moment of truth, which was to have the gravest consequences for our world, especially in the form of two atomic bombs which were dropped on Hiroshima and Nagasaki in World War II, was witnessed by Alfred North Whitehead, a famous philosopher, who likened it to a Greek drama: "We were the chorus commenting on the decree of destiny as disclosed in the development of a supreme incident. There was dramatic quality in the very staging: the traditional ceremonial, and in the background the picture of Newton to remind us that the greatest of scientific generalisations was now, after more than two centuries, to receive its first modification … a great adventure in thought had at last come home to shore."[37]

Einstein became famous all over the world for his feat in shattering the Newtonian view of the universe. But this transformation into a world citizen had a grievous toll on his personal life. He gradually became estranged from his wife Mileva, who was depressed at his cold attitude. Unrepentant at heart, Einstein dictated a bossy memorandum detailing the conditions under which he would go on living with Mileva. Of course it did not resolve the issue, and Einstein initiated divorce proceedings against his wife so that he could marry his cousin Elsa, with whom he had had a close relationship since childhood days. At this point in the jumbled-up life of Einstein, a strange letter appeared on the scene. This letter was written by Ilse, the older of Elsa's two daughters, who was serving as Einstein's secretary.

Ilse had addressed the letter to her close friend Dr Georg Nicolai with the mysterious words "Please destroy this letter immediately after reading it" scrawled across the top in big letters. In it, she related how a simple "jest" from Einstein one afternoon had suddenly escalated into a serious proposal from him that he would like to marry her instead of her mother. Einstein told her that her mother was prepared to step aside. "Albert himself is refusing to make any decision; he is prepared to marry either Mama or me," Ilse wrote. "I know that A. loves me more than any other man ever will, he also told me so himself yesterday," she went on. The feelings, however, were not reciprocated. Ilse loved Einstein like a father, but she had no desire to be close to him physically. Her instinct was not to marry him. There is no evidence that Einstein's relationship with Ilse was ever consummated. Einstein and Elsa were married the next year and remained husband and wife until her death in 1936.

Ilse's letter and the bossy memorandum to Mileva, as well as a host of other documents which shed an unflattering light on Einstein, have transformed many modern scholars' view of this great scientist. They are unapologetic about airing his dirty linen in public. "To me this makes him more human … a living, breathing personality with faults," explained Dr Schulmann, who said he still liked

Einstein, in spite of his dictatorial attitude towards his first wife, and his callous attitude concerning the question of whether he married his cousin Elsa or her daughter Ilse.

As for myself, I only have this opinion to share with my readers, after acquainting myself with the lives of these creative geniuses: not only are we ordinary mortals wiser in being an everyday creator rather than an eminent one. In addition, it makes sense for us to be wary when we are around our more famous and creative counterparts. They are not always pleasant people to be around with, in spite of their great achievement and fame. As the saying goes: good to look at, but not good to know!

Notes

1. Mumford & Gustafson, 1988.
2. Glover *et al.*, 1989; Sternberg & Lubart, 1995.
3. Mumford *et al.*, 1991.
4. Csikszentmihalyi & Getzels, 1971; Runco, 1994.
5. The National Productivity Board of Singapore, 1992.
6. *The Straits Times,* January 9, 1999.
7. Barron & Harrington,1981.
8. Mumford & Gustafson, 1988.
9. Amabile, 1996.
10. Lepper, Greene & Nisbett, 1973.
11. Amabile, 1990.
12. Csikszentmihalyi, 1996.
13. *Ibid.*
14. Richard, 1990.
15. Ericsson & Charness, 1994.
16. Ericsson, Krampe & Tesch-Romer, 1993.
17. Bloom, 1985.
18. Zuckerman, 1977.
19. Hayes, 1989.
20. Barron, 1969; MacKinnon, 1978.
21. quoted in Ericsson & Charness, 1994.
22. Kerst, 1965, quoted in Therivel, 1999.
23. Brown, 1988; Rossman, 1931.
24. Ericsson & Charness, 1994.
25. Therivel, 1993.
26. Albert, 1983.
27. Whitman, 1973, quoted in Therivel, 1999.
28. Storr, 1976.
29. quoted in Gardner, 1993.
30. Frankl, 1984.
31. Gardner, 1993.
32. Storr, 1976.
33. Simmons, 1996.
34. Westfall, 1993.
35. Storr, 1976.
36. *The Straits Times*, September 3, 1999.
37. Johnson, 1991.

chapter 2

The Nature of Asian and Western Society

Now that we have a clearer picture of what creativity is, we can proceed to examine the role of culture in creative behaviour. Many scholars have alluded to this intimate relationship between culture and creativity. For example, in his article *Creativity and Cross-Cultural Variation*, Lubart looks at how creativity is manifested in different cultures, such as in traditional China or in religious India. He also argues that in certain societies like America, the person finds it easier to be creative, because of the strong emphasis on the rights and freedoms of the individual.[1]

Arieti proposes several features which characterise the *creativogenic* society.[2] One of them is the availability of cultural means. For example, Mozart would not have been successful if he had been born in Africa instead of Austria. Another is the people's openness to cultural stimuli, i.e., not only must the cultural means be available to the creative genius, but the population (or at least a significant part of it) must also desire the result. In the case of Mozart, his music was appreciated by a wide audience in Europe, including the reigning pope and king. A third feature of a creativogenic society is its ability to incorporate new stimuli from other cultures. One reason why Meiji Japan survived the Western intrusion into East Asia, while Qing China did not, is that the former was better able to assimilate the innovative ideas and practices of modern statecraft from the West, while the latter remained a closed society.

In my own research, I have attempted to deepen my understanding of the intimate relationship between culture and creativity by looking at how different cultures affect the creative behaviour of the individual. There are innumerable cultures in this world, and it would be impossible for me to study every single one of them. So I have limited my investigation to two major cultures. One of them is found in the West e.g., America, Britain, Canada, Australia and New Zealand. These societies have been strongly influenced by the social philosophy of *liberal individualism* in their historical development. The other one is found in the East e.g., China,

Japan, Taiwan, South Korea, Hong Kong and Singapore. These societies have been strongly influenced by the social philosophy of *Confucianism* (for a detailed look at the differences between Confucianism and liberal individualism, see the boxed article at the end of this chapter).

A Comparison of Asian and Western Society

The Confucian-heritage societies of the East differ from the liberal individualistic societies of the West in several ways. To begin with, the typical Asian society is more *tightly* organised, in contrast to the typical Western society, which is more *loosely* organised. A prototypical example of a tightly-organised Asian society is Japan. In this country, social interaction between two individuals is governed by many cultural norms e.g., whether the person one is interacting with is a *kohai* (junior) or *sempai* (senior), or a male or female. In contrast, social interaction in a liberal individualistic society like Australia is less governed by such cultural norms. Second, the typical Asian society is *collectivistic*, i.e., it puts a greater emphasis on the social group than the individual. As a result, Asians tend to conform to what their ingroups say and do; in addition, they also tend to be more concerned with winning the social approval of their ingroups. This is known in local jargon as gaining *mian-zi* (face) from significant others like relatives and close friends. In contrast, the typical Western society is *individualistic*, i.e., it puts a greater emphasis on the individual than the social group. As a result, Westerners tend to follow their own goals in life; in addition, they are less likely to be concerned with *mian-zi* or winning the social approval of their ingroups.

Third, the typical Asian society emphasises social order and harmony, as well as the avoidance of conflict. In contrast, the typical Western society emphasises the open and democratic exchange of ideas, even at the risk of conflict. Fourth, the typical Asian society is hierarchical, in contrast with its Western counterpart, which is egalitarian. An example will make this clear: in Singapore, a government minister has publicly stated that Singaporeans should not be *bo tua bo suay*, i.e., Singaporeans should not be disrespectful to those who are their seniors, whether in social position or chronological age. In contrast, even the highest government official in the most powerful country in the world, the American president, has to endure stringent criticisms from his people. These basic differences between the two cultures are summarised in the following table.

EAST	WEST
• Tightly organised (many social rules and norms to regulate behaviour in public)	• Loosely organised (few social rules and norms to regulate behaviour in public)
• Collectivistic (greater emphasis on the social group vis-à-vis the individual)	• Individualistic (greater emphasis on the individual vis-à-vis the social group)
• Hierarchical (more distinction in rank and status between superior and subordinate)	• Egalitarian (less distinction in rank and status between superior and subordinate)
• Great emphasis on social order and harmony in family and society	• Great emphasis on the open and democratic exchange of ideas between individuals
• More negative view of conflict in society	• Less negative view of conflict in society
• More concern with *mian-zi* (face) or in gaining the social approval of the group	• More concern with realising one's creative potential in life

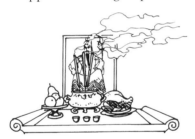

Exercise your right to vote!

A Caveat: East Is *Not* East and West Is *Not* West

Although Asian societies are fundamentally different from Western societies, it should be pointed out that Asian societies, like their Western counterparts, are not totally homogenous entities, i.e., Asian societies differ from one another in subtle ways, just as Western societies do (this will become clearer in the chapters to come, as I examine the inner workings of societies in the East and West). Another way to express this difference is via a paradoxical phrase: East Is *Not* East and West Is *Not* West.

To take an example from the East: in Singapore, there is much obeisance to the political authority, because of the autocratic and effective government. In contrast, in Japan, real power lies with the bureaucrats, rather than the government, which is seen as ineffective (however, note that the prestige of these Japanese bureaucrats has suffered in recent years because of financial scandals, such as the one involving the Japanese Ministry of Finance). Not surprisingly, Japanese politicians are not so well-respected, compared to government bureaucrats. Still, it is appropriate to classify Singapore and Japan in one cultural category, as these two societies have been very much influenced by the social philosophy of Confucianism in their historical development. Or consider this example from the West: in accordance with the cultural ethos of liberal individualism, American and Swedish society emphasise social equality between individuals. Hence it is appropriate to classify these two societies in the Western category, rather than the Asian one. However, membership in this Western category does not imply that American and Swedish society are completely alike. Indeed they are not: Americans tolerate financial inequality better than do Swedes, who are willing to be taxed at high rates so that income inequality can be reduced. This is evidenced in the ratio of income distribution of the top 20 percent to the bottom 20 percent of the working population: in America, this ratio is 9.0, while in Sweden it is only 3.0.[3] In fact, the tolerance of income inequality in America is so high that it has enabled the Microsoft chief, Bill Gates, to become the first US$100 billion dollar man in the world, with a personal fortune which exceeds the economic output of all but the 18 wealthiest nations in the world.[4]

The Conception of Selfhood in the East and West

Another way of understanding the differences between Asian and Western society is to look at the *indigenous conception of selfhood* which is operating in the society. This refers to the way of being a person in society. Every society will have its indigenous conception of selfhood, or its way of being a person in society. A person who is born into the society will be socialised to live in accordance with its indigenous conception of selfhood. As a result, the psychological make-up of the person will be shaped in a certain way. This will in turn affect the behaviour of the person. In this way, we can account for those cultural differences in behaviour which we see in the world e.g., between a conforming Asian and a creative Westerner. The following figure provides a simple model which explains this process:

The Ptolemaic Self of the West

The Western conception of selfhood is *Ptolemaic* in nature, because of its "I-ness", or emphasis on the individual.[5] The psychological challenge for a person with this Ptolemaic conception of selfhood is to free himself from the shackles of the collective, to become an independent and separate entity. Such a person is autonomous and self-determined, and pursues his own interests and goals in life, instead of conforming to what the social group says and does in society. He believes in his uniqueness as a person, and focuses on his private thoughts and feelings. He is also prone to the experience of *self-focused* emotions, like pride, anger, joy and sadness. When interacting with other people, he is frank and direct, and says what comes to his mind, instead of beating about the bush. In this way, he differentiates himself from other people, and validates his uniqueness as a person.

The Galilean Self of the East

In contrast, the Eastern conception of selfhood is *Galilean* in nature, because of its "we-ness", or emphasis on the social group.[6] The psychological challenge for a person with this Galilean conception of selfhood is to maintain his connectedness with those significant others whom he is relationally bonded to e.g., his family and relatives. Such a person is psychologically dependent on the ingroup, and conforms to it, instead of following the wishes and desires of his own heart. He believes in the importance of social order and harmony, and attempts to uphold the social rules and norms which govern proper behaviour in public. He is also prone to the experience of *other-focused* emotions, like shame, embarrassment and empathy. When interacting with other people, he is cautious and indirect, and attempts to read the other person's mind, instead of expressing his personal feelings and opinions in the matter. In this way, he connects himself with other people, and gains the approval of his ingroup. This difference in the notion of selfhood causes people in the East and West to view the world through different lenses, as shown by the following boxed article, which recounts the experience of Chinese and American audiences who watched a Hollywood movie.

Who Is the Villain of the Show?

This experience was recorded by the Chinese psychologist Francis Hsu in his book *Americans and Chinese*.[7] Hsu was watching a Hollywood movie called *Valley of Decision* with a Chinese friend. In the movie, the roles of hero and heroine were respectively played by Gregory Peck and Greer Garson. Peck acted as the son of a wealthy industrialist in one of the great steel centres of America. He had many new ideas concerning both production and labour relations. They were, however, contrary to those of his parents. Peck could get no support from his wife, who could not understand him and what he stood for. Instead, her views were entirely in line with those of his parents, and she was a woman after their own hearts. Peck found that he could relate more to Garson, who acted as a maid in the family's palatial home. During a conversation with Garson, Peck became attracted to her views, personality and sympathy.

In the meantime, labour trouble loomed in his father's plant. The workers began a strike for higher wages and better conditions of work. A group of strike breakers were then called in. Peck tried to persuade his father to call them off, and to discuss terms with the labour leaders. But while his father was exchanging views with them, a battle began between the labourers and the strike breakers. His father was killed, many men were injured, and the family's magnificent house was destroyed. Garson's father, who was one of the labourers, was also killed. After order was restored, Peck took over the management of the plant and redefined factory policies in a way that was more acceptable to the labourers and more commensurate with his own views. The movie then moved rapidly to its conclusion. Peck's unsympathetic wife demanded a divorce, which freed Peck to marry Garson, and presumably they lived happily ever after.

To the American audience, this is good drama for several reasons. There is the production conflict between new views on manufacturing methods and old-fashioned ones. There is the social conflict between liberal attitudes towards labour and the hard-fisted attempt to suppress the working men. Finally, there is the marital conflict presented by the wife who – in a creative twist of the scriptwriter's pen – could get along with her parents-in-law better than she could with her husband. These conflicts are eventually resolved in a manner that, according to the American way, is desirable. Peck and Garson, the hero and heroine of the movie, are finally triumphant, and an American audience can feel satisfied with the movie.

However, Hsu's Chinese friend was far from pleased. He understood the gigantic size and extent of American industry and wealth, and he had some comprehension of the bitterness and violence of American industrial disputes. He was also aware that Americans were usually ready to experiment with new ideas or to introduce novel methods of production. But he considered both Peck and Garson to be the *villains* of the show. Peck was shamefully unfilial because he was opposed to his parents and undid all that they had established in life. Garson was practically the sole cause of not only the breakdown of Peck's marriage but also his family's ruin and his elder's death. For when the maid first entered the picture, the family was prosperous, dignified and intact. Had she not encouraged her young master in his views, he would not have asked his father to negotiate with the labourers, and the old man would not have been exposed to their fatal attack, nor would her own father have died in the melee.

This difference in interpretation of who the villain of the show is stems from the contrasting assumptions which people in the East and West hold regarding moral behaviour. To the Chinese, steeped in filial piety and respect for the elderly, a son in conflict with his father is a bad son, and a maid who helps such a son in his unfilial ventures is a bad woman, no matter what the circumstances are. Through the same lens, the daughter-in-law is viewed as an extremely virtuous woman who suffers in malicious hands. The question of the young master's own unhappiness with his wife, as opposed to his possible happiness with the maid, should never have been raised in the first place. In contrast, to the American, the pursuit of individual liberty and happiness is considered as a valid goal of the person in society. As such, the behaviour of Peck and Garson should not arouse any moral qualms, as they were only doing what was right and reasonable given the situation.

Different Ways of Raising a Child in the East and West

We have seen that people who live in the East and West have contrasting notions of being a person in society. This difference in the notion of selfhood is reflected in the child-rearing philosophy and practices which are found in these two societies. In the Confucian societies of the East, *filial piety* is of paramount importance. This refers to the need of the child to honour, respect and obey his parents, and not do anything that will make them feel disappointed and ashamed of him. Confucius, the renowned Chinese sage of antiquity, believed that the filial piety of children, learned within the bosom of the family, was of great importance to good government. When someone asked him why he was not in public service, he replied that to be filial to one's parents was contributing to good government, and this in itself was an important service to the state (*Analects*, II: 21). The cultural emphasis on filial piety means that children from a traditional Asian family are raised in terms of whether their conduct meets some external moral criteria e.g., not being rude to one's parents or not treating them in a disrespectful manner. They are to be transformed into adults who exercise impulse control, behave properly, and fulfil their obligations – above all, filial obligations.[8] Dependence of the child on the parents is encouraged, and breaking the will of the child, so as to obtain complete obedience, is considered desirable. There is less interest in encouraging the child's expression of opinion, autonomy and independence. The Hong Kong psychologist David Y. F. Ho has termed this Asian way of raising a child as a form of *authoritarian moralism*.[9]

In contrast, the child-rearing practices in the individualistic societies of the West have been very much influenced by the views of the political philosopher John Locke (1632–1704). Locke was a stalwart opponent of patriarchy, a form of government which was favoured by Confucius, in which a benevolent ruler reigned wisely over his people. Instead, he argued that kingship could not be derived from fatherhood. In his observations on child-rearing, Locke argued that the father should firmly exercise authority early on in his child's life. However, as his child grew older, he should abandon this coercive authority, relating to him as an older but wiser friend instead. The ultimate goal was to enable his child to stand on his own two feet when he achieved independence later on. In this way, children would be able to take care of themselves, and good relationships between parents and their children could continue into the children's adulthood.[10]

Becoming a Separate Person in the East and West

This difference in child-rearing philosophy and practices means that the psychosocial task of becoming a separate person is accomplished in a contrasting manner in the East and West. Although separation and individuation are developmental milestones that must be faced by all human beings, "leaving home" in the Western sense is not. In the West, the person leaves home to become his own person in the world by totally letting go of the psychological ties that bind him to those significant others in his life, especially his parents, and also his church and community.

However, the Asian does not "leave home" in this sense: the psychological ties that bind him to his family are less thoroughly severed, even as he accomplishes the developmental task of becoming a separate being. This can be seen in the tendency of unmarried Asian children to stay in the family of origin, even when they have reached adulthood, and the continuance of close ties between married children and their parents. Indeed, the challenge facing the Asian is more one of "staying home", i.e., being around one's parents until their death and worshipping deceased parents and ancestors all one's life.[11]

This cultural difference in the phenomenon of becoming a separate person has been described by Balint in his interestingly-titled paper *Friendly Expanses/Horrid Empty Spaces*. In his paper, Balint proposed that there were two defensive reactions to the trauma of recognising that one is a separate being.[12] One reaction, which is typically found in Western society, is to see oneself as alone and relying on one's own resources. This involves a world-view of *friendly expanses*, dotted more or less densely with dangerous and unpredictable objects. To survive in such a world, the individual must develop the necessary skills to conquer such dangers as might appear, and to have confidence in the efficacy of these skills. The other reaction to the recognition of separateness is to cling on desperately to objects. In this alternative view, the world consists of objects, separated by *horrid empty spaces*. This world-view relies more on physical proximity for safety, and is more characteristic of people who live in the East.

Indeed, the traditional Chinese family has been described by a Chinese scholar as providing a relatively warm atmosphere in which the individual finds not merely economic security, but also the satisfaction of most of his social needs. Beyond this warm atmosphere lies what the individual considers as the cold and harsh world wherein his treatment and fate become unpredictable.[13] The bleakness that is conjured up in this image of the outer world is often utilised to discipline the child in Asian society.[14] For example, Japanese or Chinese parents may tell a visitor, "We don't need this boy, so please take him with you", or he may simply be locked out of the house. In contrast, the typical style of disciplining a child in the West is to ground him *inside* the house.

Cultural Emphasis on Self-Reliance in the West

The child-rearing philosophy and practices of the West produce a person who is independent and self-reliant, instead of being psychologically dependent on the social group. The term "self-reliance" goes back a long way in the history of the West. Thomas Jefferson chose in his draft of the American Declaration of Independence to strike a note of self-reliance, when he said that emigration and settlement here "were effected at the expense of our own blood and treasure, unassisted by the wealth or the strength of Great Britain", conveniently forgetting how recently the British had defended the colonists against the French and Indians.[15] Emerson in his famous essay *Self-Reliance* even declared the individual and society to be in opposition, arguing that society is everywhere in conspiracy against the manhood of every one of its members.[16]

This cultural emphasis on being an independent and self-reliant person is captured in the traditional image of the rugged and solitary cowboy eking out a living on the dangerous frontier of a virgin and fertile land, as well as in the modern image of the seasoned Caucasian with a heavy backpack on his shoulders travelling to exotic lands like Nepal and Tibet. In unison, they convey the cultural message that to be a person who can stand on his own two feet is right and good. In contrast, to be psychologically dependent on other people is weak and foolish. This dependence on others is manifested in such behaviours as gullibility, suggestibility, interpersonal yielding and compliance with others' requests and expectations. Such behaviour has its origins in the motivation to please other people, in order to seek their nurturance, support and approval.[17] Only children should be dependent, and even then, the cultural injunction is to socialise them to stand on their own two feet. As a result, training in autonomy and development in the appreciation of being alone come very early on in life. Day-old children sleep alone in their cribs, often in separate rooms from their parents. On the playground, children are taught to stand up for themselves and to fight back if necessary. Among adults, the emotional capability to break off dependent attachments to parental figures is crucial to the maintenance of individual freedom and autonomy.

To fail in this task is to be viewed as a person who is unhealthy or abnormal. This is reflected in the "Western nightmare" of failing to become one's own self by separating from others.[18]

Cultural Emphasis on Psychological Dependence in the East

In contrast, the "Eastern nightmare" involves a failure at achieving the cultural goal of connecting with others. In this culture, psychological dependence does not have a negative connotation, as it does in the West. Instead, it facilitates empathy, reciprocity and a sense of belonging; it implies that working with others is the right way of expressing and enhancing the self. This is reflected in the Japanese word for self, *jibun*, which means "the sharing of mutual life space".[19] This sense of identification and compliance with significant others is nurtured from young, via an intense socialisation process which fosters a peculiar form of closeness between the mother and child, one which is characterised by the feeling of *amae*. *Amae* refers to the sense of, or the accompanying hope for, being lovingly cared for, and involves depending on and presuming another's indulgence.[20] The child who *amaeru* develops not only an expectation of indulgence from the mother, but also an acceptance of her authority. In time this attitude becomes expanded into a need for, and reliance on, the affection and authority of the various social groups in society.[21]

This psychological dependence on the group enables the Japanese to develop *ittaikan* (feeling of oneness) with it, and gratifies his needs for social approval. It makes it difficult for him to behave in an assertive manner. This is reflected in the Japanese saying "The nail that stands out gets beaten down" (contrast this with the American saying "The squeaky wheel gets the grease"). Indeed, self-assertion in Japan is not viewed as being authentic, but instead as being immature and childish. Yielding or giving in is not a sign of weakness of character, as perceived in the West. On the contrary, it reflects tolerance, flexibility, social maturity and especially, self-control. The person's exercise of control, however, is directed primarily inward, at those inner attributes such as feelings and desires that can disturb the harmonious equilibrium of interpersonal transaction.[22]

In a similar vein, Kim has pointed out that in traditional Korea, socialisation for interdependence starts at the prenatal stage and continues throughout one's life.[23] *T'aekyo* (prenatal care) contains rigorous guidelines for pregnant women outlining desirable and undesirable attitudes, emotions and behaviours during pregnancy. These prescriptive guidelines are based upon the belief that a mother's experience during her pregnancy will directly affect the baby inside her womb and leave lasting impressions on the child. The goal of *t'aekyo* is to heighten a sense of awareness of the unique psychological and biological bonds between the mother and the child, and to nurture *chong* in the person. *Chong* arises within a closely-knit family and bosom friends who spend a long time together and are bound by a common fate. It does not develop in a contractual, commercial and rational relationship. A person with *chong* is self-sacrificial, unconditional, empathetic, caring and sincere. In contrast, someone without *chong* is conditional, selfish, hypocritical, apathetic and individualistic.

Chapter Summary

In this chapter, I looked at the differences between Asian and Western society. In general, Asian society is tightly organised, collectivistic, hierarchical and face-conscious. It also places a greater emphasis on social order and harmony, rather than conflict and confrontation. In contrast, Western society is loosely organised, individualistic and egalitarian. It also places a greater emphasis on a democratic exchange of ideas and opinions, which can lead to open conflict and confrontation. Although Asian and Western society differ in these basic ways, it does not imply that "East" and "West" are homogenous entities. Instead, "East is *Not* East" and "West is *Not* West", i.e., so-called Asian societies differ in subtle ways; this statement applies also to so-called Western societies. In the remainder of this book, I will provide examples of these subtle differences. Another way of understanding the differences between Asian and Western society is by looking at the conception of selfhood in the East and West. The Galilean self (we-ness) is promoted in the East, while the Ptolemaic self (I-ness) is promoted in the West. Due to this contrasting conception of selfhood, child-rearing practices differ between the two societies. Asian parents socialise their children to be psychologically dependent on the ingroup, while Western parents socialise their children to be independent. As a result, Asians and Westerners have different psychological make-ups; this will be examined in more detail in the next chapter. In the meantime, the interested reader can read the following boxed article, which provides an in-depth look at the social philosophies of Confucianism and liberal individualism, which have moulded the societies of the East and West respectively.

Clash of the East and West: Confucianism versus Liberal Individualism

Liberal individualism in the West emerged out of a long and bloody struggle by the people against the popes, kings and princes who ruled over them. This liberal rejection of arbitrary authority is mirrored in the intense commitment to the value of personal freedom. This can be gleaned in the rallying cry of the English philosopher John Stuart Mill (1806–1873): "Give Me Liberty or Give Me Death!" It can also be seen in the Hollywood blockbuster *Braveheart*, starring the screen heartthrob Mel Gibson, who acted as William Wallace, the coura-geous crusader for the people's freedom against an oppressive Eng-lish king in medieval Scotland.

However, it should be noted that this notion of freedom, which is so deeply ingrained in the Western psyche, is by no means intrin-sic to other cultures. Indeed, most non-Western people had no word in their language meaning "freedom" before they came into contact with the West. Of those that did, such as the Chinese, "freedom" is frowned upon as "sexual licentiousness".[24]

The philosophical roots of liberal individualism can be traced back to the writings of many Western thinkers, among whom are Thomas Hobbes, John Locke and Jean-Jacques Rousseau.[25] The mul-tifaceted ideas of these thinkers shaped the evolution of Western so-ciety in Europe during the 17th and 18th centuries, a period in the history of our world that has come to be known as the Enlighten-ment. No other places in the world have gone through an Enlighten-ment, or put in another more accurate way, in no other places did the enlightened ideas of a few philosophers become the shared under-standing of the populace at large, and in time, the general practice of reconstituted governments all over the world.[26]

The Enlightenment in the West means many things to many peo-ple – an enthusiasm for science, a desire to master nature, a belief in progress, a commitment to reform. For the German philosopher Immanuel Kant (1724–1804), it represented man's release from his self-imposed tutelage. In this context, "tutelage" means having one's understanding directed by another; while "self-imposed" means a lack of courage to rely on one's own reason. This self-imposed tute-lage of man comes from unthinking or cowardly obedience to au-thority, be it in the form of ancient custom, revealed religion or a hereditary monarch.

Not surprisingly, liberal individualism rejects any appeal to the traditional order of the past as a basis for decision-making. Instead, autonomous individuals should make use of their reasoning ability to discover the universal principles governing life in this world. Only then will there be progress and development in society. Any power or group within society that attempts to force its conception of truth or good on the individual is to be rejected.

Instead of believing in one truth or good, liberal individualism subscribes to the liberal principle that people are free to do as they please within limits set only by the personal freedom of others; le-gally all persons are equal before the law; philosophically the indi-vidual's separate existence is inviolable; and psychologically the ul-timate human condition is to be liberated from all internal and exter-nal constraints on one's desire to actualise one's self.[27] These liberal principles are enshrined in the 1948 United Nations Universal Declaration of Human Rights, and championed within the liberal polity as *individual rights*.

An individual's rights will be upheld as long as they do not infringe on the rights and freedoms of others, and do not prevent the just requirements of morality, public order and general welfare in the liberal polity.[28] At the societal level, a liberal conception of individual rights focuses on *negative rights* such as non-interference, and lacks a clear articulation of substantive goals such as the common good, collective welfare and social harmony. Consequently, liberal politics is less concerned with forging unity within the community, and more concerned with the pursuit of special interests by different groups of people, according to neutral rules. It involves the complex business of adversarial struggles, alliance building and coalition bargaining, with the aim of garnering the precious votes of skeptical electorates.[29]

If liberal individualism in the West represents a radical break from the traditional and medieval order, Confucianism in the East represents an idealisation of such a past. Confucius (551–479 BC) saw the world and all living things in it as a manifestation of *Tao* (the Way), which constitutes the very essence of the moral force that permeates order and harmony in the universe. He expounded a social and moral philosophy to maintain, reify and perpetuate this natural order.[30] *Tao* manifests itself in wider nature via the harmonious opposition of *yin* (passive, feminine principle of life) and *yang* (active, masculine principle of life). In humans it is manifested through *te* (moral excellence). It is through *te* that the person is able to follow the Way, and it is through self-cultivation that *te* can be realised.

One way in which the person can cultivate himself is via the maintenance of a state of inner equilibrium. This is achieved by establishing control over the emotions of the heart, which is regarded as a mirror which reflects an event. Once the event is over, the emotion should be gone. As the *Confucian Doctrine of the Mean and Harmony* suggests, "When the emotions of pleasure, anger, sorrow and joy are not stirred, our mind is in the state of mean and equilibrium; when these emotions are expressed, but in proper degree, our mind is in the condition of harmony." The person who cultivates himself in this way will steer away from any open expression of his inner emotions, bringing them under control via the practices of *li* (rules of propriety).[31] In this way, although he still experiences various emotions, he is not ensnared by them.

Li is the fulfilment of human impulse, the civilised expression of it – not a formalistic dehumanisation; human nature is realised rather than constrained or distorted by training and participation in *li*. This

is expressed in the traditional saying "Conquering selfishness to restore ritual propriety". In this sense, Confucius regards man as a ceremonial being. This contrasts with the situation in the West, where
people are encouraged to be "true" to themselves, by spontaneously
expressing what they are feeling inside. Apropos, it can be asserted
that to be a person in a Confucian society is to be a well-mannered
"false" self, who will not under any circumstances wear his heart on
his sleeve, so to speak.[32]

A person who has successfully cultivated himself in this manner
is considered to be a *junzhi* (sage or gentleman) who possesses *jen*
(human-heartedness). *Jen* has three related aspects. First, it consists
of loving others (*Analects*, XII: 22). Second, the man of *jen* is someone
who, desiring to establish himself, establishes others, and desiring
to develop himself, develops others (*Analects*, VI: 28). Third, *jen* is
also expressed in the social maxim that one should not do to others
what one does not wish to do to oneself (*Analects*, XII: 2).[33] The *junzhi*
who is characterised by *jen* will promote social good and harmony
wherever he treads. This is reflected in a poem entitled *Righteousness
in the Heart*:[34]

> If there be righteousness in the heart, there will be beauty in character.
> If there be beauty in character, there will be harmony in the home.
> If there be harmony in the home, there will be order in the nation.
> If there be order in the nation, there will be peace in the world.

In Confucian society, every person has *fen* (portion, place) in it.
Each *fen* is associated with a particular role and responsibility. Social
order and harmony will be maintained when everyone performs the
role and responsibility which have been allocated to him in society.
Confucian society is organised around the *wu lun* (five cardinal relations): between emperor and minister (relation of *righteousness*), father and son (relation of *closeness*), husband and wife (relation of
distinction), elder brother and younger brother (relation of *order*), and
friend and friend (relation of *faithfulness*).[35] Of the five cardinal relations, three of them are based on the family. This reflects the importance of the family in Confucian society. The primary relationship in
the family is the father–son relationship, which is based not on equality, but on *hsiao tao* (filial piety), i.e., the father expects reverence,
obedience and respect from his children. In return, his children expect love, wisdom and benevolence from their father.

The Confucian family is regarded as the prototype for society,
which is seen as its extension. Hence, like a father, an ideal ruler is a
person who utilises his power and authority for the welfare of the
people, and not for his self-interest. He must be governed, and must
govern, by *jen*. However, if the ruler is a tyrannical despot who abuses

his power, he is seen as having lost the *Mandate of Heaven* to rule. The people will be justified in removing him from power. This requirement to perform in accordance with one's role is more generally expressed in the Confucian doctrine of the *rectification of names*. That is, things in actual fact should be made to accord with the names attached to them. For example, the essence of a ruler is what the ruler ideally ought to be. If the ruler acts according to this "way of the ruler", he is then truly a ruler, in *fact* as well as in *name*, since there is an agreement between name and actuality. But if he does not, he is no ruler, even though he may be sitting on the Dragon Throne.

This Confucian doctrine of the rectification of names reminds me of an incident concerning an Australian minister which I read about in an Australian newspaper. In official name, he was a minister in charge of family affairs in the Australian government. In actual fact, a security guard had caught him swimming naked together with his girlfriend, as well as his teenage son, in the private pool of a hotel one evening. When questioned by an Australian reporter, the minister, who was divorced, replied that on returning to the hotel after he had finished work for the day, he had seen his girlfriend and teenage son having a "skinny dip" in the pool. So he decided to join the two of them in relaxing at the pool after a hard day's work. The Australian minister said that there was nothing wrong with what he had done. Instead, his behaviour underlined his belief in the beauty of the naked body.

In recounting this incident, I am not implying that what the Australian minister had done in the hotel pool that evening was wrong. I merely wish to point out that in view of the Confucian doctrine of the rectification of names, i.e., things in actual fact should be made to accord with the names attached to them, it would be extremely unlikely for a Confucian-minded minister in an Asian society, let alone one who is in charge of family affairs, to behave in this manner in public. Certainly, the Confucian-minded ministers in my country, Singapore, who regularly extol Confucian virtues to the people via the state-controlled media, would never be caught in public by a security guard with their pants down!

On a more serious note, the basic difference in philosophical outlook between the East and West – in the form of Confucianism and liberal individualism – has led to many clashes between these two societies. Two prominent examples involve the conceptualisation and practice of democracy, as well as the existence or non-existence of "Asian" as opposed to "Western" values. In the liberal polity, the rights and freedoms of the individual are championed in a Western form of parliamentary democracy, in which the government is weak and challenged vigorously by a strong opposition. In contrast, in the Confucian polity, the rights and freedoms of the individual are curtailed in an Asian form of parliamentary democracy, in which the government is strong and vigorously suppresses the weak opposition.

This latter version of democracy as practised in some countries in the East e.g., Singapore, has been dismissed by liberal critics in the West as an "elected dictatorship" or a "one-party state".[36] These Western critics argue that the existence of formal institutions associated with democratic rule in Asian societies provides no guarantee that substantive democratic practices are in fact operative. For example, an elected Parliament may be nothing but a rubber-stamp Parliament which serves as a front for an authoritarian government. In addition, they have also argued that the so-called Asian values are a myth, propagated by the ruling elite of these authoritarian states to justify and legitimise their iron grip on power.

However, instead of behaving passively like a cocker spaniel that rolls over delightedly to these charges – to paraphrase the inimitable Lee Kuan Yew, the Senior Minister of Singapore – the ruling elite has launched a counter-offensive, by accusing the other side in this debate of cultural chauvinism, of attempting to impose incommensurable "Western" values on an Asian society. These Asian critics of Western-style democracy argue that democracy is a culturally relative term. Western countries should not have a monopoly over interpretation or practice when it comes to the correct form of democratic rule.[37]

In addition, these Asian critics argue forcefully that the West should get off its own moral high horse, for it is guilty of the very same act which it accuses the East of, i.e., inventing myths to legitimise an iron order. For example, the Christian notion of the White man's burden to save the unconverted heathen from eternal damnation, has led to colonial exploitation of indigenous people in Africa and Asia. The American founding myth of individual freedom and enterprise in reality rested upon the suffering of millions, not only of Native Americans and African slaves, but also of ordinary immigrant working people, whose lives were sac-

Cultural chauvinist!

One-party dictator!

The pot calling the kettle black

rificed in the name of liberty, progress and manifest destiny. Finally, the championing of egalitarianism, mateship and giving everyone a fair go in Australia does not include Aboriginal Australians or other non-Europeans who are the original inhabitants or legal citizens of this continent-size country.[38]

Incidentally, it is not only the political leaders in Asian states who have voiced their misgivings about the Western style of parliamentary democracy, with its emphasis on individual rights and freedoms. Many eminent Westerners themselves – ancient and modern – have long felt an outright revulsion, or queasy ambivalence, towards the democratic form of political rule, even though it first took root in their cultural soil.

A notable example of the former group of luminaries is Plato (427–347 BC), the greatest philosopher of the ancient West, who advocated the reign of philosopher-kings rather than the rule of the people (NB: *philosopher-kings* are exceptional individuals in society who, having devoted themselves to study, possess the requisite knowledge to rule the people; they are somewhat like the Confucian *junzhi*, who are also highly-educated persons in society). Plato chose the philosopher-king over the people partly because he was disgusted with the fact that it was a democratic assembly of his fellow Athenians who had sentenced his teacher, the enigmatic philosopher Socrates (469–399 BC), to death by drinking hemlock. Socrates had been falsely accused of disrespecting the gods and corrupting the minds of Athenian youths by his enemies, who schemed to shut up this "gadfly of the state" once and for all.

Plato had a pupil in the Academy where he lectured, by the name of Aristotle (384–322 BC). Like his teacher, Aristotle believed that democracy was an inferior form of government, compared to a monarchy or an aristocracy.[39] He should know: at one stage in his life he was forced to flee democratic Athens, as his life was in danger. According to Aristotle, he left because he didn't want the Athenians to – as he put it – "sin twice against philosophy" (the first sin was the false charges which the Athenians had laid against Socrates).[40]

This ancient rejection of democracy is reflected in the queasy ambivalence of its modern-day advocates in the West. For example, according to the French president Georges Clemenceau, democracy is "the least intolerable of the various frightful evils", while his British counterpart, Clement Attlee, thought that "democracy means government by discussion, but it is only effective if you can stop people talking". A little kinder is the English statesman Lord James Bryce, who noted, "However grave the indictment that may be brought against democracy, its friends can answer: what better alternative do you offer?"

> Back in the philosopher's camp, John Stuart Mill – a most stalwart defender of the liberty of the individual – could find nothing better to say of the people than that their superiors were even worse, while George Bernard Shaw quipped that democracy substitutes election by the incompetent many for appointment by the corrupt few. I think Gore Vidal sums it all up best: "Democracy is supposed to give you the feeling of choice, like Painkiller X and Painkiller Y. But really, they're both just aspirin."[41]

Notes

1. Lubart, 1990.
2. Arieti, 1976.
3. Triandis, 1995.
4. *The Straits Times*, April 10, 1999.
5. Hsu, 1985; Bellah *et al.*, 1985; Etzioni, 1993; Baumeister, 1997.
6. Doi, 1973; Lebra, 1976; Tu, 1985; Markus & Kitayama, 1991.
7. Hsu, 1955.
8. Tang, 1992.
9. Ho, 1981 & 1994.
10. Bellah *et al.*, 1985.
11. Tu, 1985.
12. Balint, 1955.
13. Tang, 1992.
14. Weisz, Rothbaum & Blackburn, 1984.
15. Bellah *et al.*, 1985.
16. Emerson, 1841.
17. Bornstein, 1992.
18. Markus & Kitayama, 1994.
19. Lebra, 1976; Mente, 1995.
20. Doi, 1973
21. Rohlen, 1989.
22. Weisz, Rothbaum & Blackburn, 1984.
23. Kim, 1995.
24. Wilson, 1993.
25. Bloom, 1987; Tarnas, 1991.
26. Wilson, 1993.
27. Patterson, 1991.
28. Dworkins, 1978.
29. Vincent, 1995; Bellah *et al.*, 1985.
30. Smith, 1973.
31. Fung, 1948.
32. Tang, 1992.
33. Lau, 1979.
34. quoted in Kim, 1995.
35. Tu, 1993.
36. Lawson, 1996; Roden & Hewison, 1996.
37. Han *et al.* 1998.
38. Pan, 1990; Roberts, 1987.
39. Russell, 1979.
40. Boorstin, 1998.
41. Pepper, 1984; Stromberg, 1996.

The Psychological Make-Up of the Asian and Westerner

In the previous chapter, we have seen that there are many differences between Asian and Western society. These differences are also reflected in the contrasting conceptions of selfhood, as well as in the child-rearing philosophy and practices of the East and West. These fundamental differences between the two cultures shape the psychological make-up of the Asian and Westerner. In this chapter, I will elaborate on the nature of this psychological make-up. My investigation is divided into four parts. First, I will examine how Asians and Westerners vary in their self-construal (how they look at themselves in relation to other people). Second, I will examine how they differ in their tendency to emphasise the positive or negative aspects of themselves. Third, I will examine how they differ in their personality traits. Finally, I will examine how they differ in their personal values.

How Asians and Westerners Look at Themselves

We have seen that Asian society puts a greater emphasis on the social group vis-à-vis the person, while Western society puts a greater emphasis on the person vis-à-vis the social group. This difference in emphasis affects the manner in which individuals in these two societies construe or look at themselves, in relation to significant others, like family and close friends. Westerners tend to construe themselves in an independent manner, while Asians tend to construe themselves in an interdependent manner.[1] A person with an *independent self-construal* views himself as a unique individual who is separate and distinct from other people. Because his identity as a person derives from his ability to remain as an independent entity, he is motivated to differentiate himself from others. As a result, he behaves in an independent and autonomous manner e.g., he formulates his own goals, and follows his own interests in life, instead of conforming to the wishes of the group. In contrast, a person with an *interdepend-*

ent self-construal views himself as part of a larger web of social relations. Because his identity as a person derives from his ability to maintain a connection with significant others, he is motivated to fit in with them. As a result, he behaves in an interdependent and social manner e.g., he lets his ingroup determine his goals and interests in life, conforms to what they say and do, and strenuously avoids any social conflict with them.

Self-Enhancement in the West versus Self-Criticism in the East

The Western tendency to construe themselves in an independent manner makes them more likely to regard themselves in a positive light, especially in relation to their abilities and attributes as a person. This is in contrast to Asians, who tend to be more modest in appraising themselves. For example, a lot of empirical research has shown that Westerners are more likely to display the *false uniqueness bias*. This refers to the tendency to overemphasise the uniqueness of one's own positive attributes of the self. In one survey, it was found that over 50 percent of a representative sample of American undergraduates reported that they were in the top ten percent with respect to interpersonal sensitivity. However, this false uniqueness bias was not found in Japanese, Korean or Thai undergraduates.[2]

According to Kitayama and his colleagues, this tendency of the person to regard himself in a positive or negative manner may extend to the way he regards a common action in social life.[3] For example, a common action in social life, like buying a chair, can be regarded in a positive and self-enhancing manner, as in "buying this old-fashioned chair to brighten up my living room"; or it can be regarded in a negative and self-deflating manner, as in "buying this old-fashioned chair because it's the only one I can afford". These definitions of a social act may be differentially distributed across different cultural contexts. That is, in some cultural contexts like the West, there are more self-esteem enhancing definitions of a social act, compared to self-esteem deflating ones. However, in other cultural contexts like the East, the situation is reversed, i.e., there are more self-esteem deflating definitions of a social act, compared to self-esteem enhancing ones.

In support of this hypothesis, Kitayama and his colleagues found that their American respondents showed a tendency for self-enhancement: they chose a greater number of success situations than failure situations as relevant to their self-esteem and further, they judged that their self-esteem would increase more in the success situations than it would decrease in the failure situations. By contrast, Japanese individuals showed a tendency for self-criticism. They chose a greater number of failure situations than success situations as relevant to their self-esteem and, further, they judged that their self-esteem would decrease more in failure situations than it would increase in success situations. In addition, they also found that situations construed by their American respondents promoted self-enhancement, in that the success situations made in this culture were judged as having more influence on self-esteem than the failure situations; in contrast, situations construed by their Japanese respondents promoted self-criticism, in that the failure situations made in this culture were judged as having more influence on self-esteem than the success situations.[4]

Why Westerners Enhance Themselves and Asians Criticise Themselves

The following explanation has been proposed to account for the striking difference in the prevalence of the false uniqueness bias in the East and West, i.e., why Westerners have the tendency to enhance themselves, while Asians have the tendency to criticise themselves: individuals will be differentially tuned into evaluating positive or negative self-relevant information in accordance with the culture in which they have been socialised. The central focus of a liberal individualistic society is to encourage the person to be his own unique and spontaneous self. The pattern of socialisation in the West will seek to identify those positively-valued attributes of the self that accentuates the person's uniqueness. Hence, Western caretakers will draw attention to children's positive features, praising and complimenting them. The child may in turn develop a habitual attentional bias towards self-relevant information which is positive in nature e.g., "I am a clever boy or girl", "I can paint well", or "I can play the trumpet beautifully".

In contrast, the central focus of a Confucian society is to raise children who are filial to their parents, and behave in an obedient and respectful manner towards their elders. The pattern of socialisation in the East, which is characterised by authoritarian moralism, will seek to identify those negatively-valued attributes of the self that prevent the person from fitting in with the rest of the social group. Hence, Asian caretakers will draw a child's attention to shortcomings, problems or potentially negative features that have to be corrected to meet the expectations or norms common in a social relationship. The child may in turn develop a habitual attentional bias towards negative self-relevant information.[5]

As a result of this difference in raising a child, the substance of self-esteem will differ in the East and West: the self-esteem of the Westerner is likely to be based primarily on the affirmation that *positive* features are *present* in his or her self. In contrast, the self-esteem of the Asian is likely to be based on the affirmation that *negative* features are *absent* from his or her self. There is anecdotal evidence to support this postulation: whereas the American way of feeling good is often centred around distinguishing oneself and standing out from the rest of the group, the Japanese way of feeling good is often framed in terms of *hitonami* (average as a person), i.e., to the extent that if one is average, one is to feel relief about one's self.[6] However, this Asian emphasis on ensuring that one's child does not accumulate negative behaviourial traits may end up in a belittlement of the child, as the following boxed article shows.

The Asian Child: Feeling Belittled by Father and Mother

A number of Asian Americans in therapy reported feeling how as children they felt belittled, not only in terms of the lack of recognition given to themselves, but also by the constant references made to other people's children, and how much better these children were in comparison with themselves. This comparison left them feeling that they were not good enough. A 19-year-old Chinese American gave this account of how degraded she felt by her father. On social occasions, someone would comment on how pretty she was, but her father would reply, "No, she's not pretty but your daughter is really beautiful." She rather plaintively queried, "Why couldn't he just have said 'thank you' for once?"[7]

Maxine Hong Kingston is another person who has experienced this belittlement of the self. In *The Woman Warrior*[8], she described how as an adolescent she had this sharp exchange of words with her mother:

"And it doesn't matter if a person is ugly; she can still do school-work."

"I didn't say you were ugly."

"You say that all the time."

"That's what we're supposed to say. That's what Chinese say. We like to say the opposite."

This characteristically Asian way of raising a child – morally-toned and disciplinary in focus, with love tucked into the background – is captured in a movie, *The Joy Luck Club*, which is a dramatic and moving portrayal of the criss-crossing and interlocking relationships among four Chinese mothers who emigrated to America, and their daughters. Readers who are interested in how Asian children relate to their parents are strongly encouraged to watch this touching movie, which is based on the book of the same name by Amy Tan.[9]

Universal Dimensions of the Human Personality

Besides differing in the way they construe and feel about themselves, Asians and Westerners also differ in their *personality traits*. Personality traits refer to dimensions of individual differences in tendencies to show consistent patterns of thoughts, feelings and actions.[10] For example, if Jack is a humorous person, we know he is inclined to crack jokes with people; if Miss Lee is a shy person, we know she is inclined to keep a safe distance from others. Based on research in various countries, many psychologists are now convinced that the best representation of personality traits is the *Big Five model of personality*.[11] This pattern of covariation among personality traits is found in many cultural groups of the world, including Asians and Westerners.[12] The following boxed article describes in more detail the Big Five model of personality.

The Big Five Model Of Personality

According to the Big Five model of personality, there are five basic dimensions to the human personality. They include **extraversion-dominance, agreeableness, conscientiousness, emotional stability** and **openness to experience**.[13] Evolutionary psychologists who conduct their research within a Darwinian framework have argued that these five basic dimensions of personality evolved during our long past as hunter-gatherers; they represent an adaptation to the harsh environment which our ancestors faced as they struggled for survival in the African savanna with all the other wild animals.

The Big Five model of personality covers a vast conceptual space that encompasses the five central concerns in human society, namely power (extraversion-dominance), love (agreeableness), work (conscientiousness), feeling (emotional stability) and creativity (openness to experience). They are inherent in a wide variety of personality systems which different psychologists have developed to describe and explain human behaviour. Empirical research has found that people from different cultures invariably make use of these five basic dimensions of personality to assess the behaviour of a person. According to Goldberg, this is because people wish to know the answer to at least five types of questions, in relation to an individual X whom they are going to meet.[14]

1. Is X active and dominant or passive and submissive, i.e., will I lord it over X or will X lord it over me? (extraversion-dominance)
2. Is X agreeable and warm or disagreeable and cold, i.e., is X likely to end up being my friend or my enemy? (agreeableness)
3. Is X responsible and reliable or irresponsible and negligent, i.e., can I rely on X to do something for me or will X take this opportunity to skive? (conscientiousness)
4. Is X cool and calm or worried and anxious, i.e., is X the sort of person who will lose his cool and blame me for no reason at all? (emotional stability)

5. Is X clever and smart or stupid and dumb, i.e., when the situation arises, will I be the one who is teaching X or vice versa? (openness to experience)

The Closed Personality of the Asian versus the Open Personality of the Westerner

In what is to follow, I will look at two personality traits which differ in significant ways in the East and West. The first one is openness to experience. A person who is open to experience is characterised by a recurrent need to enlarge and examine his experiences in life, be it in the area of fantasy, aesthetics, feelings, actions, ideas or values. He likes to experiment with the new, and to surmount, cross or set new boundaries. He is unwilling to be restrained by artificial or socially-imposed boundaries.[15] In addition, he has a personal belief and value system which is not tightly compartmentalised or easily affected by contradictory information, i.e., he can live with ambiguity or open himself to various alternatives without feeling anxious. Finally, his thinking processes are creative e.g., he can think in a divergent way; he has the ability to form remote associates among radically different ideas and he relies on imaginative metaphors to represent a situation.[16]

Open mind

An example of such an open personality is the Western philosopher Jean-Jacques Rousseau, whose autobiography contained prototypical examples of openness. According to McCrae, so active was the imagination of Rousseau that his novels captivated Europe; so attuned was he to beauty that as a self-taught composer his single opera transformed French musical taste. The effusive emotions of Rousseau ignited the whole Romantic movement, and his utter disregard for conventional behaviour – late in life he dressed in an Armenian caftan and cap – scandalised the peasants he lived among.[17]

Research has indicated that the open personality is the product of a socialisation style that is warm, supportive, and relatively constraint-free, and that nudges the child to engage in various kinds of trial-and-error learning, which is crucial to the development of a sense of initiative and mastery during childhood.[18] This socialisation of the open person contrasts sharply with the early experience of the closed person, who tends to be nurtured by authoritarian and overprotective parents. These parents often rely on social discipline to imprint restrictive and conforming values on their offspring. In addition, they reinforce the dependence behaviour of their child, at the same time that they prevent him from developing autonomous forms of behaviour.[19]

The open personality is more likely to take root in the loosely-organised, individualistic and liberal society of the West. In such a society, there are few rules and regulations which one must obey and follow. Instead, the person is encouraged to be original, and to innovate and explore. In contrast, the closed personality is more likely to take root in the tightly-organised, collectivistic and hierarchical society of the East. In such a society, there are many rules and regulations which must be followed. Failure to fall into line will lead to social sanctions. As a result, the person will find it difficult to be open, original and innovative.[20]

The Constrained-Submissive Personality of the Asian versus the Extraverted-Dominant Personality of the Westerner

Besides being more open to experience, Westerners also tend to be more extraverted and dominant, in comparison to Asians. The extravert is a very familiar character in the personality landscape: to many people, it conjures up the image of a person who is socially poised and confident, as well as energetic, bold and assertive. The typical extravert is emotionally exuberant, carefree and easy-going. This enables him to mix around well with other people in lively settings such as parties and discotheques. In addition, the extravert is likely to experience frequent and intense *self-focused emotions*, such as frustration, anger, pride and joy.[21] These emotions involve his internal attributes (needs and desires) as the primary referent. They result from the blocking or satisfaction/confirmation of this set of internal attributes e.g., "I was treated unfairly" or "I perform better than others". Experiencing and expressing a self-focused emotion reinforce the particular self-defining attribute, and lead to additional attempts to assert the emotion in public and confirm it in private, thereby validating the unique self of the individual.

In contrast, a person who is not so extraverted and dominant does not have frequent and intense experiences of self-focused emotions. He is also likely to refrain from displaying these emotions in public. Instead, he prefers to conduct himself in a reserved and detached manner, rather than to give in to these emotions. He does not crave for social stimulation, like the extravert, and avoids acting on the spur of the moment. Unlike the extravert, who is upbeat, active and constantly on the move, the introvert engages in more passive and sedentary activities like reading books; he prefers a well-ordered life to one which is filled with change, chance and risk.

Dominant extraverts are more likely to take root in the liberal individualistic society of the West. In such a society, the person has been socialised from young to behave in a spontaneous and exuberant manner, by asserting himself, as well as differentiating himself from the wider sociocultural environment. In contrast, in the Confucian society of the East, the person has been socialised from young to fit into the social group, and to observe and respect the plethora of social norms and customs in society, which regulate social behaviour, and bring order and harmony.

Several empirical findings concerning the personality attributes of people in Asian and Western cultures support this contention that Westerners are more extraverted and dominant than Asians. For example, one comprehensive review of the empirical research into the Chinese personality has concluded that Chinese people in general are more restrained, cautious, patient and self-contained, and less impulsive, excitable, spontaneous and natural, than Americans. This difference in behaviour has been traced to genetic and cultural differences between the Chinese and Americans.[22] Similarly, another study has found that Chinese students are chiefly distinguished from Americans by their lack of extraversion; they display a low score on all the six facet scales of extraversion, which include warmth, gregariousness, assertiveness, activity, excitement seeking and positive emotion.[23] This difference in extraversion belies a basic difference in approach to reality in the East and West: in the case of the Asian, he shapes his internal needs and desires in order to maximise the goodness of fit with an existing reality (in the form of other people and external circumstances). Psychologists have termed this psychological phenomenon as *secondary control*.[24] In contrast, in the case of the Westerner, he relies on *primary control* to establish a feeling of psychological control, i.e., he attempts to shape an existing reality so that it will fit in with his personal needs and desires. For a look at how cultural artifacts like paintings and poems reflect this basic difference in approach to reality in the East and West, see the boxed article at the end of this chapter.

The Conservative Value System of the Asian versus the Open/Hedonistic Value System of the Westerner

One final difference between the Asian and Westerner is in terms of the personal values which they subscribe to in life. The term "personal value" refers to the belief that people hold about desirable ways of behaving or desirable end-states of life e.g., to be an honest person or to seek happiness. Another way of putting this point is that the personal values which we subscribe to in life have an "oughtness" quality about them, so that obeying them feels right, while disobeying them feels wrong.[25] Personal values function like psychological needs to influence goal-directed behaviour. An important way in which they exert their influence is by way of the positive or negative valences (attraction or aversion) that become attached to objects and events within the person's psychological environment. Following the activation of a particular value, certain objects, actions and outcomes are seen as attractive, or *positively-valenced*, whereas others are seen as aversive, or *negatively-valenced*. For example, a person who values openness and change will see an innovative course of action as attractive, while another person who values order and harmony will regard it as disruptive.

Every society will strive to promote those values which are conducive to its longtime survival. It does so by socialising its members to accept the naturalness, desirability, goodness and correctness of that particular value, so that behaving in accordance with the value will create *positive affect* in the person, while deviating from it will create *negative affect*.[26] Given that there are so many diverse societies with their own unique beliefs and traditions in this world, the inevitable question arises: do people who live in different societies have a common understanding of human values?

Empirical research has given an affirmative answer to this question. That is, people who live in different societies have a common understanding of what a particular value means. There are many values in this world, but they can be organised into ten value types. These ten value types are **power, achievement, hedonism, stimulation, self-direction, universalism, benevolence, tradition, conformity** and **security**. These value types are shown in the *circular structure of values* in the following figure and table. The circular structure of values captures the notion that the personal values which we subscribe to can be compatible or in conflict, de-

The Circular Structure of Values

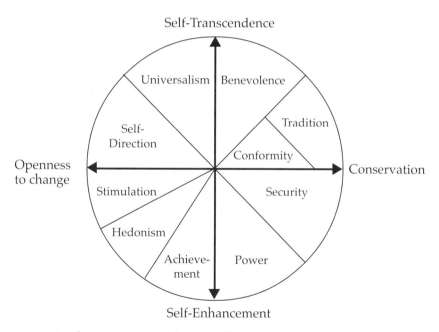

Reprinted with permission from Schwartz (1992), *Universals in the Content and Structure of Values: Theoretical Advances and Empirical Tests in 20 Countries.*

CHAPTER 3

Ten Universal Dimensions of Values

	Definition (example of value)
Power	Social status and prestige, control or dominance over people and resources (*social power, wealth, authority, preserving public image*)
Achievement	Personal success through demonstrating competence according to social standards (*success, ambition, capability, influence*)
Hedonism	Pleasure and sensuous gratification for oneself (*pleasure, enjoying life*)
Stimulation	Excitement, novelty and challenge in life (*varied and exciting life, daring to try new things*)
Self-Direction	Independent thought and action – choosing, creating, exploring (*creativity, freedom, independence, curiosity, choosing own goals*)
Universalism	Understanding, appreciation, tolerance and protection for the welfare of all (*broadmindedness, wisdom, equality, unity with nature, a world of beauty, a world at peace, social justice, protecting the environment*)
Benevolence	Preservation and enhancement of the welfare of people with whom one is in frequent personal contact (*honesty, loyalty, helpfulness, forgiveness, responsibility*)
Tradition	Respect, commitment and acceptance of the customs and ideas that traditional culture or religion provides the self (*respect for tradition, humility, accepting one's portion in life, devotion, moderation*)
Conformity	Restraint of actions, inclinations and impulses likely to upset or harm others and violate social expectations or norms (*self-discipline, obedience, politeness, honouring of parents and elders*)
Security	Safety, harmony and stability of society, of relationships, and of self (*family security, national security, reciprocation of favours, social order, cleanliness*).

Reprinted with permission from Schwartz (1992), *Universals in the Content and Structure of Values: Theoretical Advances and Empirical Tests in 20 Countries.*

pending on how closely aligned they are. Those values that are located next to each other in the circle will be compatible e.g., conformity, tradition and security values. Those values that are located on opposite ends of the circle will be in conflict with each other e.g., self-direction and security values. In turn, these ten value types are grouped into four different clusters, according to the similarity in content of the values. These four clusters are **self-transcendence, self-enhancement, conservation** and **openness to change**.[27]

Although empirical research has shown that people who live in different societies have a common understanding of what a particular value means, this does not imply that they subscribe to the same values. Instead, the values which a person subscribes to will depend on the society that he or she grows up in. Hence, in the liberal individualistic society of the West, open values which emphasise change and the freedom to choose one's direction in life will serve as channels of behaviour for the Westerner. Hedonistic values which focus on the satisfaction of personal needs and desires will also be emphasised. In contrast, in the Confucian society of the East, conservative values which emphasise the importance of tradition, conformity and security will serve as the corresponding channel of behaviour for the Asian.[28]

Chapter Summary

In this chapter, I explored the psychological make-up of the Asian and Westerner. Asians tend to see themselves as being a part of the social group, while Westerners tend to see themselves as being separate and independent persons. Because of this difference in self-construal, Westerners are more inclined to enhance themselves, while Asians are more inclined to criticise themselves. Westerners also tend to be more open to experience and extraverted, compared to Asians. In addition, they differ in their value system as well: Asians subscribe to conservative values, while Westerners subscribe to open and hedonistic values. **It should be stressed that these differences in the psychological make-up of the Asian and Westerner are a matter of degree only.** There are within-culture variations in each of these psychological characteristics of the self. For example, there are Asians who score on the high ends of, say, openness to experience, just as there are Westerners who score on the low ends of, say, independent self-construal. However, the empirical evidence supports this psychological sketch of people in the East and West. With this in mind, we can now proceed to look at why Asians are less creative than Westerners in the subsequent chapters.

The Artist and Poet in the East and West

There is a basic difference in the Eastern and Western approaches to reality. This difference is reflected in the way in which the Asian and Westerner gain a feeling of psychological control vis-à-vis their environment. In the East, the person attempts to attain *secondary* control, i.e., he fits himself into the environment to achieve harmony; while in the West, the person attempts to attain *primary* control, i.e., he asserts himself to master the environment.

This basic difference in approaching reality can be seen in the tradition of painting in the East and West. In the West, the human form is the point of central interest throughout most of its history, from the sculpture of the ancient Greeks to medieval and Renaissance paintings of the Holy Family and classical figures, to the Dutch interiors and portraiture of the 17th and 18th centuries in the French and English schools. Landscape as a major theme emerged comparatively late, in association with the romantic movement. In China, it is otherwise. Although Man is the main focus of Confucian philosophy, Chinese artists from the eighth century or earlier found their inspiration in Nature as a whole. Landscape painting – *shan shui* or "mountain-water" – enables the artist, who has Taoist rather than Confucianist leanings, to feel a sense of communion with Nature, and to know himself as part of an orderly cosmos.[29]

Not surprisingly, the traditional Chinese artist paints in a way which is different from his counterpart in the West. The eye of the Western artist takes in the scene from the level of the average man five or six feet above the ground. In contrast, the Chinese artist works from a raised viewpoint, on a hillside opposite the scene, as it were, so that he is delivered from too much teasing detail in the foreground, and can obtain an overview of the whole. Or it may be said that he has no fixed viewpoint and that his gaze can rove at will, both horizontally and vertically. For what matters to the traditional Chinese artist is not that he should render accurately what is before his eyes at any given moment, but that he should capture the essential aspects of his subject: not Mount Hua as seen from the east on a stormy winter afternoon, but Mount Hua as the typical embodiment of the very idea of a mountain, and as a visible manifestation of the life-giving spirit that animates nature.

This does not mean that the traditional Chinese artist will not make studies of individual rocks and trees on the spot. But it does mean that he is not overly concerned with the particular, or with accidents of time and place, in his finished work. This neglect of the particular is a result of his desire to make a general statement about nature in its eternal aspect in his painting. Such Western techniques as shading, casting shadows and one-point perspective, which fixes the time of day, direction of the sun and position of the viewer, by forcing him to particularise, would defeat his purpose. Instead, the goal of the traditional Chinese artist is to achieve what has been called by Sullivan as "a totally convincing effect", so that the viewer can almost imagine that he is not looking at a picture at all, but wandering in the landscape, which the continuous perspective of the long handscroll makes compellingly real.[30]

In contrast, Western artists are concerned with capturing the particular in a concrete moment of time. In their paintings, the human being, rather than the background, is invariably the focus, because the painting is aimed at revealing the mental state of the subject – joy, reverie, distress, agony, lovesickness, ecstasy, sorrow or wretchedness, at that particular instant of time. The background on the canvas, such as a house, furniture, trees or skies, is important only insofar as it adds realism to the human being who is being portrayed.[31] In modern Cubist paintings like the work of the Spanish artist Pablo Picasso, the human figure is even reduced to basic geometric shapes in a tortured and twisted way, fractionating familiar reality into a thousand pieces e.g., in his world-famous painting entitled *Guernica*, which attempted to capture the horror and anguish of a small Spanish village which is ravaged by all-consuming war.

As another example of how cultural artifacts in the East and West differ in accordance with this basic difference in approaching reality, contrast these two poems from the East and West. The first one is by the 19th-century English poet, Tennyson, while the second one is by the 17th-century Japanese poet, Basho. Each poet is describing a similar experience: his reaction to a flower he sees while taking a walk. Here is what Tennyson wrote:

> *Flower in a crannied wall,*
> *I pluck you out of the crannies,*
> *I hold you here, root and all, in my hand,*
> *Little flower – but if I could understand,*
> *What you are, root and all, and all in all,*
> *I should know what God and man is.*

Translated into English, Basho's *haiku* runs something like this:

> *When I look carefully*
> *I see the nazuna blooming*
> *By the hedge!*

The difference in these two poems is striking. Tennyson reacts to the flower by wanting to dominate it. He plucks it, root and all. And while he ends with an intellectual speculation about the flower's possible function for his attaining insight into the nature of God and man, the flower itself is killed as a result of his interest in it. Tennyson in this particular poem may be compared to that most productive – or destructive? – of species to emerge out of the Enlightenment of the West, namely, the scientist, who seeks truth via the dismembering of life. Basho's reaction to the flower is entirely different. He does not want to pluck it; he does not even touch it. All he does is "look carefully" to "see" it. In this seeing, what Basho would like to do is not just to look at the flower, but to be at one, or to "one" himself with it – and to let it live.[32]

Notes

1. Markus & Kitayama, 1991.
2. Markus, Kitayama & Heiman, 1996.
3. Kitayama, Markus & Lieberman, 1995.
4. Kitayama, Markus, Matsumoto & Norasakkunkit, 1997.
5. Markus, Kitayama & Heiman, 1996.
6. Markus & Kitayama, 1991.
7. Tang, 1992.
8. Kingston, 1977.
9. Tan, 1989.
10. McCrae & Costa, 1995.
11. McCrae & John, 1992.
12. Yik & Bond, 1993; McCrae, Costa & Yik, 1997.
13. McCrae & Costa, 1996.
14. McAdams, 1992.
15. McCrae, 1993–1994; McCrae, 1994; McCrae & Costa, 1997.
16. McCrae, 1987.
17. McCrae, 1996.
18. Harrington, Block & Block, 1987; Dollinger, Leong & Ulicni, 1996.
19. Bornstein, 1992; Ho, 1994.
20. Chan, Gelfand, Triandis & Tzeng, 1996; Pelto, 1968.
21. Markus & Kitayama, 1991.
22. Yang, 1986.
23. McCrae, Costa & Yik, 1997.
24. Weisz, Rothbaum & Blackburn, 1984.
25. Feather, 1992; Schwartz, 1996.
26. D'Andrade, 1984.
27. Schwartz & Bilsky, 1990; Schwartz, 1992 & 1994.
28. Ng, 1999.
29. Morton, 1995.
30. Sullivan, 1979.
31. Hsu, 1955.
32. Fromm, 1976.

Culture, Creativity and Individuated Behaviour

The Basic Conflict Between Creativity and Conformity

So far, we have seen that the creator is a passionate person who has an unconventional view of the world, due to a set of unusual thought processes. By dint of a strong personality, he attempts to shape the rest of society to be in accord with his alternative vision of life, sometimes in the face of strong opposition. The uneasy relationship between the creator and society is reflected in the basic conflict between creativity and conformity with the social group. In *Self-Reliance*, Emerson commented on this antipathy: "The virtue in most regard is conformity. Self-reliance is its aversion. It loves not realities and creators."[1]

Conformity is a change in a person's behaviour or opinions as a result of real or imagined pressure from a person or group of people.[2] It involves a loss of self-reliance, which undermines the person's creativity by reducing his confidence in himself as a person who can exercise his creativity. Instead of marching in accordance to his own internal drumbeat, the conformist engages in a copious imitation of the majority. By engaging in this psychological propping up of the self, the conformist avoids nakedly exposing himself to the challenge of the creative act, for fear of not being able to measure up to it. In such cases, group pressures towards conformity may actually come as a welcome relief to him, serving as a defensive form of "escape from creativity".[3]

The Emotional Side of Creative/Critical Thinking

The antipathy between creativity and conformity has received empirical support from research which indicates that *critical thinking* – which the creator excels in – is not simply an intellectual challenge, but an emotional one as well. Critical thinking is a problem-solving process that is not restricted by habit or convention, but is free to be uncommon to what seems normal or natural.[4] An open attitude is as important to this process as one's intellectual knowledge and skill. This attitude comprises zeal, objectivity, flexibility, decisiveness, intellectual skepticism and open-mindedness, as well as respect for another person's point of view.

Empirical research has indicated that such an open attitude is lacking in conforming and group-dependent individuals, who show a great psychological need for social approval, nurturance, deference, order and control. These individuals typically refrain from any spontaneous and exuberant behaviour which casts attention on themselves. Instead, they place a clamp on what they are thinking and feeling inside. By yielding their personal autonomy to the social group in this way, they gain its approval, as well as preserve its internal unity and harmony. However, conducting themselves in this restrained and somewhat self-deprecating manner will limit their capacity for creative/critical thinking.[5]

This is in marked contrast to the non-conforming and group-independent individuals, who show a psychological need for autonomy, independence and separation from the social group. These individuals typically behave in a spontaneous and exuberant manner, so as to satisfy their personal needs and desires. By behaving in this carefree and self-gratifying manner, they risk the censure of the group, as well as threaten its internal unity and harmony. However, maintaining their personal autonomy from the group enables these individuals to engage in creative/critical thinking.

Creativity As a Form of Individuated Behaviour

Rather than identifying and complying with the social group and wider society, the creator engages in *individuated behaviour*.* Individuated behaviour, in contrast to conforming behaviour, is characterised by its differentiation from other parts of the sociocultural environment e.g., using a new paradigm to understand and perform a task, and taking a stance that is in opposition to the rest of the group.[6] People vary in their tendency to publicly differentiate themselves from others in their social environment. Some people are comfortable with it, and even use it to make a living. For example, the American singer Michael Jackson glides and slides in strange costumes on stage, and appears in public wearing only one glove instead of two.

Other people who are shy and modest will shrink from any individuated behaviour that puts them in the spotlight. For example, the Chinese diaspora has led to the proliferation of many self-made millionaires who prefer to stick to their traditional and spartan forms of living, away from the public eye.[7] I stayed in the house of one of these self-made millionaires for a period of time. He was an elderly Taiwanese businessman with companies in China, Taiwan and Indonesia. In spite of his great wealth, he is a frugal and modest person who dresses simply, drinks plain water and has a simple meal of rice, vegetable and fruit for dinner.

≈≈

* Note that although creativity is by definition a form of individuated behaviour, the reverse is not necessarily true, i.e., not all individuated behaviour is creative. The British phenomenon of streaking falls into this category. These British streakers, who run in the buff across sporting fields, grab the attention of both crowds and competitors with their antics. In one case at Wimbledon, the Russian tennis player Anna Kournikova giggled bashfully into her towel as a naked man danced in front of her. Painted on his gyrating body were the words "the balls should bounce" – an allusion to a bra advertisement in which Anna had said, "Only the balls should bounce." The authorities have threatened these streakers with instant arrest without success. But they have managed to come up with a profile of the British streaker. First, he likes a drink or two for Dutch courage before going into action. Second, he does not believe in doing his deed by halves, like running in his G-string or socks. However, he believes in good "form", i.e., hiding his dangling modesty with a foreign object, like a winner's trophy. In one classic photo of streaking, a bearded man was seen being led off the field by an English bobby, who used his famous plastic helmet to hide the offender's "little brother" (as this hairy organ is called in the East). Finally, by their perseverance at their craft, these streakers have defied the pundits' prediction that the fad would die out. This is especially so in the case of Roberts, a 35-year-old father of three, who has more than 150 naked runs to his credit, and who was dubbed "Great British Streaker" by the press. Perhaps Roberts' most memorable performance was his impromptu act on the green at the recent Golf Open. Painted on his back was an arrow pointing to his posterior bearing the words "19th hole". For this hilarious antic, Roberts was prevented from catching a plane to attend the handover ceremony of Hong Kong to China. In retaliation, he has threatened to streak at the next US Superbowl (*The Straits Times*, August 9, 2000).

≈≈

According to Brewer, individual differences in the tendency to engage in creative and individuated behaviour derive from a fundamental tension between the human need for validation and similarity with the social group and wider society on the one hand, and a countervailing need for uniqueness and differentiation from the social group and wider society on the other. These psychological needs for similarity with and differentiation from the group and society are shaped by the culture which the person has grown up in.[8]

In the loosely-organised, liberal and individualistic culture of the West, the person is socialised from young to stand apart from the rest of the social group and society, by asserting his uniqueness, and behaving in a spontaneous and exuberant manner. As a result of living in this type of culture, the psychological make-up of the Westerner assumes a certain form, i.e., he is extraverted and dominant, construes himself in an independent manner, and possesses a hedonistic set of personal values (for a review of these psychological constructs, see Chapter Three). Because of this psychological make-up, the Westerner has the tendency to engage in creative and individuated behaviour. This type of behaviour will meet his psychological needs for uniqueness and differentiation from the social group and society.[9] This is shown in the figure below, while the boxed article which follows looks at the creative flair of Richard Branson, the head of the Virgin business empire as well as the most famous entrepreneur in Britain.

A Cultural Model of Creative and Individuated Behaviour

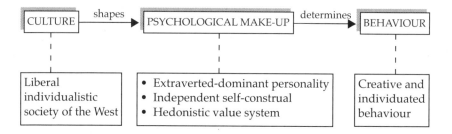

How a Billionaire Businessman Lost His Virginity in Britain

An example of a Westerner who behaves in a creative and individuated way is the British entrepreneur and bearded billionaire Richard Branson. In my opinion, he is the creative businessman par excellence, with a flair for individuated and outrageous behaviour that feeds his insatiable appetite for publicity. His headmaster in the public school he attended had once predicted that he would either end up in prison or become a very rich and famous man. Richard Branson chose the second option, and in his autobiography *Losing My Virginity*, he tells readers about his rise to fame and fortune.[10]

It began with a cut-price mail-order record publishing business named Virgin because, according to Branson, he was a complete virgin in business. His record business became successful with several hits. However, impatient for further success, he sold it off for £700 million as a springboard for establishing Virgin Atlantic, a new airline operator that shook up the cosy world of less-than-competitive national carriers. Starting with just one plane and one route – London to Newark, New Jersey – Virgin Atlantic took off quickly. It now has 29 airplanes and an ever-expanding departure board of destinations. So successful was Virgin Atlantic that British Airways (BA), another airline operator in the United Kingdom, became concerned. The competitive relationship between the two airline operators took a turn for the worse, with Virgin accusing BA of dirty commercial tricks, and BA making some offensive remarks about Virgin's safety as an airliner. This led Branson to mount the biggest uncontested libel action in British legal history. The bearded buccaneer – as the press dubbed him – agreed to the terms of £500,000 in damages for himself and £110,000 for his airline. Among the messages of congratulations was one from the late Princess of Wales: "Dear Richard, Hooray! Love, Diana."

The sky's the limit

While his most successful business is Virgin Atlantic, Branson also owns a railway franchise and a TV station in Mexico, as well as businesses in canned cola, vodka, hotels, radio, computer games and wedding wear. This billionaire businessman is not afraid of standing conventional business models on their heads. His maverick and nonconformist attitude is seen in his chucking aside of the standard suit-and-tie uniform of the working world, in favour of more exotic wear, all for the cause of publicising his numerous ventures. For example, to market his vodka venture, he appeared as a Russian dancer; to publicise his wedding-wear business, he shaved off his beard and dressed up as a bride. For the launch of *Losing My Virginity*, Branson took off everything, with only a copy of his book as a fig leaf to protect his "little brother" from the eyes of the camera. Branson's marketing stunts have captured the attention of the major presses in the world and made him the best-known tycoon in Britain.

In addition to these regular exposures to the media, Branson also has an indefatigable appetite for adventure, escaping many times from the jaws of death in the process. For example, he has tried out a motorised flying tricycle, and landed safely, though when its inventor tried it the next day, it crash-landed and killed him. Branson has also braved the altitudes in his bid to be the first man to fly non-stop around the world in a hot-air balloon. This project has seen several mishaps. For example, at one time the balloon, which was resting on a stretch of Arabian desert, took off before Branson could get on it, due to the strong desert winds. At another time, it drifted illegally into the airspace of Communist China, and then sank down to the bottom of the Pacific Ocean.

It also appears that Branson is a good loser: when two balloonists from a rival team thwarted his ambition to be the first person to circle the globe, a reporter asked him how he felt about it. Instead of feeling peeved because he had been defeated by his balloonist rivals, he congratulated them heartily. He even said that he was looking forward to flying to Switzerland to join in their celebration of victory. In the interview, Branson reflected philosophically that as an entrepreneur, he had "tried lots of things, and some we achieve and some we don't … And if somebody else beats us at something, I think we're reasonably experienced at picking ourselves up and moving on."

Branson told the reporter that his next ambition was to sponsor a round-the-world balloon race. "A whole new sport can be born," he told Reuters. "Such a race would captivate the world." He was prepared to utilise his Virgin Group to sponsor the central costs of the race, including the prize money. Branson suggested that this ballooning race could be held once every two or three years, and predicted that it would attract up to 30 crews. In addition, he also expressed hopes that this global race would eventually become an Olympic sport, with Virgin paying towards the rescue costs of balloonists who experienced troubles during their arduous journey across the sky.

If these hopes and ambitions eventually materialise, it will be a testimony to our world of how this bearded buccaneer creatively transforms a personal defeat into an Olympic challenge that brings the world closer together. In view of his vast and varied contributions to the British business fraternity, Richard Branson was recently knighted by Queen Elizabeth, earning him the name of Sir Virgin King.[11]

The Lack of Creativity in Asian Society

One would be hard-pressed to find a successful Asian businessman with the histronic, flashy and individuated style of Richard Branson. This is because in the tightly-organised and collectivistic societies of the East, the person has been socialised from young to fit into the social group and society. As a result, he is psychologically dependent on the group, and has the tendency to conform to what it says and does. Behaving in this manner will enable the Asian to meet his psychological need for validation and similarity with others, rather than uniqueness and differentiation from them.[12] The Asian possesses a psychological make-up which facilitates this form of conforming and uncreative behaviour: he is constrained and submissive, construes himself in an interdependent manner, and subscribes to a conservative set of personal values which emphasise tradition, conformity and security. This connection between Confucian culture, Asian self and uncreative and conforming behaviour is shown in the figure on the next page.

A Cultural Model of Uncreative and Conforming Behaviour

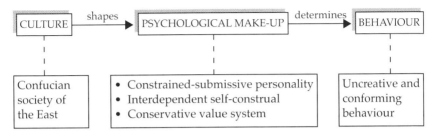

The Case of the Japanese

The lack of creative flair is evident in Asian society: in contrast with the Americans, the Japanese have made relatively fewer contributions to basic science, and only a few Japanese have been singled out for Nobel Prizes, in spite of its technologically-advanced society and the high education level of its people. In *The Who's Who of Nobel Prize Winners 1901–1995*, there were only eight entries in the Japanese category, while there were over 200 entries in the American category.[13] One of the Japanese Nobel laureates, Leo Esaki, argued that people in his country lack the American penchant for original creations and inventions, because they fear the loss of the psychological security that comes from standing apart from the group to challenge the unknown.[14]

This argument is supported by cross-cultural research which indicates that among the countries in the world, the Japanese score highest in *uncertainty avoidance*.[15] A person who avoids uncertainty attempts to steer away from the vagaries and ambiguities in life. One way of doing this is to seek psychological refuge in the social groups in society. This psychological identification of the Japanese with his ingroup is scrutinised by Chie Nakane, a Japanese anthropologist, in her book entitled *Japanese Society*.[16] In this classic work, Nakane observes that different individuals can be categorised into certain social groups in terms of their common *attribute* e.g., X and Y are academic scholars; or in terms of the mutual *frame* which they occupy e.g., X and Y lecture in a certain university. An attribute is formal and universal: as long as you possess a certain qualification, you are automatically a member of the social category in question. On the other hand, a frame is personal and particular: you feel a deep sense of belonging to the social institution in which you work. According to Nakane, the Japanese have a strong tendency to identify themselves on the basis of frame rather than attribute, in comparison with individuals from other societies, i.e., in Japan, whether a person possesses a PhD is less important than which university he obtains his PhD from. As a result of this strong group identification, the Japanese will strive to fit in with the social group, rather than stand out as an individual, i.e., he will engage in uncreative and conforming behaviour, rather than creative and individuated behaviour.

In a book entitled *Inside the* Kaisha: *Demystifying Japanese Business Behaviour*, Noboru Yoshimura (a *kaisha* insider) and Philip Anderson (an American business professor) provided another reason to explain why the Japanese avoid creative and individuated behaviour: the fear of social embarrassment.[17] Their basic argument can be summarised as follows. In Japan, to behave in the correct way in a certain situation is very important. Correct behaviour is learned by emulating a model. Modelling starts in early childhood, as young Japanese learn appropriate behaviour through imitating their parents. Once they enter school, teachers become models for correct conduct. As they enter the workplace, a junior Japanese *kohai* (salaryman) will model his behaviour on his *sempai* (mentor/senior), learning to do things in the context of the particular *kaisha* (company). To the average Japanese, these models are very important because they provide the predictability and stability that he needs to avoid embarrassing himself in a social situation. Unlike in the West, in Japan, people who behave in socially unacceptable ways and bring embarrassment to themselves are considered to be poorly brought up or educated.

The drive to avoid embarrassment can seriously hamstring Japanese firms. In one particular case recounted in *Inside the* Kaisha, a group of middle managers gave up their pursuit of a creative idea which would have reaped untold benefits for the firm if it had been carried out. And the reason? None of them could be 100 percent sure the plan would be approved by the company's board of directors. If it were not approved, everyone involved in the project would be extremely embarrassed. So the idea was never brought up to the board, and the project died before it was born. Here is Yoshimura and Anderson's analysis of this case: "The middle managers believed their idea would have a dramatic impact on the company. Their proposal to bring the plan before the board was politically astute; it would have created a context in which the strategy almost certainly would have been approved. Yet even the *threat* of social embarrassment was impossible to overcome. The managers simply had no model to follow telling them how to promote such a new idea. Western managers might say, 'Let's give it a shot', but this kind of thinking is uncommon among salarymen, because they fear failure and because their companies are not used to and don't appreciate unexpected behaviour."

I have argued that in general, the Japanese are not creative. Some may beg to differ, pointing to the likes of competitive Japanese companies like Toyota, Sony and Sega Toys, household names in the automobile, electronic appliances and electronic games industries which are giving their Western counterparts a run for their money with their clever inventions (e.g., Sega Toys came up with popular gadgets like Poo-Chi and Aibo, two robotic pet dogs which can respond to light, touch and sound). Although it cannot be denied that the Japanese have scored notable triumphs in industry, which are acknowledged by the rest of the world, these have come about *not* via independent scientific discoveries and technological breakthroughs, but rather through efficient borrowing or ingenious adaptations of the foreign technology of the West.[18] This ability of the Japanese to creatively synthesise existing technologies into a new hybrid is facilitated by the Japanese tendency to work and learn in a group: in the *kaisha*, members of a quality control circle (QCC) spend many hours together discussing how they can improve a certain product, which is known as *kaizen*, or continuous improvement. A typical Japanese innovation in such a QCC is a coffeemaker with a grinder and a timer built in. Yoshimura and Anderson put it in this way: "Americans start with a big picture and craft it according to the needs of customers. Japanese start with pieces and add something new according to the needs of customers."

Evidence for this difference in innovative style can be seen in studies comparing American and Japanese research and development (R&D) strategies. These studies found that Japanese *kaishas* are more likely than their American counterparts to invest in applied versus basic research; preexisting products and technologies developed by other firms versus new technologies; and imitation versus first-mover innovation. Commenting on these findings, Yoshimura and Anderson observed that Japanese firms have many engineers, and Japanese business models suggest that they must be kept busy. This leads to the situation where a reflective observer starts to question whether it is technical employment which drives research investment or the other way round (as the case should be). As an American executive employed by the US-based research subsidiary of a Japanese firm commented: "On a practical basis, new distinct topics get funding, and the R&D organisation will tend to introduce many topics in deference to many middle managers supporting many engineers who are commanded to generate 'new ideas'. Applied research is about researchers learning a new topic, but not researching it in great depth or in any large numbers. In middle-down management and in the presence of nebulous top-down direction, the R&D budgeting process tends to produce breadth, but not depth."[19]

The Global Entrepreneurship Monitor (GEM) also reinforced this image of the Japanese as "reluctant innovators"; ten countries were surveyed in this study by the London Business School and US-based Babson College, including America and Japan.[20] Interviews were conducted with 10,000 adults in these countries; in addition, data from international organisations such as the World Bank were also included. The researchers found that level of entrepreneurship, which accounted for a third of the difference in a country's economic growth, varied sharply between these ten countries, from one in 12 American respondents who affirmed that they had tried to set up new firms, to less than one in 50 Japanese respondents who made a similar affirmation. In addition, the researchers also noted that Japan lacked many of the qualities which were vital to encouraging entrepreneurship, including public respect for this type of business e.g., just 8 percent of Japanese respondents said they regarded this type of economic activity highly, in comparison to 80 percent of American respondents, who held entrepreneurship in high regard. The study concluded that promoting entrepreneurship and enhancing the entrepreneurial dynamism of a country should be an integral element of any government's commitment to boosting economic well-being. With the burst of the Japanese bubble economy and the advent of a new global economy based on Information Technology, Japanese firms are realising that they have to change their business practices and institutions in order to survive in the competitive marketplace. In this major reinvention of the Japanese corporation, Sony is the trendsetter in abandoning traditional Japanese practices to be an entrepreneurial firm: it recruits staff on the strength of their talents and not their alma mater, and it rewards them on the basis of their contribution, not their seniority. It has also shifted its focus from hardware to software, where it believes its future lies. This can be seen most clearly in its acquisition of Columbia Pictures, a major Hollywood studio.

The Case of the Chinese

The lack of creative flair is also evident among the Chinese people. For example, in *The Who's Who of Nobel Prize Winners 1901–1995*, there were only three entries under the Chinese category, and all three scientists had made their scientific contributions while they worked and resided in the West. In studies of creativity among ordinary people, one piece of research found that American students scored higher in creative fluency than Chinese students in Hong Kong.[21] Another study found that Chinese respondents performed better in convergent thinking tasks, compared to American respondents, who did better in divergent thinking tasks.[22] A third study, which investigated developmental aspects of ideational fluency, flexibility and originality (three measures of creative thinking) across five age groups (ranging from nine to 60 years) in two cultures, found that the American scores were uniformly higher than the Chinese scores.[23] A psychologist on Chinese cognition has attributed this pattern of finding to the standard of social regulation in the East, which is so acute and pervasive that it may actually constrain the verbal and ideational fluency of the individual.[24] Another psychologist has suggested that the emphasis of the Chinese on respecting and obeying their superiors, be they parents, employers or government officials, uses up cognitive capacity which may otherwise be devoted to a creative task, and this may be a reason why Chinese norms for some creativity tasks fall below American norms.[25]

This assertion is supported by a lot of empirical research and anecdotal observations. For example, in one particular study, Hong Kong respondents were compared with French and American respondents in their tendency to defer without question to conventional authority, and to accept conventional norms and values unthinkingly. The Hong Kong respondents were found to have a stronger tendency to defer to authority, in comparison with the French and Americans.[26]

This tendency to defer to political authority is especially evident in Singapore. Four decades of authoritarian government under the People's Action Party (PAP), as well as continual reminders by the Confucian ministers in this hierarchically-run city-state that they should not be disrespectful to their elders have made university students here so politically apathetic that Mr Goh Chok Tong, the Prime Minister of Singapore as well as the leader of the PAP, actually had to suggest to them in a recent campus talk that they might want to consider form-

I don't want to get involved!

ing political associations affiliated with political parties to generate more interest in political issues on campus.[27] In contrast, in response to the newly-elected government of John Howard announcing that the education budget for tertiary students would be cut, the students in the Australian university where I studied unfolded a defiant banner which declared publicly that it was John Howard's throat that should be cut!

This submissive and deferential attitude of the Chinese to authority is a product of Confucian ideology. Or as Mao Zedong put it once to the American journalist Edgar Snow, it was hard for his people to overcome the habits of more than 2,000 years of emperor-worshipping tradition. Support for this assertion – that Confucian socialisation is positively linked with a deferential and uncreative attitude – comes from one particular line of research, which shows that the Chinese way of raising a child, which emphasises the importance of filial piety and fitting in with the group, may encourage the development of *cognitive conservatism*, a constellation of attributes which leads the person to adopt a passive, uncritical and uncreative orientation to learning and to hold fatalistic, superstitious and stereotypical beliefs; as well as to be authoritarian, dogmatic and conformist. In one study, Boey administered a set of psychological tests measuring rigidity and cognitive complexity to university students in Hong Kong. He found that the student's father's attitude to filial piety was positively correlated with the child's scores on tests of rigidity, and both the father's and mother's attitudes to filial piety were negatively correlated with the child's scores on cognitive complexity.[28]

This line of research associating the child-rearing philosophy and practices in a Confucian-inspired society with rigid and closed-minded thinking reminds me of the stinging criticisms launched by the intellectual vanguards of the May Fourth Movement in Chinese history. These intellectuals, led by the passionate writer Lu Xun, denounced the outmoded ideology of Confucianism, which confined every living Chinese to rigid family and clan roles, creating a stagnant and backward society of the past which could not keep up with the changing times of the emerging world order, and which simultaneously allowed foreign aggressors to cut up the country like a piece of raw meat. Lu Xun denounced the old China as a culture of people eaters, in which "beggars eat scraps by the roadside, half-starved children are sold for eight coppers a pound, and in the countryside men are starving to death. Our vaunted Chinese civilisation is only a feast for the rich and mighty."[29] He was especially vitriolic in his attack on the cruel and archaic conventions of the China that he experienced first-hand e.g., in its custom of foot-binding, an excruciatingly painful ordeal in which "the foot became so compressed that the woman usually hobbled about with difficulty or had to lean on a wall, cane or another person for support. One result of this virtual crippling … was to confine women to the boudoir. They were thus physically prevented from moving about freely and unchaperoned and were rendered immune from the social disease of conjugal infidelity …"[30]

Asians *Can* Be Creative

Although I have highlighted the lack of creative flair among Asian people vis-à-vis their Western counterparts, three caveats are in order. Let me start with the easiest caveat: Asians are *more* creative than Westerners in terms of their culinary skills. I arrived at this conclusion while enjoying reunion dinner with my relatives during the recent Chinese New Year, and saw the sumptuous spread of homemade delicacies on the dinner table. They included chicken curry, fried meat rolls, steamed fish, Hokkien noodles, lean meat stewed in black sauce, flour-coated shrimp, stir-fried vegetables and assorted soups. Admittedly, this assertion of mine – that Asians are *more* creative than Westerners in terms of their culinary skills – is quite subjective, and will depend to a large extent on the taste buds of the individual. But if the reader would care to catch the opening scene in the delectable Taiwanese movie *Eat, Drink, Men, Women*, and observe the master chef making dinner for his three daughters; or if the reader were to take a look at the food that the average Asian can find at the hawker centre (an endless assortment of cooked food like steamed buns, fried rice, chicken rice, duck rice, fish-ball noodles, wanton noodles), and compare this with the food that the average Westerner can find in the fast-food restaurant (variations of burgers and fries), he might conclude that Asians are indeed more creative than Westerners in terms of their culinary skills.

The second caveat is this: the Asian mind can be very creative indeed, if it is freed from the conformist and sycophantic ideology of Confucianism. Nothing illustrates this point better than the Taoist impulse of the Asian mind, which revels in the dynamic flux of life in the Tao. Many Asians in the past (including Confucian scholars) have been seized by this expansive, holistic impulse of the Tao, and they have left their artistic mark on our world. These include but are not limited to the following: the *shan shui* (mountain-water) or landscape paintings of those celebrated Chinese artists living during the Tang and Sung dynasties, who present rustic scenes to the viewer on a long silk scroll, which are serene yet evocative of the Tao (examples are Li Cheng's "Buddhist Temple in the Hills After Rain" and Xu Daoning's "Fishing in a Mountain Stream"). The philosophical musings of Chuang Tzu ("Am I a person dreaming that I'm a butterfly, or am I a butterfly dreaming that I'm a person?") permit flights of fancies from our humdrum and socially-constrained world to the bosom of the Tao. The well-loved novel of the Chinese people, *Xi You Ji* or *Journey to the West*, was written by a Confucian scholar infused with the irreverent spirit of Taoism. According to Dennis Bloodworth, "without resorting to the acid satire of a Voltaire, this delightful Taoist-Buddhist fable takes a light-hearted and entertaining dig at the highbrow side of Confucian-inspired living, with its dreary rules and regulations, its wanton hypocrisy and pious humbug, its sycophantic attitude towards authority".[31] Finally, the Taoist poet Tao Chien's ode to the Tao is, in my opinion, without equal, as the reader can judge for himself by reading the following poem, which evokes the mystique of Nature in simple yet elegant verse:

> *I built my hut in a zone of human habitation*
> *Yet round me there sound no noise of horse and carriage*
> *Would you know how this is possible?*
> *A heart that is distant creates a wilderness round it*
> *I pluck chrysanthemums under the eastern hedge*
> *Then gaze long at the distant summer hills*
> *The mountain air is fresh at dusk of day*
> *The flying birds two by two return*
> *In all these things there is a deep meaning*
> *Yet when I would express it*
> *Words suddenly fail me*[32]

The West's Debt to the East

Finally, it should be pointed out that one of the greatest untold secrets of history is that the "modern world" which we live in, filled with Western inventions like the telephone, the desktop computer, the automobile and the airplane, is actually a unique synthesis of Asian and Western ingredients. In fact, according to Temple, author of *The Genius of China: 3,000 Years of Science, Discovery and Invention*, possibly more than half of the basic inventions and discoveries upon which the modern world rests, come from China.[33] Yet ironically, few people know this, especially the Chinese themselves, who would be surprised indeed to learn that *modern* agriculture, *modern* shipping, the *modern* oil industry, *modern* astronomical observations, *modern* music, decimal mathematics, paper money, umbrellas, fishing reels, wheelbarrows, multistage rockets, guns, underwater mines, poison gas, parachutes, hot-air balloons, manned flight, brandy, whisky, the game of chess, printing, and even the essential design of the steam engine, all came from China!

The West's debt to the East is great indeed: without the importation from China of nautical and navigational improvements such as ships' rudders, the compass and multiple masts, the great European voyages of discovery could never have been undertaken; Columbus would not have sailed to America, and Europeans would never have established colonial empires. Without the importation from China of the stirrup which enabled the rider to stay on horseback, the armoured knights of medieval Europe would never have ridden on their white horses to rescue damsels in distress, and there would not have been an Age of Chivalry, as well as the irresistible notion of True Love in our modern world.* Without the importation from China of guns and gunpowder, these European knights would not have been knocked from their horses by bullets which pierced their metallic armour, bringing the Age of Chivalry to an end. Finally, without the importation from China of paper and printing, Europe would have continued for much longer to copy books by hand, literacy would not have become so widespread, and democratic revolutions would not have spread like wild fire across Europe and America. Johann Gutenberg did not invent movable type. It was invented in China. William Harvey did not discover the circulation of blood in the body. It was discovered – or rather, always assumed – in China. And Isaac Newton was not the first to discover his First Law of Motion. It was discovered in China.

Science and Civilisation In China

According to Temple, the discovery of Chinese inventiveness is the result of a series of incidents in the life of the distinguished scholar Dr Joseph Needham. In 1937, Needham, at 37, was one of the youngest Fellows of the Royal Society and a biochemist of considerable distinction at Cambridge. He had already published many books, including one on the de-

≈≈

* Many of us believe that True Love exists, and it consists of these components. First, True Love requires the free choice of the individual; it cannot flourish in the context of submission to family, social or religious authority. Second, True Love is based on mutual admiration and regard between a matching couple. Finally, True Love is not an idle diversion in life; instead, it is the *raison d'etre*. This irresistible notion of True Love has enabled many Hollywood directors to make a lot of money from romantic movies e.g., James Cameron's *Titanic*. However, True Love does not exist. Instead, it is socially constructed. It has its origin in the medieval doctrine of courtly love, which was developed by the aristocratic ladies of southern France in the 11th century. According to the historian Anthony Esler, medieval knights, who were supposed to obey the code of chivalry, did not hesitate to beat their wives, and often saved their sexual passion for mistresses and prostitutes (much like the rich and famous in our modern society). Some noblewomen responded to this state of affairs by broadening the concept of chivalry to incorporate the notions of courtesy and tenderness to the fairer sex. According to this medieval doctrine of courtly love, the perfect knight must be a faithful lover who displays courtesy, dresses elegantly, talks wittily and washes more often! From this doctrine originates the irresistible notion of True Love in our modern world. What differs in our case is that the "modern knight" should have a good and secure job; he should also make his declaration of love with a bouquet of red roses and a diamond-studded ring. Readers can get carried away when they imagine such a strange scene in our modern world. To bring them back to reality, i.e., to make them realise that True Love is a social construction which does *not* have to be the case, consider this account of a "primitive" society, which finds our notion of True Love to be rather strange: "By and large, the clanship structure and social life of most 'primitive' societies provide wholesome intimacy … most 'primitive' peoples fail to see any great difference between individuals, and hence do not become involved in unique connections in the Western fashion … trained observers have commented on the ease of their detachment from love objects, and their candid belief in the interchangeability of loves. Dr Audrey Richards, an anthropologist who lived among the Bemba of Northern Rhodesia in the 1930s, once related to a group of them an English folk-fable about a young prince who climbed glass mountains, crossed chasms, and fought dragons, all to obtain the hand of a maiden he loved. The Bemba were plainly bewildered, but remained silent. Finally, an old chief spoke up, voicing the feelings of all present in the simplest of questions: Why not take another girl?" (Morton M. Hunt, quoted in Branden, 1980).

≈≈

finitive history of embryology. One day he met and befriended some Chinese students. One of them was a young woman from Nanking whose father had passed on to her his unusually profound knowledge of the history of Chinese science. Needham began to hear tales of how the Chinese had been the true discoverers and inventors of this and that important thing, and at first he could not believe it. But as he investigated further, evidence began to come to light from Chinese texts, hastily translated by his new friends for his benefit. Needham became obsessed with this subject, as he freely admitted. Not knowing a word of Chinese, he set about learning the language. In 1942, he was sent to China for several years as Scientific Counsellor to the British Embassy in Chungking. He was able to travel all over China, learn the language thoroughly, meet men of science everywhere he went, and accumulate vast quantities of priceless ancient Chinese books on science. These were flown back to Britain by the Royal Air Force and today form the basis of the finest library, outside China, on the history of Chinese science, technology and medicine, at the Needham Research Institute in Cambridge.

In July 1946, Needham stated in a lecture to the China Society in London, "I personally believe that all Westerners, all people belonging to the Euro-American civilisation, are subconsciously inclined to congratulate themselves, feeling with some satisfaction that, after all, it was Europe and its extension into the Americas which developed modern science and technology. In the same way, I think that all my Asian friends are subconsciously inclined to a certain anxiety about this matter, because their civilisation did not, in fact, develop modern science and technology … What is really very badly needed is a proper book on the history of science and technology in China, especially with reference to the social and economic background of Chinese life. Such a book would be by no means academic, but would have a wide bearing on the general history of thought and ideas." When he returned to Cambridge, Needham did exactly as he said, i.e., he started to write about the history of science and technology in China. The result was the monumental set of books entitled *Science and Civilisation in China*.

At this stage, a question may arise in the reader's mind: if the Chinese were so advanced in antiquity and in the Middle Ages, how was it that the Scientific Revolution, the coming of modern science into the world, happened in Europe, and not in China? This was precisely the question which presented itself forcefully to Dr Needham when he first met the Chinese scientists who came to Cambridge in 1937. According to Dr Needham, distinctively modern science, which was a mathematisation of hypotheses about nature combined with relentless experimentation, is a phenomenon with multiple and overlapping causes, which included the Protestant Revolution, as well as the rise of entrepreneurial capitalism. As a result, how one looks at the primary causative factor depends on one's background.

For example, if one were a theologian, he would probably think that the liberation of the individual from the clutches of the Catholic Church during the Protestant Reformation was responsible for the Scientific Revolution in the West. If one were a philosopher, he would probably think that it was the analytical thinking as favoured by the Western mind, rather than the holistic thinking as favoured by the Chinese mind, which was responsible for the growth of modern science in Europe. Finally, if one were a Marxist, he would probably think that the economic and social changes in the European world of the 17th to 19th centuries bore the main responsibility. In Dr Needham's own opinion, the bureaucratic organisation of China in its earlier stages helped science to grow. However, as the country gradually turned inward during the Ming and Qing dynasties, due to the sheer conservatism of the Confucian bureaucracy, which was against the creation of a bright future based upon overseas expansion and commerce, but was instead concerned with preserving and recapturing the ancient and glorious past, the further development of science and technology in China was curtailed.[34]

Chapter Summary

In this chapter, I argued that creativity is a form of individuated behaviour which is influenced by culture. I began by making two related observations: first, there is a basic conflict between conformity and creativity; second, there is an emotional side to creative/critical thinking, i.e., the creative/critical thinker must be independent and self-reliant, instead of being psychologically dependent on the group. Having made these observations, I then argued that creativity is a form of individuated behaviour (although I was also careful to note that the reverse is not necessarily true, i.e., not all individuated behaviour is creative). At this juncture, I presented a model of creative and individuated behaviour which is influenced by culture. This model makes the assertion that Westerners are more likely to engage in this type of behaviour. In comparison, Asians like the Japanese and Chinese are more likely to engage in behaviour which is uncreative and conforming. Even so, I argued that Asians *can* be creative. Their creativity is displayed in their culinary skills, as well as in their painting, poetry and literature. In addition, I pointed out that the West owes the East a great debt in the West's march towards modern science and technology. I also made the observation that when freed from the sycophantic ideology of Confucianism, the Asian mind can be very creative indeed. This point is taken up in the following boxed article, which makes the interesting assertion that in order to be creative, we should all be butterflies dreaming that we are human beings.

A Taoist Critique of Confucianism, or Why We Should All Be Butterflies Dreaming That We Are Human Beings

The founder of Taoism is the mystical figure of Lao Tzu (Old Master). According to tradition, he was an older contemporary of Confucius, who instructed the latter for a brief period of time. Legend would have it – and many Chinese paintings like to depict it – that before this quasi-legendary founder of Taoism and teacher of Confucius disappeared into the misty mountain ranges, never to be seen or heard of by anyone again, he reluctantly agreed to the request of a philosophic and persuasive guard of the Hankukuan Pass to deposit his wisdom for our world. This came in the succinct form of some 5,000 Chinese characters, as the mystic and obscure *Tao Te Ching*, which is described by Lin Yu Tang as a "concentrated essence of old roguish wisdom", and which is reputed to have been translated into more languages than any other book, except the Holy Bible.[35]

More in accordance with historical fact, the Taoist school of thought originated in the same crucible of social upheaval that gave birth to Confucianism, i.e., the declining years of the Chou Dynasty (1027–221 BC). During this period of the Warring Kingdoms (403–221 BC), various schools of thought competed for the people's attention. Confucianism, with its doctrine of propriety and social status, and its emphasis on human culture and restraint, is one such school of thought, and represents the classical strand in Chinese philosophy. In contrast, another school of thought, Taoism, with its emphasis on going back to nature, and its disavowal of human restraint and culture, represents the romantic strand in Chinese philosophy.[36]

This tension between Confucianism and Taoism can be seen in the manner in which they regard the supernatural: Confucianism offers no Heaven and Hell for its adherents, nor any formula for immortality of the soul. In the *Analects*, the disciples of Confucius noted that the Master seldom talked about what would happen when a person died. When he was asked this question, his famous reply was: "When I do not understand life, how can I understand death?" Hence, as Lin Yu Tang pointed out, although Confucianism may have solved the problems of human nature and social order, it has left out of consideration the meaning of life and death, as well as the riddle of the supernatural. This left a large gap in its philosophy. It is here that Taoism steps in to capture the popular imagination via its provision of a world of unknowables, which Confucian good sense has banished from its province of ideas (Confucius and his disciples encouraged people to revere the dead, but not to engage in any metaphysical speculation about their ontological status).

Starting out with the dualistic notion of *yin* and *yang*, already current in the period of the Warring Kingdoms, Taoism soon added to its territory the fairies of the ancient Shantang barbarians, who dreamed of a fairyland out on the high seas, to which place the first emperor of China, Shi Huang Ti, actually started out with 500 boys and virgins to seek his immortality. The Taoist hold on the imagination – especially when fertilised by Buddhist philosophy, which seeped into the Celestial Kingdom via Arab traders on caravans plying the Silk Road in the early years of the Christian era – became irresistible. A prime example is *Xi You Ji* or *Journey to the West*, a fantastic novel written in the 16th century, which, unlike John Bunyan's fictional account of a spiritual journey in *Pilgrim's Progress*, is based on the real-life experience of Hsuan Tsang, the Chinese monk who made a holy pilgrimage to India in AD 629.

In this well-loved fable of the Chinese people, the reader comes across many strange and wacky characters. The most memorable of them all must be Shi Mo Kong, the mischievous Monkey God who had such magical powers as the ability to jump 108,000 *li* in one bound (a *li* is one-third of a mile), as well as the capacity to summon aid when in a tight spot by plucking out one of his own hairs, chewing it up, and spitting out the pieces, which immediately turned into an army of monkeys. This celestial rebel in an absurdly bureaucratic Heaven, which was a mirror reflection of misgovernment on earth, caused many a stir in myriad places with his mischievous pranks, including in the underwater palace of the Dragon King, which was filled with imaginative creatures like dragon children, shrimp soldiers, crab generals, whitebait guardsmen and eel porters (note that this was over 500 years before the assortment of sea characters paraded themselves in the Hollywood animated movie *The Little Mermaid*). The Dragon King made a complaint to the Jade Emperor in Heaven, who already had his Peaches of Immortality stolen by Shi Mo Kong. He roped in the Supreme Buddha to help him to deal with this monkey business. And the solution of the Supreme Buddha? He sent Shi Mo Kong on a noble mission to accompany Hsuan Tsang on his pilgrimage to the Holy Mountain of Buddha in India. Shi Mo Kong was joined in this role of escort, disciple and protector by Chu Pa Jia, a former Marshal of Heaven who had been transformed into a fat, lazy and amorous pig after getting drunk and making hay with the Moon Goddess, as well as Friar Sand, a heavenly general who used to be in charge of lifting the curtain for the Jade Emperor but who was subsequently demoted because he had carelessly smashed some jade and crystal. Their task was to protect Hsuan Tsang from evil spirits and demons, who could not wait to make a meal of this pious monk, as consuming his flesh would grant them immortality.

In our modern times, the Taoist influence can be detected in many ordinary aspects of Chinese life. One is the traditional Chinese funeral, which consists of a strange mix of sacred and profane activities, giving rise to a myriad of sights and sounds ranging from ear-splitting clanging cymbals, Taoist chanting and wailing women in mourning robes determined to rouse up the underworld with their ceremonial cries, to the shuffling of mahjong chips and the merry laughter of wanton, carefree children. Such a kaleidoscopic mix of sight and sound in the vicinity of the dead, cannot help but be a completely out-of-this-world experience for the Westerner, who would no doubt be horrified by the pragmatic practice of the Chinese to revere their dead while enjoying a game of mahjong (a popular form of gambling) in a roadside funeral parlour. Another example of Taoist influence is the latest made-in-Hong Kong movie, which invariably pits a senior Taoist priest against a terrible blood-sucking vampire. This saviour in Taoist gown comes complete with his magic wooden sword, vampire-searing incense paper, and supernatural incantation, as well as a company of bumbling disciples, who understandably are more interested in pursuing a fair maiden than being pursued by the vampire.

Taoism looms over Confucianism in its zany appeal to the ordinary folks in society. For with its idyllic stance, its romantic escape from the world and its flights of fancy and wonder, as well as its solicitations of the supernatural – the Chinese request their gods to perform all sorts of miracles, from winning the lottery and increasing their customer base to curing them of cancer and improving the grades of their children – it successfully revolts against the artificiality and sterility, the responsibilities and obligations of Confuciandom. Of the two cardinal Confucian virtues, benevolence and righteousness, Lao Tzu has contemptuously asserted: "*No* character, *then* benevolence; *no* benevolence, *then* righteousness." One witty Taoist poet even compared the *junzhi* (Confucian gentleman) treading cautiously in his precipitous path of righteousness to a small and obnoxious bug creeping along the narrow seams of a man's trousers. As Lin Yu Tang has remarked, it is all so easy to make fun of these poker-faced Confucian bureaucrats who seldom smiled. For Confucianism, with its classicist emphasis on ceremonialism and anxiety over the distinctions of mourning periods and the thickness of coffin panels, and with the intense desire of its followers to seek official positions and save the world, lends itself easily to caricature by the expansive and irreverent impulse of Taoism. This Taoistic impulse is well captured in this famous poem by Li Bo, one of the most romantically exuberant poets that China has to offer to our world, who is recounting his experience of drinking with his shadow and the moon:

> *A pot of wine amidst the flowers,*
> *Alone I drink sans company.*
> *The moon I invite as drinking companion,*
> *And with my shadow we are three.*
> *The moon, I see, she does not drink,*
> *My shadow only follows me.*
> *I'll keep them company a while,*
> *For spring's the time for gaiety*
> *I sing: the moon she swings her head;*
> *I dance: my shadow swells and sways.*
> *We sport together while awake,*
> *While drunk, we all go our own ways.*
> *An eternal, speechless trio then,*
> *Till in the clouds we meet again!*[37]

This Taoistic impulse is most intense in Chuang Tzu, dubbed by one Chinese scholar as the World Philosopher at Play,[38] who challenges the Confucian assertion that the individual's primary moral obligations are to social institutions, such as family and state. When a ruler who had heard of his renown sent emissaries to the river where Chuang Tzu was fishing to ask him to administer his state, Chuang Tzu held on to his fishing pole and, without turning his head, said, "I have heard that there is a sacred tortoise in Chu that has been dead now for 3,000 years. The king keeps it wrapped in cloth and boxed, and stores it in the ancestral temple. Now would this tortoise rather be dead and have its bones honoured? Or would it rather be alive and drag its tail in the mud? ... Go away! I will drag my tail in the mud."

As Berling has pointed out, to accept such an honoured post would pull Chuang Tzu into the realm of the socialised self; he would be devoting his energies and his vitality to improving social institutions.[39] This effort would exhaust him and cut him off from the natural world of which he was a part, i.e., the dynamic flux of life in the Tao. Instead, like Western individualists, Chuang Tzu advocates freedom from the restrictions of public obligations, and raises a standard against wan conformity. However, Chuang Tzu's argument for freedom does not entail either legal rights or a psychological notion of self-expression or personal choice, like the Western concept of liberal individualism. His position is not a call for the rights of the indi-

vidual at all, but for a shift of attention from social and political issues – common in his time, especially among the Confucianists,
Mohists and Legalists – to another dimension of life altogether. This
alternative dimension of life is encapsulated in Chuang Tzu's view
that a human being has not only a body, but a mind as well, i.e., he or
she has a unique capability to transcend the limits of physical existence and imagine himself or herself in another place, time or form.

Chuang Tzu challenges us to take full advantage of our imaginative potential by not limiting our capacity for empathy and openness. He questions the normativeness of the human point of view,
which Confucianism encourages: "Monkeys pair with monkeys, deer
consort with deer, and fish wander with fish. Men think that Mao-
ch'iang and Lady Li were beautiful, but if fish saw them they would
swim away, and if deer saw them they would run off. Of these four,
which knows the true beauty of the world?" These words humor-
ously show that humans have the capability to see Mao-ch'iang and
Lady Li from the viewpoint of a monkey, a deer or a fish, i.e., we are
not limited to the human perspective.

Chuang Tzu also records experiences which transcend the limits of the body. Almost all people have dreamt that they were an
animal, but Chuang Tzu goes on to question whether he is a person
dreaming he is a butterfly, or a butterfly dreaming he is a person. He
has the courage and imagination to suppose that he might *be* the
butterfly; in that imaginative act, he transcends both his humanness
and his identity as someone called Chuang Tzu. This is not threaten-
ing or distressing to him: whether as Chuang Tzu or as the butterfly,
he is very much alive and endowed with wit and grace. To conclude,
Taoism represents the fanciful, creative and playing mood of the Chinese people, just as Confucianism represents its conforming, obedient and working mood. Which accounts – according to Lin Yu Tang
– for the fact that every Chinese is a Confucianist when he is successful, and a Taoist when he is a failure: the naturalism of Taoism is the
balm that soothes the
wounded Chinese
soul.

Am I a person dreaming that I'm a butterfly?
Or am I a butterfly dreaming that I'm a person?

Notes

1. Emerson, 1841.
2. Aronson, 1992.
3. Crutchfield, 1962.
4. Zechmeister & Johnson, 1992.
5. Perkins, 1993.
6. Whitney, Sagrestano & Maslach, 1994.
7. Pan, 1990.
8. Brewer, 1991.
9. Barbaranelli, Caprara & Maslach, 1997.
10. Branson, 1998.
11. *The Straits Times*, January 1, 2000.
12. Bond and Smith, 1996; Hui & Villareal, 1989.
13. Schlessinger & Schlessinger, 1996.
14. quoted in Weisz, Rothbaum & Blackburn, 1984.
15. Hofstede, 1980.
16. Nakane, 1973.
17. Yoshimura & Anderson, 1997.
18. Sakaiya, 1993.
19. Yoshimura & Anderson, 1997.
20. *The Straits Times*, June 23, 1999.
21. Ripple, 1989.
22. Dunn, Zhang & Ripple, 1988.
23. Jaquish & Ripple, 1984–1985.
24. Liu, 1986.
25. Liu & Hsu, 1974.
26. Bloom, 1977.
27. *The Straits Times*, May 12, 1999.
28. Boey, 1976; Ho, 1994.
29. quoted in Gibney, 1992.
30. Levy, 1970, quoted in Baker, 1979.
31. Bloodworth, 1967.
32. Fung, 1948.
33. Temple, 1986.
34. Kennedy, 1988.
35. Lin, 1936.
36. Fung, 1948.
37. Lin, 1936.
38. Wu, 1982.
39. Berling, 1985.

Culture, Creativity and Motivated Behaviour

Creativity As a Form of Motivated Behaviour

In the previous chapter, I argued that creativity is a form of individuated behaviour which is influenced by culture, i.e., Westerners tend to behave in a more creative and individuated manner, while Asians tend to behave in a less creative and individuated manner. In a similar vein, in this chapter, I will argue that creativity is a form of motivated behaviour which is influenced by culture. More specifically, a creative person has the tendency to be *task*-involved in an event / activity; this type of task-involved and creative behaviour is encouraged in the West. In contrast, an uncreative person has the tendency to be *ego*-involved in an event / activity; this type of ego-involved and uncreative behaviour is encouraged in the East.

The essential difference between task- and ego-involved behaviour is the presence or absence of an inner sense of psychological freedom to

Task-Involved

Ego-Involved

create. When a person is task-involved, he is an *origin* of action, i.e., he perceives himself as being the cause of his own behaviour. As a result, he experiences an inner sense of psychological freedom to create. An example is the interior designer who decorates a new house for a recently-married couple with a given budget. He will feel challenged and intrinsically motivated by this task. In contrast, when a person is ego-involved, he is a *pawn* to the action, i.e., he does not perceive himself to be the cause of his own behaviour. Instead, he feels controlled by extraneous and alien forces, which include external contingencies such as rewards and punishment, or introjects such as guilt, anxiety and shame. Needless to say, a person who feels himself to be under the control of such extraneous and alien forces will fail to experience an inner sense of psychological freedom to create. An example is the employee who goes to work reluctantly every morning to a boring job with a demanding boss, because of his need to earn enough money to feed his wife and children.

Creating Under Task- and Ego-Involved Conditions

The association between task-involved and creative behaviour on the one hand, and ego-involved and uncreative behaviour on the other, springs from the empirically-established fact that the quality of the creative product will be higher under conditions of task involvement than ego involvement. According to Crutchfield, this is because the creative solution consists of the emergence of a new and fitting reorganisation of the elements of the problem.[1] Invariably this first necessitates setting aside an earlier and more conventional approach to the problem. This task is especially difficult when the person is ego-involved in the activity. In such a psychological state of ego involvement, there are extraneous and powerful controlling forces which suppress the more creative forms of problem-solving. They include forces like evaluation pressure, contracted-for rewards, external surveillance, deadlines and the need to seek approval from the ingroup, which undermine interest in task engagement and consequently have a detrimental effect on creative performance. Conversely, the sense of freedom when undertaking an activity for the sheer pleasure that it offers is *autotelic*, i.e., it leads the person to complete involvement with the task at hand. In such a psychological state of task involvement, the person finds it easier to think in a more flexible and less rigid manner. This will result in a much deeper conceptual processing and integration of information.

A lot of research supports this postulation that creative behaviour is task-involved, while uncreative behaviour is ego-involved. In one study, it was found that subjects working for an external reward had a more difficult time in thinking in a flexible manner when doing water-jar puzzles than did non-rewarded subjects.[2] In a second study, it was found that subjects who were told that their work would be evaluated produced artistic collages that were rated as less creative than those produced by subjects who did not expect evaluations.[3] In a third study, it was found that citation frequency, a reasonable index of the quality of scientific research, was highest for those research psychologists who were high on task- and low on ego-involvement scales. However, the number of publications, which was less likely to indicate quality of accomplishment, was slightly positively associated with the ego-involvement scale.[4]

Psychological Characteristics of the Task-Involved Creator

We have seen that creative behaviour is task-involved, while uncreative behaviour is ego-involved. What are the psychological characteristics of the task-involved creator? Deci and Ryan have shed some light on this issue by empirically investigating the differences between the task-involved and creative individual on the one hand, and the ego-involved and uncreative individual on the other. They found that task-involved and creative individuals are self-actualised, are at a mature stage of ego development, are high in private self-consciousness and score high on various measures of creativity.[5] They believe in their ability to determine their own fate, attribute their success to individual ability or effort as opposed to luck, and do not experience feelings of boredom. They also possess a high level of self-esteem, rarely derogate themselves, and experience low levels of guilt. In contrast, ego-involved and uncreative individuals are found to adopt an extrinsic, pressured and time-conscious approach when performing an activity, and to report that it is very important to do well in achievement situations. They also have the tendency to experience hostile feelings. In addition, when they persist vigorously at a task in the absence of external controls, this persistence does not seem to reflect intrinsic motivation, insofar as it is not related to self reports of interest and enjoyment. Rather, it seems to reflect a form of ego-involved self regulation.

Let the Creative Juices *Flow*!

But perhaps the most trademark characteristic of the task-involved creator is his experience of *flow* during the creative problem-solving process. The association of flow with creativity is established by Csikszentmihalyi, who described his research in *Creativity: Flow and the Psychology of Creativity and Invention*.[6] In this book, Csikszentmihalyi reported his findings concerning the question of why creative individuals in different domains (e.g., chess players, rock-climbers, dancers and composers) devoted so much time to their craft. From his interviews with these creators, Csikszentmihalyi discovered that what kept them motivated in their activity was not the hope of winning fame or making money, i.e., ego involvement, but instead the fact that they enjoyed what they were doing, i.e., task involvement. This feeling of enjoyment did not arise when they were relaxing, or taking drugs or alcohol, or indulging in the expensive privileges of wealth. Rather, it arose when they were engaging in painful, risky or difficult activities which involved an element of novelty / discovery and stretched their capacity. Csikszentmihalyi used the term *flow* to describe this optimally enjoyable experience, as many of the respondents indicated the feeling when things were going well as an almost automatic, effortless, yet highly-focused state of consciousness. The flow experience was described in similar terms, regardless of the activity that produced it, and it did not vary much by culture, gender or age. The following boxed article shows, first, a subjective and personal description of flow, by a poet whom Csikszentmihalyi had interviewed, and second, an objective and scientific description of flow, based on the empirical findings of Csikszentmihalyi.

The Psychology of Flow

A Poet's Description of Flow

"Well, you're right in the work, you lose your sense of time, you're completely enraptured, you're completely caught up in what you're doing, and you're sort of swayed by the possibilities you see in this work. If that becomes too powerful, then you get up, because the excitement is too great. You can't continue to work or continue to see the end of the work because you're jumping ahead of yourself all the time. The idea is to be so ... so *saturated* with it that there's no future or past, it's just an extended present in which, you're, uh, making meaning. And dismantling meaning, and remaking it."

Nine Psychological Dimensions of Flow

1. There are clear goals every step of the way – the person knows what needs to be done next.
2. There is immediate feedback to one's actions – the person knows how well he is doing.
3. There is a balance between challenges and skills – the person's abilities are matched to the opportunities for action.
4. Action and awareness are merged – the person's concentration is focused on what he is doing.
5. Distractions are excluded from consciousness – the person's thoughts do not wander away from the activity.
6. There is no worry of failure – the person is too involved in the activity to be concerned with failure.
7. Self-consciousness disappears – the person doesn't make a distinction between self and environment.

8. The sense of time becomes distorted – hours seem like minutes or even seconds to the person.
9. The activity becomes autotelic – the person does the activity for the sheer pleasure it gives him.

Moving with the flow!

The Creative and Task-Involved Westerner

The creative and task-involved person is more likely to be found in a Western society rather than in an Asian society. This is because Western society is more loosely organised, individualistic and egalitarian, and puts a greater emphasis on realising one's potential in life, in contrast with Asian society. It enables the person, from childhood, to develop an inner sense of psychological freedom to act. In addition, it supports and facilitates the individual's freely-chosen behaviour. As a consequence of living in this type of society, the Westerner is imbued with a set of psychological attributes which increases his tendency to behave in a creative and task-involved manner. These attributes include an openness to experience, an inclination to view himself as a separate and independent person, and a high level of perceived ability which enables him to take up a challenging task, as well as an adherence to a set of open values which is autonomous and self-determining in nature. A person with this psychological make-up is creative and task-involved. This is depicted in the figure below, while the boxed article which follows takes a look at the American movie director James Cameron and his life-long passion: directing Hollywood blockbusters.

A Cultural Model of Creative and Task-Involved Behaviour

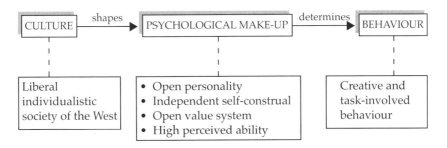

CULTURE	shapes	PSYCHOLOGICAL MAKE-UP	determines	BEHAVIOUR
Liberal individualistic society of the West		• Open personality • Independent self-construal • Open value system • High perceived ability		Creative and task-involved behaviour

James Cameron and the Making of *Titanic*

An example of the Westerner who behaves in a creative, task-involved and autonomous manner is James Cameron, the famous American movie director behind *Titanic*, the extravagantly expensive but critically-acclaimed romantic movie of the 1990s, which won innumerable awards, including the Oscar for Best Picture.[7] This tragic love story, which had audiences all over the world reaching for their handkerchiefs, catapulted Leonardo DiCaprio and Kate Winslet to international stardom in their respective roles as Jack and Rose, the ill-fated lovers on the *Titanic*, which in its day was not only the largest moving object ever made, but also the most opulent, well-appointed and reputedly unsinkable luxury liner. This turned out to be human hubris, as the *Titanic* struck a huge iceberg on the early morning of April 15, 1912, split into two pieces and plunged two-and-a-half miles to the bottom of the Atlantic Ocean, taking with it 1,500 of its passengers.

The movie *Titanic* is a realistic recreation of the last hours of this so-called unsinkable luxury liner. Representing years of Cameron's passion and dedication, it is undoubtedly this extraordinary filmmaker's most ambitious undertaking to date. This talented writer-director had actually vowed not to make *Titanic* unless he could successfully dive to the wreckage himself, and bring back motion picture footage for use in the film. It took a couple of years to set up, but Cameron finally put together the world's first Hollywood deep-diving expedition. It comprised the following components: one Russian research ship, *Akademik Mstislav Keldysh*, the biggest of its kind in the world; two submersibles, *Mir 1* and *Mir 2*, two of only five manned vehicles worldwide that could go to the depths of the *Titanic* wreckage (which was discovered in 1985); and one remote-operated vehicle (ROV) named Snoop Dog, built for the film but functional at the *Titanic* depth. In addition, it also included a specially designed motion picture camera and pressure housing for underwater filming, as well as a brace of powerful underwater lights to penetrate the icy darkness that covered the ocean floor.

However, being able to film the actual wreckage was one thing; constructing a life-sized model of the *Titanic* was another. To do this properly, 20th Century Fox acquired 40 acres of waterfront property south of Rosarito in Baja California, Mexico, to build its full-service motion picture studio. This consisted of a 17 million-gallon tank, which would become home to the exterior ship set, and a five million-gallon enclosed tank, which would house her lavish interiors. Two more non-flooding soundstages, a wet/dry soundstage and a support infrastructure equivalent to a small town completed the facility. The construction of the replica was based on the original blue-prints of the *Titanic*, and assembled from, among other things, three-and-a-half million pounds of steel, 15,000 sheets of plywood, several tons of paint and 30,000 rivets (the actual ship itself had three million rivets). The whole movie set was equivalent to a 70-storey skyscraper on its side.

However, the greatest challenge in making *Titanic* was not the deep-diving expedition. Neither was it the construction of the life-sized replica of the luxury ocean liner, or the painstaking reproduction of its opulent interior. The greatest challenge was the fact that it was very difficult to make a movie about a story which was so well known and researched. What can you say about the *Titanic* that had not been said before? After musing for a long while on this question, Cameron came to the conclusion that "the only territory that had been left unexplored in prior films about the sinking of the *Titanic* was the territory of the heart. I wanted the audience to cry for *Titanic*. Which means to cry for the people on the ship ... But the death of 1,500 innocents is too abstract for our hearts to grasp ... To fully grasp the tragedy of the *Titanic*, to be able to comprehend it in human terms, it seemed necessary to create an emotional lightning rod for the audience by giving them two main characters they care about ... Jack and Rose were born out of this need, and the story of *Titanic* became their story."

And so this was how *Titanic* became a magnificent canvas on which to paint a love story which could offer the full spectral range of human emotions, from love to hatred, joy to grief, bravery to cowardice and terror, as Cameron wove the passionate love story of Jack and Rose from the stern to the bow of the *Titanic* and through every interesting place and event in between, permitting his audience to experience the optimism and grandeur of the ship in a way that most of her actual passengers never did. The story is made even more real by enabling the two ill-fated lovers to share the stage with Captain Smith (who piloted the ship) and Thomas Andrews (who designed it), both of whom met their fates with the *Titanic* at the bottom of the North Atlantic Ocean. By telling the story in this way, Cameron hoped that his audience would be able to empathise with Jack and Rose as they fell in love with each other. Then they would "move from watching them ... to seeing through their eyes as they live out one of the most horrific nights of the 20th century. And then the film comes full circle, from being a film about the *Titanic*, to being a love story that happens merely to be set on the *Titanic*, back to being about the emotional truth of the *Titanic* after all. By feeling the fear, the loss, the heartbreak of Jack and Rose, we finally can feel for the 1,500." Judging from the enthusiastic response to *Titanic* (it made US$600 million at the box office and double the amount worldwide; a lot of teenage girls who could not get over Leonardo DiCaprio went to see the movie many times; one lady from New Zealand was reputed in the Internet to have watched it 47 times), Cameron had certainly found his mark.

The Face-Conscious, Ego-Involved and Uncreative Asian

While the task-involved and creative individual (like James Cameron) is more likely to be found in Western society, the uncreative and ego-involved individual is more likely to be found in Asian society. Such a society is more tightly organised, collectivistic and hierarchical, in comparison with its counterpart in the West. In addition, it is also more face-conscious. The term "face" refers to the social reputation which is achieved by getting on in life through success and ostentation.[8] Put more simply, face is a measure of the social recognition accorded by society to oneself. The concern for face is so prevalent in Asian society that the Chinese scholar Lin Yu Tang has referred to it as one of the "three sisters" who control Chinese life (the other two are fate and favour): "Their voices are soft, their ways are gentle, their feet tread noiselessly over the law courts, and their fingers move silently, expertly, putting the machinery of justice out of order while they caress the judge's cheeks."[9]

Because of the importance of face in his society, the Asian will go to great lengths to behave in ways designed to display and protect both the image and reality of that position in life which he has achieved. For example, many wealthy Chinese in Singapore, Hong Kong and Taiwan splurge on branded cars like the BMW or Mercedes Benz in order to show off their wealth to their relatives and friends. Wedding couples in these Asian communities typically host their invited guests to expensive ten-course dinners in five-star hotels in order not to lose face on this auspicious day of their lives. In the case of Japan, not only people, but companies, universities, political parties, clubs and governmental ministries possess status too. These organisations are ranked in regularly published lists, so that everyone in society knows who's who. It can be intimidating, especially for members of the lower-ranked organisations. In his book *Reading the Japanese Mind: The Realities Behind Their Thoughts and Actions,*[10]

Robert March, a Western professor at a major Tokyo university, observed that young men who have graduated from universities that are not in the top ten can be snubbed by young women. For example, Hosei University in Tokyo, originally a private specialist law college, has a fine reputation, although it is not in the top ten. A young male Hosei graduate confided to Robert March that young women have rebuffed his invitations after learning he was "only" a Hosei graduate. It appears that for these young women, a young man is not an individual with his own personality, but a branded product.

Why does the Asian behave in this face-conscious manner? He does so because other people in his society have a strong tendency to use considerations of hierarchy and status in making socially evaluative judgments about an individual.[11] As a result, the Asian is very sensitive about the social position which he occupies in the status hierarchy. He attempts to move up the rungs of the socioeconomic ladder by acquiring those material goods in his society which will "inflate" his face in the community e.g., branded car, private condominium and country-club membership. Only by acquiring them will he be able to feel a sense of satisfaction. This way of feeling good about oneself is known as *contingent self-esteem*. It is to be differentiated from *true self-esteem*, which is not reliant on the feelings and opinions of other people. Instead, true self-esteem is based on a feeling of inner worth, which arises when the person behaves in an autonomous and self-directed manner.[12] For example, a creative painter who sets for himself the meaningful goal of assisting a group of students from a disadvantaged background to discover their drawing potential, and achieves this goal after much personal sacrifice, will experience true self-esteem.

In the case of the face-conscious Asian, his behaviour is controlled by his desire to enhance his face in his community, i.e., to increase his contingent self-esteem. Behaving in this manner will prevent him from being creative. This is because creativity requires the person to stand on his own two feet, free from the shackles of the collective. This quality of character is lacking in the face-conscious Asian, who is dependent on the opinions and evaluations of others in order to feel good about himself. The face-conscious Asian who relies on his social group to supply his esteem needs will end up as an "ego-involved hostage", i.e., the social pressure to conform to the materialistic majority arouses extrinsic motives in the face-conscious Asian. His main efforts in life are directed towards the acquisition of those material goods which enables him to win the approval of the social group. This is shown in the cultural model of behaviour on the next page. This model indicates that Asians who live in a Confucian-heritage society will tend to develop a closed personality, an interdependent self-construal, a conservative value system, and a strong inclination to identify with their ingroup. As a result of such a psychological make-up, the typical Asian behaves in an uncreative and ego-involved manner.

A Cultural Model of Uncreative and Ego-Involved Behaviour

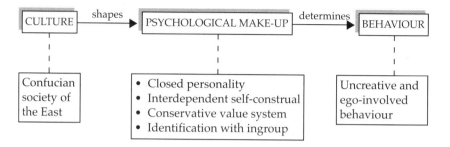

Can Money Buy You Happiness?

The successful acquisition of material goods will enable the Asian to increase his face before everyone in his community. He and his family can take pride in what he has achieved. However, there are hidden costs associated with this materialistic and ostentatious pursuit of success. This can be seen clearly in the following incident, reported in the local newspaper, of a Chinese family whose new Mercedes Benz was repeatedly scratched by a vandaliser. Indignant and frustrated, the owner of this glossy and expensive car – a successful chemicals company manager – decided to track down the culprit himself. He spent about S$15,000 on video-recording equipment, and he and his wife took turns to stay up into the wee hours of the morning, hoping to catch the vandaliser red-handed on film. His efforts paid off, but he got a nasty shock: the culprit turned out to be none other than his next-door neighbour, who was seething with rage and jealousy at the sight of his new Mercedes Benz![13]

The moral of the story is this: money may inflate the face of the Asian, but it cannot buy him happiness. Over the last few years, a lot of empirical evidence has been amassed, which supports this notion that happiness is simply not for sale.[14] Instead, those individuals for whom material affluence is a priority in life are more likely to experience behaviourial problems, like smoking and drinking, as well as a lower level of subjective well-being, like anxiety and depression, compared to their counterparts who wish to develop closer relationships, become more self-aware, or contribute to the community. For example, it was found that university students who emphasised the importance of physical appearance, financial success and popularity were lower in well-being and self-esteem. Those who aspired to affluence were also found to have more transient relationships, watched more television and were more likely to use cigarettes, alcohol and other drugs than were those who placed less emphasis on extrinsic goals like money or social status. The detrimental effects of an extreme focus on extrinsic goals like money or social status appear not to be limited to any one culture in particular. This can be gleaned in a large-scale study by Dr Richard Ryan and Dr Tim Kasser, who collected data from respondents in 13 countries, including Germany, Russia and India. They found that the neurotic link between obsessive wealth and subjective (mental) health holds, regardless of the nationality of the person.

Dr Ryan hypothesised that unhappy people are more likely than others to go after money and fame in order to compensate for something more meaningful which they lack in their personal lives, such as being connected in an authentic manner to significant others like family and friends. The empirical support for this hypothesis comes from a provocative study by a group of psychologists in America who discovered that 18-year-olds for whom financial success was especially important turned out to be disproportionately likely to have mothers who were not very nurturing. When parents are "cold and controlling", the researchers wrote, "their children apparently focus on attaining security and a sense of worth through external sources". This seems consistent with anecdotal accounts of very wealthy men who grew up in troubled homes. Such stories are sometimes cited as evidence that they made the best of a bad thing, turning out well in spite of their childhood. The problem with this interpretation, according to the researchers, is that they might not have turned out so well; instead, they just became rich, that was all.

Whatever the cause of this neurotic link between obsessive wealth and subjective health, one thing is clear: money cannot buy you happiness, whether you are an Asian or Westerner. If you really desire to attain personal fulfilment in life, then you should not pursue materialistic goals. Instead, you should go after those creative and meaningful goals which reflect genuine human needs, like wanting to feel connected with others, becoming more self-aware, contributing to the community and helping the poor and needy. Otherwise, you may end up like the businessman in the following poem:[15]

> *I asked no quarter and I gave none,*
> *I fought it out until eighty-one.*
> *Intelligence guided my efforts,*
> *Cynicism dictated my business reports.*
>
> *I played one off against another,*
> *Keeping my head well above water.*
> *I transmuted my blood to steel,*
> *Early conquering the realm of feeling.*
>
> *I taught ruthlessness by example,*
> *And hard work and steadfastness.*
> *Now that the hated grave approaches,*
> *I wish for the love I could not give.*

Chapter Summary

In this chapter, I argued that creative behaviour is task-involved and free, while uncreative behaviour is ego-involved and controlled. Westerners are more likely to behave in a creative and task-involved manner, because their individualistic culture encourages them to pursue their own chosen goals in life. In contrast, Asians are more likely to behave in an uncreative and ego-involved manner, because their collectivistic culture encourages them to be face-conscious, i.e., to seek the approval of the social group by pursuing material wealth. Research has shown that an obsessive pursuit of wealth has negative effects on psychological health. But in spite of the fact that money is no guarantee of happiness, many Asians still strive after it. This is illustrated in the boxed article on page 91.

The reader who reads the article might get the impression that Asians (especially Singaporeans) are an unkind and ungracious group of people, in comparison with their Western counterparts. However, I would like to temper this harsh critique of the Asian way of life (especially its concern with materialistic goals) with two caveats. First, not all Asians behave in this manner, i.e., not all Asians are excessively concerned about enhancing their own face in the community by the acquisition of material goods: it depends on how the individual Asian has been socialised from young.

For example, if the Asian grows up in a family which promotes an inquisitive rather than a materialistic mindset, then he will probably be task-involved and creative. Or if he grows up in a family which promotes love and harmonious living, then he will probably be kind-hearted and agreeable. Here, I am reminded of a good friend in Singapore, who took no-pay leave from his organisation to assist in the relief operation for the victims of the recent earthquake in central Taiwan. He went in spite of the fact that it was not completely safe to do so – there were many aftershock tremors in the disaster area. What's more, he went with his wife's blessing, even though she had just given birth to their first child.

The second caveat is this: not all Westerners behave in a task-involved and creative manner; it depends on how the individual Westerner has been socialised from young. For example, if he grows up in a family which promotes a hedonistic streak in the character, then he will probably be egoistic and self-centred (very much like the face-conscious Asian). Indeed, the Western emphasis on individual rights and freedoms has the potential not only to nurture individuals who are task-involved and creative, but also who are egoistic and self-centred (see the book *The Culture of Narcissism* by the American sociologist Christopher Lasch). This has led to many social problems in Western society, including a high divorce rate, single parenthood, juvenile delinquency, and an obsession with sex and violence. These problems have cost much individual and collective anguish within Western society, and occupy the hearts and minds of its intellectuals and policy-makers.[16]

In making these two caveats, I wish to impress upon the reader one thing: I am not trying to take sides with the East or the West in this book. In my view, both sides have their good and bad points; they have lessons to offer each other, concerning the twin challenges of how a society should be organised and how the individual should live in society. Since I am an Asian who is interested in promoting creativity in my society, I will focus on what we in the East can learn from our counterparts in the West (see the boxed article at the end of Chapter 9). Perhaps one day, a learned scholar from the West will write a similar book about what his or her society can learn from my kind of society in the East. This mutual attitude of learning from each other is, in my opinion, more laudable than the highly-politicised and value-laden discourse which characterises communication between ideological foes in the East and West.

Singapore: A *Kiasu*, Materialistic and Uncreative Society with No Soul

In spite of the fact that money is no guarantee of happiness, many Asians still strive after the status symbols of their society. But because these material goods are what similar others in society desire as well, and the demand is more than the supply, the person is forced to be one step ahead of the others, so that he will not lose out to them. In Singapore, a person who behaves in this manner is said to be *kiasu*, or to be afraid to lose out.[17] This *kiasu* syndrome of Singaporeans can be seen in a broad spectrum of behaviours, which range from a mad rush for free textbooks and buffet food to overnight queues for limited editions of Hello Kitty dolls offered by McDonald's.[18]

The *kiasu* reasoning is this: if so many people are going after the same thing, then it must be good, or else why are they going after it? So better to play it safe by getting it first, otherwise later there will be no more. A herd mentality is developed which results in everyone going after similar things in life, especially the Five Cs (cash, car, condominium in a private estate, country-club membership and credit card). No one wants to be different, and choose the path which is less trodden by. The end result is a *kiasu*, materialistic and uncreative society with no soul, inhabited by a people who are characterised by their uncharitable preoccupation with making money.[19] For example, Singaporeans are one of the greatest speculators in real estate in the world, i.e., they treat their homes as financial investments which they can release into the resale market for a tidy profit after a couple of years of living in it, which is highly ironic, considering that their government spends a lot of time, money and energy in pushing the notion of "home ownership".

This Singaporean addiction to Mammon is resilient even in the face of the Asian economic crisis: an estimated US$3.2 billion was spent in 1998 on legalised gambling alone, the same amount as in 1997, before the economic crisis hit the country.[20] It also seems to transcend national boundaries, as can be seen in a mass arrest of 200 Singaporeans by Malaysian policemen. And their crime? Instead of enjoying their holiday in Gelang Patah in Johor, which is the nearest Malaysian state to the island of Singapore, separated by a one-kilometre causeway, these Singaporeans dabbled in illegal bookmaking (a form of gambling) at the holiday resort. An irate commentary which appeared subsequently in a Malaysian newspaper questioned the double standards of Singaporeans, who are law-abiding citizens in their own country but become litterbugs, speed monsters and convicted gamblers once they cross the causeway to a foreign land.[21]

The materialistic dream and ungracious behaviour of Singaporeans are mirrored by their lack of involvement in voluntary activities: only one out of every ten Singaporeans serves as volunteers for the weak and unfortunate in their society, in comparison to nearly one out of every two Americans,[22] which led the Senior Minister of Singapore, Mr Lee Kuan Yew, to comment in public that he wished his countrymen and women could become more like Americans in their grassroots volunteerism.[23] Besides this laudable involvement in community service, many Americans are also dedicated to the cause of the environment, which can range from rescuing the blue whale and the Amazon rainforest to saving the ozone layer. To realise this environmental cause, they are prepared to break the laws of their state e.g., at a recent meeting of the World Trade Organisation (WTO) at Seattle, they successfully prevented the WTO delegates from enacting trade liberalisation measures which would, in their view, result in further exploitation of the environment by the devouring system of capitalism. For their anarchic behaviour, which included street demonstrations and acts of vandalism, many of these environmental fighters ended up being arrested by the Seattle police.

In the case of *kiasu* Singaporeans, they also ended up on the wrong side of the law, *not* because they were dedicated to an altruistic cause like saving the environment, but merely because they could not get their hands on limited editions of Hello Kitty dolls. These Hello Kitty dolls were offered by McDonald's Singapore for every purchase of its Extra Value meal.[24] These limited editions of the soft toys came in six different designs, the Millennium, Malay, Romantic, Japanese, Korean and Chinese designs. These soft toys were so popular that many *kiasu* Singaporeans sacrificed their sleep to queue up overnight at various McDonald's outlets for them. Some of these *kiasu*

Singaporeans even turned ugly when they failed to lay their hands on these dolls, in spite of their overnight wait. In one incident, three men were arrested for rioting at a McDonald's outlet at 4:30 a.m. The trio, aged between 19 and 22, had thrown stools at officers, injuring a sergeant's right wrist. The Singapore Civil Defence Force said it received at least nine phone calls about fights and people fainting in queues near McDonald's outlets. A Cisco (a public security agency in Singapore) spokesman said that 64 of its officers were deployed for crowd control at 24 outlets from 4 a.m. at McDonald's request.

Garbage left behind by the Hello Kitty crowds prompted officials from the Ministry of Environment to book 15 litterbugs in the queues, as well as to instruct McDonald's to do a thorough clean-up of its premises, and to provide more litter bins at its various outlets during its next toy sale. The Federation of Merchants' Association, which represents about 6,000 small and medium businesses, said the long queues at McDonald's for Hello Kitty collectibles were disrupting business in housing estates, and wanted McDonald's Singapore to stop selling the soft toys and stick to selling burgers. Mr Edmund Baker, executive director of the Consumers Association of Singapore, said in a television interview that McDonald's Singapore should have foreseen the crowd problems from its experience in Hong Kong: "It would have saved them a lot of the fire-fighting problems which they are now going through." An anguished writer to the local newspapers summed it best when he commented that the ugly antics of these *kiasu* Singaporeans had brought shame to Singapore, an assertion which I could not help but agree with. The fact that Singaporeans have had more than 20 years of national courtesy campaigns to encourage them to behave civilly to one another added to the irony of this situation.[25]

Notes

1. Crutchfield, 1962.
2. McGraw & McCullers, 1979.
3. Amabile, 1996.
4. Helmreich *et al.*, 1980.
5. Deci & Ryan, 1985; Sheldon, 1995.
6. Csikszentmihalyi, 1996.
7. Marsh & Kirkland, 1998.
8. Hu, 1944; Hwang, 1989.
9. Lin, 1936.
10. March, 1996.
11. Bond, Wan, Leung & Giacalone, 1985.
12. Deci & Ryan, 1995.
13. *The Straits Times*, January 12, 2000.
14. *The Straits Times*, Feb 4, 1999; Kasser & Ryan, 1996.
15. O'Malley & Thompson, 1977.
16. Sacks, 1997; Etzioni, 1993; Bellah *et. al.*, 1985.
17. Chan, 1994.

18. Low, 1998.
19. Chan, 1994.
20. *The Straits Times*, April 4, 1999.
21. *The Straits Times*, October 2, 1999.
22. *The Straits Times*, June 12, 1999.
23. *The Straits Times*, May 7, 1999.
24. *The Straits Times*, January 7, 22 & 28, 2000.
25. Nirmala, 1999.

How Asian and Western Students Strive for Success

In the previous chapter, we have seen that creativity is a form of motivated behaviour. More specifically, creative behaviour is task-involved, while uncreative behaviour is ego-involved. Task- and ego-involved behaviour have been studied by educational psychologists under the rubric of *learning goal*. This refers to the goal which motivates a student to work hard in his studies. For example, some students may focus on their performance in tests and exams, while other students may focus on mastering the topic. The first group of students is said to adopt a performance goal, while the second group of students is said to adopt a mastery goal.

Performance and Mastery Goals

The student who adopts a *performance goal* in his studies is concerned with getting good grades in tests or exams. He gauges his success in the classroom by looking at how well he fares in comparison with the rest of his classmates. A lot of importance is attached to doing better than them in the test or exam, i.e., although high marks in a test or exam are good, to be first in class is even better. In contrast, the student who adopts a *mastery goal* in his studies is concerned with developing a deep understanding of a topic which he has a lot of interest in. Unlike the performance-oriented student, the mastery-oriented student does not gauge his success in the classroom by looking at how well he has fared in tests and exams compared to the rest of his classmates. Instead, success for him is measured in terms of whether he has mastered the topic by his own individual efforts. A lot of importance is attached to developing new skills and knowledge in what interests him.[1]

Research has indicated that students who adopt performance and mastery goals are different in many ways. The mastery-oriented student appreciates the intrinsic value of learning, has a stronger belief that effort leads to success, prefers to take up more challenging tasks, has a higher degree of self-confidence, utilises more effective task-performance strategies, processes information at a deeper and more conceptual level, maintains higher satisfaction and interest throughout the learning activity and possesses an intrinsic view of the purpose of education, i.e., he believes in education as an end in itself, such as to understand the world around him. He is also good at divergent thinking.[2] In contrast, the performance-oriented student experiences positive feelings after low-effort success, and processes information in a shallow and superficial manner. He has a preference for less challenging tasks, is disturbed by many task-interfering thoughts and feelings (as a result of being too unduly concerned with whether he has done well in the eyes of significant others, like family and friends) and possesses an extrinsic view of the purpose of education, i.e., he believes in education as a means to an end, such as to earn a higher salary later on when he goes out to work. When faced with failure on a task, the performance-oriented student with a low perceived ability has been found to display a helpless behavioural pattern, i.e., he gives up the fight and becomes dejected and demotivated, instead of seeing what he can learn from his failure, like the mastery-oriented student.[3] In addition, it has been found that the autonomous student is likely to adopt a mastery goal, while the controlled student is likely to adopt a performance goal; furthermore, the autonomous student reacts to failure in a mastery-oriented fashion, while the controlled student reacts to failure by being ego-involved.[4]

Contextual Influences on Task Performance

Research has indicated that the type of learning goal which is adopted by the student is affected by the situation which he is in. For example, when social comparison has been emphasised in the classroom, students have focused on their relative abilities and performance in the task. In contrast, when absolute standards, self-improvement and participation have been emphasised, they have focused more on mastering the task.[5] In another study, it was found that students who experienced the classroom climate as being more "pawn-like" evinced less curiosity, desire for challenge, and independent mastery orientation than students who experienced their classroom climate as being more "origin-like".[6] Other research has shown that when people received rewards that were designed to elicit a certain behaviour, such as monetary payments, good-player awards or prizes, they tended to lose interest in the activity after the rewards were terminated, a phenomenon known as *overjustification*. Similarly, external events explicitly designed to control people, including deadlines and imposed goals, have been found to decrease intrinsic motivation for the task.[7]

In an illuminating and well-designed study, Reeve and Deci have explored the possibility that winning a competition can be experienced either as controlling (if the interpersonal context emphasises the importance of beating one's opponent), or as informational (if the interpersonal context does not pressure one to win). They found, as predicted, that both groups of winners – those in the non-pressured context and those pressured to win – felt highly competent, relative to the losers. However, compared to the non-pressured winners, the pressured winners showed a marked reduction in perceived self-determination, which, in turn, undermined their intrinsic motivation. In their discussion, Reeve and Davis noted that "winning a competition may not undermine intrinsic motivation if the interpersonal context does not add undue pressure to win. Unfortunately, it seems that the unyielding focus of our society on winning – whether in athletic competition or school performance, for example – may be creating a pressuring context that can have quite negative effects on individuals' experience and motivation."[8]

Albert Einstein: Students Need to Be Free

Perhaps the most prominent example of the deleterious effects of controlling and pressurising forces on the creative work of a person, and the positive consequences that can arise once these extraneous forces are removed, is given in the case study of Albert Einstein. The social psychologist Amabile, in examining the life of this eminent scientist, noted a recurrent theme in his life: his interest in science was undermined by external forces that exerted control over his work.[9] As a youth, Einstein attended a regimented and militaristic school in Germany, where the exam pressures so overwhelmed him that he temporarily lost his interest in science. Partly in an attempt to escape from such a strictly regimented learning environment, Einstein left Munich for Zurich when he was 15, hoping to enrol in the polytechnic institute there. To his dismay, however, he failed the entrance examination, and was required to enrol in a Swiss school for remedial coursework.

This episode has been regarded as a key turning point in Einstein's scientific thinking. In sharp contrast to what he had known before, the Swiss school was humanistic in orientation, focusing on the individual's unencumbered search for knowledge. There was little emphasis on memorisation, much emphasis on individual laboratory work and student-initiated investigation, and a concentration on the development of relaxed, democratic exchanges between students and teachers. Ironically, it was in this school for remedial coursework that Einstein devised his first *Gedankenexperiment* (thought experiment) – imagining that he was travelling on a beam of light – that would eventually lead him to his famous theory of relativity. In his autobiography, Einstein noted: "It is in fact nothing short of a miracle that the modern methods of instruction have not yet entirely strangled the holy curiosity of inquiry; for this delicate little plant, aside from stimulation, stands mainly in need of freedom; without this it goes to wreck and ruin without fail."

George Bernard Shaw: The School Is Worse Than a Prison

Another eminent creator who had experienced the deleterious effects of a controlling and regimented environment, and lived to tell us his story, is the author and humorist George Bernard Shaw. This famous playwright, who titillated the world with such witty and delectable plays like *Pygmalion* on which the musical *My Fair Lady* was based, had the misfortune of being a student in a regimented and stifling school system in the West. He provided us with a humorous account of his educational experience as a young lad in "A Treatise on Parents and Children", preface to *Misalliance* (1909):

> … and there is, on the whole, nothing on earth intended for innocent people so horrible as a school. To begin with, it is a prison. But it is in some respects more cruel than a prison. In a prison, for instance, you are not forced to read books written by the warders (who of course would not have become warders and governors if they could write readable books), and beaten or otherwise tormented if you are not able to remember their utterly unmemorable contents. In the prison you are not forced to sit listening to the turnkeys discoursing without charm or interest on subjects that they don't understand and don't care about, and are therefore incapable of making you understand or care about. In a prison they may torture your body; but they do not torture your brains; and they protect you against violence and outrage from your fellow prisoners. In a school you have none of these advantages. With the world's bookshelves loaded with fascinating and inspired books, the very manna sent down from Heaven to feed your souls, you are forced to read a hideous imposture called a school book, written by a man who cannot write. A book from which no human can learn anything. A book which, though you may decipher it, you cannot in any fruitful sense read, though the enforced attempt will make you loathe the sight of a book all the rest of your life.

The Asian Education System

The reflections of Einstein and Shaw concerning their negative schooling experience will strike a chord among those of us who have undergone a similar experience, but this time in the Asian educational system, which is considerably more instrumental, regimented, pressurising, competitive and performance-oriented, compared to its counterpart in the West. This has enabled the Asian educational system to produce hardworking and disciplined students who have consistently ranked among the world's best in all fields of academia. For example, in the Third International

Mathematics and Science Study reported in 1996, eighth-graders from Singapore, Japan and Korea were the three top-scoring participant countries in mathematics among the 41 countries that participated in the study. The three top-scoring countries in science were again Singapore, Japan and Korea. Other studies, including the First and Second International Mathematics Study, confirmed these extraordinary accomplishments, and attested to the broad level of excellence of Asian students.[10]

However, in spite of this achievement, the Asian educational system has been lambasted by its critics for various ills, which range from the inculcation of selfish attitudes in students to the production of uncreative thinkers. In the case of Singapore, a highly competitive and pressurising system of education has resulted in many rich and bright but selfish scholars on prestigious government scholarships worth hundreds of thousands of dollars, who indicated (anonymously) to a local reporter that they viewed these government scholarships as a "money contract", "a trophy that looks good on the resume", which would enable them to "build a contact base from which I'll be able to land a more lucrative job". These government scholars indicated to the reporter that they did not intend to serve out their bonds, and would spend only two to four years in service, which led the scholarship bodies in Singapore to issue a rare joint statement to the local press, with this sharp message to these bright but selfish scholars: rethink your stance, or give up your scholarship now, because scholarships are not just financial contracts but moral obligations, and a scholar who "secretly harbours such intentions at the very outset, and worse, to brag anonymously about them, is deceitful, dishonest and reveals a basic character flaw".[11]

In Taiwan, Professor Lee Yuen Tseh, the Nobel laureate who chairs a commission which looks into educational reform in Taiwan, is highly critical of the examination system in his society, which fails to identify and encourage original talent. Professor Hiroyaki Yoshikawa, the president of Tokyo University, laments that Japanese students returning from the West are at first full of enthusiasm and ideas, but their enthusiasm tends to be crushed by the Japanese system.[12] In his provocative book *Dragon Gate: Competitive Examination and Their Consequences*,[13] Zeng Kang Min argued that the competitive systems of education in Japan, Korea and Taiwan have resulted in an ever-growing cram or tuition industry, as well as a religious interest in evoking the help of a supernatural power. Zeng also examined such tragic and alarming issues as the increasing levels of youth suicides and the dramatic rise in cheating, raising some fundamental questions about the Asian educational system as a whole. Other critics of the Asian educational system have decried its emphasis on rote-learning and memorisation, which produce students who are good at passing examinations, but who flounder when it comes to creative thinking. The following boxed article provides an in-depth look at the educational system in Japan.

Getting an Education in Japan

According to Yoshimura and Anderson, the ultimate aim of education in Japan is to enable the average Japanese (whom they call "Hiro" for reference) to join a big and prestigious company like Hitachi (in the private sector) or the Ministry of Finance (in the public sector). Becoming a "salaryman" or junior executive in such an organisation will provide Hiro with long-term job security. But to achieve this goal, Hiro has to be a new graduate of a top-ranked Japanese college. To get into such a college, he has to work hard to get into a "good" high school (grades ten to 12). A good high school is simply one with a high percentage of graduates who enter top-ranked colleges like Tokyo University.

The ticket to such a high school is a "good" junior high school (grades seven to nine), again defined as one that channels a high percentage of its graduates to good high schools. One way to get into a good junior high school is to enter a private after-hours preparatory school called the *juku*. Admission to such a preparatory school, which typically starts in the fourth grade, is based on the results of an examination. In Hiro's day, the early 1970s, it was still unusual for elementary school students to attend a preparatory school. By 1985, however, 16.5 percent of them were enrolled in such schools, a figure that increased to 23.6 percent by 1993.

Hiro attends extra classes at the preparatory school four weeknights plus Saturday evenings every week for a year. Every Sunday, along with 2,000 students from different preparatory schools, he takes a test, after which every student is ranked from first to last according to test scores. Most children study past midnight, believing that this is the only way to pass the extremely competitive examinations administered by elite junior high schools, which are known in local jargon as the "entrance exam hell". A maxim which every school-age student in Japan will understand reflects this diligent attitude towards one's studies: "pass with four, fail with five", i.e., if one is sleeping five hours a night, one is probably not studying hard enough to pass the examination.[14]

According to Yoshimura and Anderson, Hiro will aim for one of the top ten junior high schools in Japan, ranked according to the number of students in each class admitted to Tokyo University, the apex of Japanese education. He will know exactly which school to target because many leading Japanese magazines produce special issues ranking high schools according to the percentage of students who pass the entrance examinations of Japan's most prestigious colleges. Hiro passes the examination of his first-choice high school, which spares him another gruelling round of examinations after ninth grade. Through junior high and high school, he finds himself near the bottom of his class of 180, based on constant examination and feedback. However, although these scores are revealed to him, it is not published for everyone to see. Consequently, Hiro is treated no differently from other students who have done better than him. For all that matters is that Hiro is a student in a very prestigious high school, whose ranking is known to all. Without question, in terms of prestige and career prospects, it is better to bring up the rear at such a place than to be first at a high school that does not get many students into Tokyo University. Thus it is that Hiro absorbs one important lesson: membership in a prestigious organisation is everything in Japan.

Like hundreds of thousands of other students, Hiro will take a sham examination at the end of high school to decide which university examination to take. His score suggests that he will not get into Tokyo University, so he enters one of the colleges in the elite tier behind *Todai* (the unofficial name for Tokyo University). This severely diminishes his chances of becoming a high-level government bureaucrat, but it leaves him well-positioned to become a salaryman at the end of four years in the university. In the university, Hiro will focus more on extracurricular activities than on academic work, because he knows that what he learns will seldom be tied directly to his future job. Joining extracurricular activities, on the other hand, shows that he is cooperative and team-oriented. Making it to captain or vice-captain of a team is even better: it signals to his future employers that he has good relationship skills. However, this development of good relationship skills comes at great personal cost: Hiro gradually loses his individuality, spontaneity and creativity, as he becomes more and more adept at conforming and fitting into the social group.

The Historical Context of Learning in the East

The emphasis on competition and getting good grades in national examinations is not restricted to Japanese students alone. Instead, it is a characteristic feature of the educational system in other Asian societies, such as China, Taiwan, South Korea, Hong Kong and Singapore. There is a historical reason to explain why the educational system in the East has turned out the way it has, i.e., a highly instrumental, regimented, pressurising, competitive and performance-oriented regime which produces disciplined and hardworking students who regularly outperform students in other countries at international competitions, but who nevertheless lack confidence in themselves and fail to go on to win Nobel Prizes.[15]

After World War II, the East Asian region contained a number of countries which were among the poorest in the world. Characterised by high levels of illiteracy and ravaged by the aftermath of wars and civil wars, the region's prospects were not viewed with optimism. It was countries in Africa and Latin America that were thought to be on the threshold of rapid development.[16] Resource-scarce countries like newly-independent Singapore were regarded as a "political joke" in some quarters. However, this scenario proved fallacious. From 1965 to 1990, the 23 economies of East Asia grew faster than all the other regions of the world, and most of this was a consequence of the growth in Hong Kong, South Korea, Singapore, Taiwan, Japan, China, Malaysia, Indonesia and Thailand. These nine countries have been described by the World Bank as the high-performing Asian economies. The speed and unanticipated nature of this development need underlining e.g., it took Britain 58 years to double real per capita income from 1780, while America achieved this feat in 47 years from 1839. In contrast, Japan took 34 years from 1900, while South Korean took 11 years from 1966.

Several scholars have argued that a crucial factor in East Asian countries transforming their sleepy and backward villages into modern cosmopolitan cities was the coming to power of strong, authoritarian and "brook-no-nonsense" governments. These governments were committed to improving the lot of their people, by introducing wide-ranging investment-friendly policies that could stimulate the economy, earn foreign currencies and provide jobs for workers.[17] A key characteristic in this all-out drive to improve living standards was the emphasis on the role of high-level manpower in economic development, and the consequent investment in human capital.[18] This was seen in the sequential nature of educational expansion: in the early stages of growth and industrialisation, the expansion of primary education took priority. Subsequently, due to changes in the economy, first secondary and then tertiary education became the foci for expansion.

The school curriculum in these Asian societies is strongly controlled by the state, and this has resulted in a uniform national curriculum, unlike the situation in many Western countries, where a decentralised curriculum exists. A national system of assessment is established in parallel with this centralised curriculum. This national assessment system plays a critical role in selecting and allocating pupils through highly competitive and norm-referenced public examinations to elite institutions of higher learning. Where provision of education is universal, like in the lower levels of schooling, these public examinations serve the function of determining the stream of education which the student enters e.g., in Singapore, students take a streaming examination at the end of Primary Four and Primary Six, to determine their educational stream in the competitive school system.

The pattern of teaching and learning has been shaped by, and has also shaped, this competitive and pressurising ethos: the knowledge and skills transmitted to pupils focus on what is perceived to be necessary for the public examination. Pupils are encouraged to remember information, and the key to success is diligence. The ultimate objective is to graduate with distinction, as a good academic track record is correlated with higher lifetime earnings. This career-motivated mentality of the typical Asian student makes sense within a socio-economic context where public provision for the disadvantaged is minimal, in comparison with the generous provision in the West. In addition, it is accentuated by the efforts of both state and family alike to place the Asian student in more instrumental disciplines like business, engineering and computing. In the case of the state, it is to ensure that there will be enough workers to run the new knowledge-based economy; in the case of the family, it is to ensure that their ward can find a job when he finally completes his education.

The Cultural Context of Learning in the East

The strong emphasis on education in Asian society is in turn reinforced by the importance which Confucian culture has traditionally placed on education. For example, the opening sentence of the *Analects* (I:1) refers to the significance and joy of learning: "Is it not pleasant to learn with a constant perseverance and application?" In fact, close scrutiny of the *Analects* reveals that the term "learning" pervades the whole literature, thus qualifying it to be called a book of learning. Similarly, in the *Three Characters Classic*, a major elementary guide to knowledge for Chinese students over the past 600 years, there is a poem about the significance of education:[19]

> *Men, one and all, in infancy are virtuous at heart.*
> *Their natures are much the same, the practice wide apart.*
> *Without Instruction's aid, our instinct grow less pure.*
> *By aiming at thoroughness only can teaching ensure.*
> *… To feed the body, not the mind – fathers, on you the blame!*
> *Instruction without severity, the idle teacher's shame.*
> *If a child does not learn, this is not as it should be.*
> *How, with a youth of idleness, can age escape the blight?*
> *… Diligence has its reward, play has no gain.*
> *Be on your guard, and put forth your strength.*

The traditional emphasis on education in the Confucian society has an internal and external dimension. Internally, education is important for personal development and human perfectibility. Externally, it is important for social mobility. There is a firm belief that these two ends of education are achievable by whosoever has a heart to try. Coupled with this reliance on one's efforts, willpower and concentration of the mind is the strong emphasis on education across all strata of society, from the individual student to his parents/teachers and employers. This has contributed to a cultural context of learning in the East which can be described in the following way. First, there is a high degree of parental involvement in and commitment to the education of their children. Second, teachers occupy a relatively high status in Asian society, and there is a strong commitment on their part to teaching and to involvement in their students' overall development. Third, the premise of egalitarian access to the rewards of successful learning permeates all levels of society. Fourth, there is a strong assumption that it is effort rather than innate ability which yields rewards in schooling (or as Confucius has put it, "by nature close together, in practice far apart"). Finally, the occupational system in the East values education as appropriate preparation for work, as seen in the emphasis of employers on the academic track record of the student.[20]

The Competitive and Performance-Oriented Student in Asian Society

The confluence of historical and cultural forces has shaped the development of the Asian educational system, which is highly instrumental, regimented, pressurising, competitive and performance-oriented, as we have seen in the example on Japan. Such a system does not provide a conducive climate for creativity, which requires a lot of room for individual experimentation. The lack of creativity of the Asian student is reflected in many aspects of his behaviour. One of them is his tendency to take a competitive and performance-oriented approach in his studies, which leaves him with little time for intellectual meandering in the wilderness of the mind. In Singapore, entire schools have been smitten with this *kiasu* desire to be first, as can be seen in the following incident. In the 1990s, the Ministry of Education decided to carry out an annual ranking exercise for secondary schools. In this ranking exercise, all the secondary schools in Singapore would be ranked from first to last, in terms of their students' performance in the national examination for those examinable subjects which they were enrolled in. Not long after this annual ranking exercise was put in place, there was a report in the local newspapers about how students in some rank-conscious schools were being discouraged from enrolling in those examinable subjects which the school was traditionally weak in, especially subjects in the humanities like literature and history. Instead, their students' choices were directed towards the study of subjects in the hard sciences like Maths, Science and Biology which the school as a whole excelled in, and which would *ipso facto* improve its standing in the annual ranking exercise, if the majority of its students offer them as examinable subjects.

The Reliance of the Asian Student on Model Answers

The obsession of the Asian student with grades and doing well in national exams accounts for his habit of buying self-help books and "model answers" to past-years examination questions. These study aids, which aim to improve a student's performance in a national exam, sell like hot cakes among parents and students alike. For example, in Singapore, exam papers from top primary schools are in such demand that they are being sold illegally for as much as S$60 a set, causing concern among the schools about copyright infringement. However, if these parents are bothered by their unlawful behaviour, they are not showing it. Instead, they argue that the exam papers are worth the money because they are better than any assessment book which they could buy in a bookshop. Said Mrs Karen Ong, 36, a housewife, "My daugher goes to an average school. I am afraid the standard is too low. That's why I paid over $100 for some papers."[21]

Model answers!

The Lack of Passion of the Asian Student for What He Studies

The desire of the Asian student to do well in tests and exams is mirrored by a lack of passion for what he studies. This lack of passion is not surprising, considering that when the Asian student picks a course to study, he typically chooses one with good market value, i.e., which can assist him in finding a good job later on when he graduates. Hence business, engineering and computer-related courses are popular with Asian students, compared to courses in the humanities like literature, history or philosophy, which have less market value. The inflexibility of the Asian education system in forcing him to take up compulsory units in a certain course or programme also contributes to the lack of interest in what he studies. For example, in the case of Japan, its educational system is so regimented that by the decree of the Ministry of Education, every second-grader in the nation must be taught to appreciate Beethoven's Turkish March, while leading Japanese universities in Tokyo and Kyoto regularly select their students based on a competitive entrance examination.[22]

In contrast, Western students who are applying for places in esteemed universities can improve their chances by demonstrating a talent for say, grinding telescope lenses or writing Latin verses. They also seem to be more passionate about what they learn, in comparison with their Asian counterparts. For example, while I was doing my postgraduate studies in Australia, I met a Caucasian undergraduate who chatted with me in accented Mandarin, and informed me that he would like to do further research in Jungian psychology because the topics in this branch of psychology e.g., dreams, the collective unconscious and the spiritual side of life, fascinated him. Meanwhile, another Caucasian undergraduate doing her Honours in anthropology had just come back from a research stint in Brazil. She informed me that after she graduated, she would like to work in an organisation that advances the cause of disadvantaged minorities, like the Aboriginals in Australia. But the Asian undergraduates whom I met invariably enrolled in engineering or business courses, and hoped to find well-paid and secure jobs in big multinational organisations when they graduated. This applies not only to those Asian students who had come a long way from home to invest in a degree, but also to their counterparts who were Australian citizens e.g., Chinese students who were born in Australia or whose families emigrated when they were young.

If the Asian student decides to do something different, chances are his intention will raise many eyebrows. For example, many years ago, when I informed my parents that I was going to take up psychology in the university, instead of the usual disciplines (e.g., medicine, law, engineering, business and computer science), they told me that I was mad, because it was going to be very difficult for me to find a job when I graduated. It would appear that such ingrained mindsets are hard to break, as can be gleaned in this second example about Ms Ang Geok Ling, the youngest member of the recent Singapore expedition to Antarctica. One team, which Ms Ang belongs to, will attempt to scale Mount Vinson Massif, the highest peak in Antarctica at 4,897 metres, while another team will trek 1,100 kilometres to the South Pole on foot, hauling sledges that weigh 160 kilograms each. Ms Ang, who graduated from a local polytechnic in 1997 and is working now as a staff nurse, told reporters: "My parents found out that I was in Antarctica 2000 only after my pictures appeared in the papers. I explained to them what the expedition was about and they said the usual things like 'What are you going to gain from this?' and 'Why can't you behave more like a girl?' But I told them I wouldn't give up this trip for anything."

The Silent and Passive Student in Asian Society

The lack of passion of the Asian student for what he studies is mirrored by his unwillingness to take charge of the learning process. Instead, Asian students expect their teachers to give them explicit instructions on what to study, what materials they should read and when to read them, what tasks and assignments they should complete and how to do them. They feel uneasy about unstructured situations in which they have to decide what to do for themselves. They hesitate to ask questions and do not participate actively in class, unlike their Western counterparts. In discussion groups, Asian students typically take a long time to warm up, looking at one another with nothing much to say. Professor Ho and his colleagues have termed this the phenomenon of *silence* and *passivity* in their insightful paper "An Investigative Research in Teaching and Learning in Chinese Societies".[23] They argued that this phenomenon has its roots in Confucian socialisation, in which exercising caution in speech is a virtue, while opening one's mouth exposes one to various dangers, such as invoking the anger of, and retribution by, authority figures; appearing immodest; or ridicule by one's peers. In educational settings, this phenomenon of silence and passivity results directly from role definitions, i.e., the teacher imparts knowledge while the student listens.

The *Kiasi* Student in Asian Society

Not surprisingly, the silent and passive student in Asian society is averse to failure, and will avoid it at all costs, by taking a *kiasi* (afraid to die) approach, instead of a risk-oriented approach in the learning process. The *modus operandus* of the *kiasi* Asian student when preparing for an important test or exam is as follows. First, he will attempt to get clues from the teacher on what topics would likely be set. At the same time, he will try to guess which questions are likely to be asked, based on the trend of previous test or exam papers. Relying on the information which has been gathered, he will "memorise like mad" a few selected topics, using model answers as a guide. Then in the actual test or exam, he will pick only those "safe" questions which he has crammed for, while avoiding those "risky" questions with no straightforward answers. The *kiasi* student may do well with this approach, but there are two nagging concerns. The first concern is that he has not really *understood* the topic, but is merely being "exam-smart". The second concern is that he does not have the opportunity to experience and learn from failure, since he has been so *kiasi* in the learning process. A student who behaves in such a cautious manner may do well in exams, but he will find it difficult to be creative. This is because in order to be creative, one must dare to take risks and face failures, as the following boxed article on the *investment theory of creativity* indicates.

The Investment Theory of Creativity: Buying Low and Selling High

The investment theory of creativity was developed by Sternberg and Lubart,[24] and uses the stock market as a metaphor. A new investor in shares is advised to "buy low and sell high". In other words, buy when the share prices of a company are dropping, sell when they are going up. This sounds pretty sensible advice to take, except for one thing: it requires boldness on the part of the investor to "buck the trend" and buy shares which nobody else seems to want. A creative person is like the bold investor, who is willing to "buy low and sell high", in the realm of ideas. "Buying low" for the creator means pursuing ideas that are unknown or out of favour, but that nevertheless have growth potential. Often, when these ideas are first presented, they encounter resistance, for they challenge the established way of doing things. The creative person persists in the face of this resistance and eventually "sells high" when his idea catches on with the rest of the field.

The investment theory of creativity underlines the fact that the creative act involves an element of risk in it. Risk is the chance that the gamble which one has taken on an idea or proposal will not work, or will not be accepted by the community. This will result in a net loss, instead of a net gain, for the person. Because of the inherent risk, many people refrain from the creative act, sticking to what is familiar instead. These people are risk-averse, pursuing a policy of "buying high", i.e., they prefer to work with those ideas which are well developed and accepted. This may seem odd, but anyone who has withstood the isolation and ridicule of going against the mainstream knows just how difficult it is to blaze one's own trail in life.

Risk aversion can ultimately be traced to a low tolerance for failure. Research has shown that failure tolerance declines as children progress through school, i.e., the longer they have been students in school, the more reluctant they are to expose themselves to situations where they can fail. According to Sternberg and Lubart, the main reason why students have a low tolerance for failure is that they have been subjected to an educational regime in which failure is punished, whereas good work is rewarded. For example, if they fail in a test, they may be scolded by their teacher, whereas if they pass, the teacher will praise them. So by the time students graduate from university, their tolerance for failure is at the trough. This reasoning can account for a certain phenomenon in our society: entrepreneurs who embark on risky business ventures are not highly educated, while university graduates typically work in big, stable and secure organisations.

The risk-averse person with a high fear of failure will never succeed as a creator. Neither, however, will the person who takes crazy
risks. To be a successful creator, you need to take *sensible* risks, i.e., to
use your intelligence and knowledge to balance your tendency to
take chances. An example of such a creator is the Swiss immunolo-
gist Dr Jean F. Borel, who is employed by Sandoz Ltd., a longtime
leader in pharmaceutical innovations. Dr Borel was working on developing a drug that could safely suppress the human immune system, thereby allowing transplanted organs to survive. He narrowed
his search down to cyclosporin A, but preliminary tests revealed that
it could not be absorbed in human blood. If so, then it was worthless
as a rejection remedy for transplant operations. It looked like the
research project, which had already cost the company much time
and money, was going to be axed. However, Dr Borel would not give
up. He was sure that the negative result was due to a technical problem. He based this inference on years of observing the easy absorp-
tion of cyclosporin A in the blood of rats and rhesus monkeys.

He asked permission from his company to conduct an official
experiment on himself. He knew that an animal could not be killed
with one dose of cyclosporin A, and he intended to take it in much
the same way. Permission was granted, and so Dr Borel mixed himself a cocktail containing 500 milligrams of cyclosporin A, and drank
it down. Two different bioassays a few hours later detected a significant level of cyclosporin A in his blood, proving that it can indeed be
absorbed in pharmacologically active concentration. The research
project was not axed, and eventually came to successful fruition when
the US Food and Drug Administration (FDA) gave its formal approval to Sandoz to market cyclosporin A as a revolutionary rejection remedy. In the first two years after the FDA approval, the number
of liver transplants doubled, while heart and pancreas transplants
tripled; survival rates for all transplant operations have continued
to increase as more is learned about how to use cyclosporin A. Dr
Borel's gamble had paid off.[25]

Parental Support for the Hardworking Student in Asian Society

Another notable characteristic of the Asian student is that he studies very
hard. One study has compared the performance of Asian-American students to their counterparts from other minority groups in the United
States, and found that the former group did much better than the latter
group. The good performance of these Asian-American students was attributed to their willingness to spend extra hours in study, reinforced by
parents who believe in the values of education.[26]

The major role of the family in the education of the Asian child is confirmed in a separate study, which involved first- and fifth-graders, as well as their families in Japan, Taiwan and America.[27] The researchers of this big cross-cultural study reported that the Asian families attached greater importance to their children's academic achievement than the American families. They "dedicated themselves to their child's school-work"; this dedication was demonstrated by the amount of space, funds and time which was allocated to the child.

In contrast, the researchers reported that "American families did not show the same commitment to academic achievement for their children and they did not spend a large amount of time helping them". American parents were also found to be more easily satisfied with their children's academic performance, and they reported being more concerned with their children's psychological well-being and all-round development than only with their academic achievement, in comparison with the Asian parents in the study.

The willingness of Asian parents to provide extra resources for their children to do well, as well as the willingness of the children themselves to put extra effort into their studies, is reflected in the thriving tuition industry in Asian society, which is worth tens of millions of dollars. For a good example of how far Asian parents and children are willing to go to secure the right set of academic results, see the following boxed article.

Interestingly enough, the results of a recent study conducted on over 400 Singaporean students of equal ability indicate that those who spent more hours on private tuition did more *poorly* in their year-end examinations, compared to those who had fewer hours of instruction by private tutors. The researcher cited two reasons to explain this surprising and provocative finding. First, it could be that students were "overstudying" a subject to the point that they got turned off by it. Second, it could be due to the poor quality of the tuition which they received. The study also found that parents played an important role in how their students fared. Those students who described their mothers as encouraging had better grades, leading the researcher to suggest that instead of wasting their money on hiring tuition teachers, parents should provide a good educational environment for their children in the house.[28]

Spending The New Year By Checking Into A Hotel To Study For Exams

The desire to do well in entrance examinations is so intense for some Japanese students and their concerned parents that they are willing to sacrifice huge amounts of time, effort and money, so as to make it through these "examinations from hell". One such case was reported in *The Straits Times*, under the headline "Swotting It out in Hotel – over the New Year".[29] According to this newspaper article, the New Year holiday in Japan is also a time for some parents to lock their children up in a hotel, so that they could study ten hours a day for a private school entrance examination.

These students, aged between 11 and 17, were enrolled in the six-day New Year Special Training Course, which was offered by the Japan Institute for Tutors, a company with 75,000 private teachers across the nation. Six of the most experienced tutors would stay at the hotel and teach the children during the crash course, which did not come cheap: excluding hotel-room charges and meals, the fee for the six days was about US$5,400 for 36 hours of one-to-one study with a tutor. There was an additional charge of about US$400 for enrolment and counselling. One family was even reported to be spending about US$9,400 for the intensive course, because three relatives were staying at the hotel, along with the studying child.

The rationale, according to Mr Noboru Furukawa, the president of the Japan Institute for Tutors, was to create an environment in which the entire family faced "exam war". Mr Furukawa, who nick-named himself Dr Owl, said that Japan's economic woes have not discouraged Japanese parents from spending money on education, and dismissed the criticism that a prestigious school didn't guarantee a good life. Instead, he argued that higher education was an asset that parents could give their children, and spending on education was like making savings that would not diminish. The crash course began with a Shinto ritual in the hotel classroom, in which a priest recited a prayer for the success of students, in front of an altar with traditional offerings such as rice, salt, dried squid, vegetables, fruit and fish. After this religious ceremony, the children, together with their parents, raised their fists in the air and shouted slogans pledging success at the entrance exam. Their youthful heads banded with the phrase "Sure to Pass the Exam", the students then retreated with the experienced tutors to tiny rooms in the hotel for two-hour-long teaching sessions. Ten of the 22 children would remain overnight at the hotel to "increase concentration on studies", while others would commute to the hotel daily for the next six days.

For one student named Takuma, this exam cramming was his first experience of spending nights away from his family and friends. He was reported as feeling "very grateful" to his parents for sending him to this crash course, and admitted that he was suffering a skin rash "under the pressure", a point which was confirmed by a tutor named Watanabe, who acknowledged that the mental pressure sometimes triggered physical ailments e.g., one of her students had become so stressed that he became blind when sitting at his desk. As for Tomomi, aged 12, it was not skin rashes or temporary blindness which afflicted her, but the understandable regret of a child that she could not enjoy this holiday season. "Please, please tape the television music programmes while I'm away," she was reported to have asked her mother.

Why It Makes Sense for the Asian Student to Work Hard

We have seen that Asian students work extremely hard, and they have supportive parents to cajole them to put in the requisite effort. The question inevitably arises: why does it make sense for the Asian student to work so hard (and for his parents to push him to work so hard)? The answer can be stated as follows: it makes sense for the Asian student to work hard now and do well in his studies, as this will enable him to find a good job in a big, stable and reputable organisation later on when he goes out to work. These good jobs are hard to come by, and there are many graduates each year who compete for them. If the Asian student does not work hard now and do well in his studies, he is likely to lose out to these graduates with star-studded academic track records. He is then left with the less attractive job opportunities in smaller companies, which neither pay well nor offer a stable and secure career track. He may not even get a job if the economy is not doing well. In a face-conscious society in which welfare provision is miniscule, this will really be the worst possible scenario. This is unlike the situation in the West. For example, in the United States, there are many different paths to joining a big company. The American student can spend years pursuing his talent and interest in drawing, but during or even after university, he can change his mind and decide to go into business. However, according to Yoshimura and Anderson, if you meet a Japanese salaryman, you can know with certainty that his career did not just suddenly materialise out of the blue. Instead, he can be a salaryman only because he has been on the right track for a long time.[30]

I quit! I'm going to Hollywood to become an actor!

My personal experience testifies to the freedom that the Western student enjoys in his studies. When I was in Australia, I met three Caucasian students. The first student was a young Australian lady who was also doing her PhD in psychology. She told me that after she had got her PhD (or become "permanently head-damaged", as the joke goes among graduate students), she was going to take a year or so off to travel around the world; she would support herself by doing some odd jobs (e.g., bartendering) in these foreign countries. I remember thinking at that time that my mother would be shocked if I told her that I was going to serve beers and liquors to strangers after I got my PhD!

The second student was a brilliant science graduate who gave up his PhD scholarship midway through his research to take up a four-year basic dentistry course as an undergraduate, because according to him, undergraduate science was okay, but he could not stand doing science at the postgraduate level; besides, he liked the idea of poking around in people's mouths. The third Australian I met was a student who had done extremely well in his high school, but performed dismally in the first year of his engineering degree. As a result, he decided to take time off from his studies to do what he liked best in life: surfing the waves on the Gold Coast of Australia, while pondering the meaning of life, as he put it to me. The Vice-Chancellor in his university, I was informed, supported his decision.

The Inspiration Behind the Asian Student

One additional point to observe about the Asian student is that his family serves as an important source of motivation for him, i.e., his desire to do well in school springs from an internalised wish to fulfil the expectations of significant others, especially his parents, who have made a lot of sacrifices for him. This is known as socially-oriented achievement motivation (SOAM).[31] A person who is infused with SOAM is not so much concerned with expressing the latent talent in himself, as with achieving the goal which his family has set for him. To this end, he will persevere day and night. But once he has achieved the goal which has been set, the intense achievement motivation formerly evident may vanish.

This analysis fits many anecdotal observations indicating that once admitted into the university of their choice, or hired by their preferred company, Japanese students who have been extremely competitive and performance-oriented are no longer interested in achievement.[32] In contrast, the desire to do well in school for the Western student does not spring from an internalised wish to fulfil the expectations of his family. Instead, it springs from an autonomous desire to achieve personal standards of excellence. This is known as individually-oriented achievement motivation (IOAM). A person who is infused with IOAM is self-reliant, and pursues his own goals in life. This will facilitate his creativity as a person.

The Meaning of Success in the East and West

This basic difference in achievement motivation between the East and West is seen in the contrasting way in which the Asian and Westerner construe the meaning of success.[33] In the case of Americans, the concepts of free will and individualism are emphasised as being major components of success; however, these concepts are less emphasised by the Japanese and Chinese. Instead, they often emphasise the driving force of a social group when explaining their achievement motivation. For example, one study which analysed the content of achievement-related stories, which have been specially written to motivate young Chinese children to work hard, found that they invariably focused on collective goals rather than individual goals;[34] another study found that the strength of achievement motivation was positively correlated with family and filial piety;[35] a third study found that Chinese achievement needs reflected a desire to fulfil the expectations of ingroups such as family or clan.[36]

Chapter Summary

In this chapter, I looked at how Asian and Western students strive for success. I began by making a distinction between performance and mastery goals, and looking at their contextual influences. Then I surveyed the views of two famous creators (Albert Einstein and George Bernard Shaw) on education. Both suffered negative experiences while in school. At this juncture, I shifted my focus to the competitive, pressurising and regimented educational system in Asian society. I described the historical and cultural context of the Asian educational system. I then delineated five characteristics of the typical student in an Asian society. He is competitive and performance-oriented, lacks passion in what he studies, is silent and passive, and adopts a *kiasi* (afraid to die) attitude in the learning process. He is also an extremely hardworking student who receives much parental support to score good grades. I explained why it makes sense for the Asian student to behave in this manner, given the type of society he lives in. I pointed out that the main inspiration behind the Asian student is the family, unlike his Western counterpart who is more individually motivated. In addition, I noted that success in the East is more socially oriented, while success in the West is more individually oriented. The following boxed article looks at how the Asian student compares with his Western counterpart.

How Does the Asian Student Compare with His Western Counterpart?

Having looked at how students strive for success in the East and West, the inevitable question arises: how does the Asian student compare with his or her Western counterpart? The best way to answer this question is to look at the experiences of those educators who have taught students in the East and West. An example of such an educator is Dr J. Devan, a lecturer who has six years of undergraduate teaching in the humanities at a well-regarded American university and before that, at Singapore universities. He recorded his experience in an essay entitled "Comparing the Singaporean Undergraduate with the American".[37]

In his essay, Dr Devan began with the observation that most distinctions made between American students (who are popularly acknowledged as articulate, critical and independent) and Singaporean students (who are almost always described as hardworking but passive and dull) mistake appearances for truth. What is not commonly realised, according to Dr Devan, is that although American students are generally more articulate than their Asian counterparts, they are also intellectually conservative. As accepting of the ethos of their society as Singaporean students are of theirs, they are equally the product of a culture which is skilled at encouraging ideological conformity. The Frenchman Alexis de Tocqueville, a keen observer of American society, arrived at a similar conclusion more than 100 years ago, when he pointed out that the American refusal to accept established opinion on the one hand, and conformity to the opinions of one's peers on the other, are actually two sides of the same coin. This is because when one can no longer rely on tradition and authority, one inevitably looks to others for confirmation of one's judgments.[38]

Dr Devan observed that the nature of the American classroom hinders the recognition of this conservatism. The presence of debate and the lively atmosphere of the classroom – although commendable, as it encourages the student to engage in creative thinking – can nevertheless mask the absence of genuine inquiry, as students expend a good deal of time and energy in arriving at conclusions which they already hold. In addition, the openness of discussion in the American classroom does not in itself guarantee educational excellence: Dr Devan has discovered – much to his surprise – that the American students whom he had taught knew very little. In fact, as surprising as this may sound, the average American undergraduate at a major university is probably less knowledgeable in a given field of learning than his average Singaporean counterpart. This assertion is congruent with the anecdotal observation made by another American lecturer at a Hong Kong university, concerning the Chinese and American students whom he had taught: " … in the West, most university students have strong opinions and these opinions may or may not be based on knowledge. In Asia, the students are mostly very knowledgeable, but few have opinions on issues."[39]

Dr Devan then pointed out a paradox of the American system of education: although the average undergraduate disappoints, the very best are incomparable. He believed that this gap – or "shocking difference", as he calls it – between the average and the superlative, and not liveliness or independence of mind, is what distinguishes the American undergraduate from the Singaporean. He posed this twin puzzle: how does a system that seems to generate a low average produce individuals that are so exceptional? And why does the system in Singapore, that manages a better average, fail to produce incomparable talents as often as the high average might lead a person to expect?

Dr Devan suggested that the answer to this twin puzzle can be found in the different educational systems in Singapore and America. The Singapore system manages to achieve a high average among its students by applying a constant and incessant pressure that forces them to meet established common standards. At periodic intervals in the student's life, he must cross formidable hurdles in the form of mass examinations, before proceeding to the next stage. So by the time the average student arrives at the university, he has successfully negotiated a slew of stringent exams. Augmenting the traditional investment in education, this constant and incessant pressure ensures that the average undergraduate in Singapore can excel academically, even when institutions or teachers are flawed. In contrast, nothing like this constant and incessant pressure exists in the American educational system. Lacking a set of universally applied standards, schools in various parts of the country find their own levels of educational excellence. As a result, according to Dr Devan, American students typically arrive at major universities undeserving of the educational excellence of their institutions. Yet, it is precisely this lack of a standard process and a fixed structure that has enabled the unusual American student to soar much above the level of his peers.

Dr Devan illustrated this paradox by describing a personal encounter with such a student. His name was Andrew, and he was an intellectually gifted young man of 16, who was enrolled in the first year of undergraduate study. After a few weeks of classes, it became clear to Dr Devan that the only way he could adequately teach this student was to conduct another seminar outside class, with a different syllabus, just for him. By the end of the semester, the lecturer found that he had to involve his colleagues in Andrew's studies, because this student had begun to examine issues which were not altogether familiar to him. At semester's end, Andrew wrote an outstanding term paper, of a quality which was comparable even to the peer-reviewed articles written by senior professors in established journals. Dr Devan noted that remarkable as Andrew was, his outstanding term paper could not have been conceived without extracurricular nurturing. He was helped ungrudgingly; everyone was eager to teach him; nobody, including his peers, complained. This is possible in the flexible educational system of America, which permits students to work at their own pace, instead of passing them through an "academic conveyor belt", as in the educational system of Singapore, in which all students are assessed by a uniform set of criteria involving common examinations in a level-playing field.

Dr Devan believed that Singapore students can benefit from this type of flexibility, based on his encounter with certain average or above-average students from Singapore who, after they have been transplanted into an American university, turn into fine academic swans. Without losing their disciplined habits, they become adventurous, confident and intellectually expansive. Dr Devan concluded that the Singapore educational system should find an optimal balance between maintaining common standards in educational excellence and being flexible, like its American counterpart, by allowing more exploratory freedom for its students, as the Andrews of this world cannot be processed according to a fixed structure.

To achieve this laudable goal of producing flexible and creative thinkers rather than rigid and achievement-oriented conformists, the educational system in Singapore needs to be overhauled; a revolution from the very top, which permeates the whole rank-and-file, is needed to rejuvenate the bureaucratic system. No less a person than the Prime Minister of Singapore has ignited this revolution via his challenge to educators to build "Thinking Schools, Learning Nation".[40] Since that major policy speech which he made in 1997, fundamental changes have been introduced in the educational system in Singapore. To begin with, the Ministry of Education (MOE) has given more autonomy and resources to its principals to run their own schools. For example, every principal can now make use of the annual Edusave grant to hire specialist instructors to coach their students in dance, music and life-skills, which are not in the exam syllabus. The goal here is to turn out well-rounded students who possess talents other than scoring good grades. To enable Singapore students to engage in creative and critical thinking, the school curriculum has been reduced by 20 percent. With this content reduction in the curriculum, it is hoped that Singapore teachers will have more time to assist their students to complete interdisciplinary project work, which is designed to develop their creative problem-solving abilities. Other changes have also been introduced, including the IT Masterplan, whose goal is to harness the power of the Internet to teach and learn creatively in the Singapore classroom, as well as the proposed change in the university admission criteria to include Scholastic Aptitude Test (SAT) scores of potential candidates, which reflect their critical reasoning abilities.[41] With these changes and more, perhaps the belief of Dr Devan can be proven, i.e., average students in Singapore can transform themselves into fine academic swans when nurtured in the right environment.

There is a good basis to believe that when nurtured in the right environment, Asian students can excel in a creative manner. In an article headlined "Of Asian Descent, They Are US' First Teamers",[42] it was reported that Asian-Americans of Chinese and Indian origin dominated the top 20 students picked by *USA Today* for its High School Academic First Team. These students were selected from 4,339 students nominated by their schools. As First Teamers, they were academic stars, who averaged a 3.98 grade-point average on a scale in which 4.0 denotes all "As". Seven out of the 20 scored the maximum 1,600 on the SAT. Three were in the top ten in the Inter-Science Talent Search, while four were winners of the National Council of Teachers of English Achievement Awards in Writing.

But excelling in the academic arena was not enough. Judges also considered activities, leadership and how students translated their scholarship into action. For example, among those on the roll of honours were Wei Wang, who came up with a practical method to help prevent water-main breaks in New York City by extending the life of copper alloys in pipes; Chia Jung Tsay, who not only conducted research on the chemical effects of marijuana in rats, but also made her Carnegie Hall piano solo debut at 16; Vimal Bhalodia, who exposed the vulnerability of the world's most popular cryptosystem; and Feng Zhang, who found a replication mechanism that may be used to prevent Aids and Aids-like viruses. What made these students excel? According to their teachers and mentors, they could grasp meaning quickly and make connections with ease. They also worked exceptionally hard e.g., Ms Chia, the acclaimed pianist, has been known to practise at all hours of the night. Finally, they created their own opportunities. Mr Tom Curley, president and publisher of *USA Today*, summed it up: "These students stand out for their brilliance, hard work and dedication to using their talents to benefit others. We honour them to send a message that their skills are what we as a society value most."

Notes

1. Nicholls, 1984; Ames, 1992; Dweck, 1986
2. Nicholls *et al.*, 1989; Butler, 1987; Deci *et al.*, 1991.
3. Dweck & Leggett, 1988.
4. Koestner & Zuckerman, 1994.
5. Ames & Archer, 1988.
6. Ryan, Connell & Grolnick, 1992.
7. Amabile, 1996; Deci & Ryan, 1987.
8. Reeve & Deci, 1996.
9. Amabile, 1996.
10. Stevenson, 1998.
11. *The Straits Times*, July 12, 2000.
12. *The Economist*, September 21, 1996.
13. Zeng, 1999.
14. Markus & Kitayama, 1991.
15. Ng, 2000a.
16. Morris & Sweeting, 1995; Morris, 1996.
17. Rowen, 1998.
18. Morris & Sweeting, 1995; Morris, 1996.
19. On, 1996.
20. LeVine & White, 1986.
21. *The Straits Times*, June 10, 2000.
22. Yamada, 1991; Shoji, 1995.
23. Ho, Chan & Peng, 2000.
24. Sternberg & Lubart, 1995.
25. Diebold, 1991.
26. Peng & Wright, 1994.
27. Stevenson & Lee, 1990.
28. *The Straits Times*, June 15, 1999.
29. *The Straits Times*, January 4, 1999.
30. Yoshimura & Anderson, 1997.
31. Yu & Yang, 1994.
32. Markus & Kitayama, 1991.
33. Yu & Yang, 1994.
34. Blumenthal, 1976.
35. Yu, 1974.
36. Pusey, 1977.
37. Devan, 1994.
38. Bellah *et al.*, 1985.
39. *Asiaweek*, May 22, 1998.
40. Goh, 1997.
41. Quah & Ho, 1998.
42. *The Straits Times*, May 13, 2000.

chapter 7

How Asians and Westerners Deal with Conflict

Conflict: A Paradoxical and Culture-Based Phenomenon

In the previous chapter, I argued that the typical manner in which the Asian student strives for success in the educational system does not facilitate his creativity as a person. In this chapter, I will argue in a similar vein that the typical manner in which the Asian handles conflict with a significant other does not facilitate his creativity as a person. Conflict is a paradoxical phenomenon that penetrates all forms of social relations in society. It is capable of lowering us to our basest instincts, a state of existence which is "nasty, brutish and short", to paraphrase the English political philosopher Thomas Hobbes (1588–1679). Yet, out of conflicting encounters, we often derive our most noble and lasting achievements, recognised in such international awards as the Nobel Prize for Peace, which is given out annually to those outstanding individuals who contribute to making our world a better place to live in.

Relational Contractualism: The Me-First Philosophy of the West

Conflict is conditioned by the cultural context in which it occurs, i.e., living in a certain society will influence the way the person deals with an interpersonal conflict. We have seen that in the liberal individualistic society of the West, a greater emphasis is put on the person rather than the group. Individuals who live in such a society lack a conception of what is the common good; instead, they have an abiding belief that the individual should be placed before society. For example, an American study which attempted to find out from its respondents what was special about the United States got answers such as "Individualism and the fact that it is a democracy and you

Freedom of the people

can do whatever you want" and "We really don't have any limits". The authors of this study concluded, "Consistent with the priority they place on personal happiness, young people reveal notions of America's unique character that emphasise freedom and license almost to the complete exclusion of service or participation. Although they clearly appreciate the democratic freedoms that, in their view, make theirs the best country in the world to live in, they fail to perceive a need to reciprocate by exercising the duties and responsibilities of good citizenship."[1]

The ethic of individualism in Western society implies that the person puts his needs and desires in a relationship first and foremost. The needs and desires of the other party are considered a secondary element in the relationship. Bellah and his colleagues have termed this model of relationship *relational contractualism*.[2] In this calculative model of relationship, separate but equal individuals rely on a form of cost-benefit analysis to determine whether they are getting what they are entitled to in the social relationship. If the answer is not in the affirmative, then the person will assert himself to obtain what is lacking, or withdraw and seek psychological gratification in another relationship. Behaving in this manner towards a significant other enables the person to feel a sense of equity, i.e., what he puts into the relationship is matched by what he gets out of it. However, at the same time, it leaves the relationship unstable. This is because each side has the tendency to look at a matter from his own perspective, as well as to focus on his own subjective needs and desires. The following boxed article provides a good example of this calculative approach towards close relationships in the West.

Till Death Do We Part? Let Me Count the Cost First, Darling!

In the West, the individualistic emphasis on the "I-ness" rather than the "we-ness" of the relationship can be seen in the phenomenon of "pre-nups" and "post-nups". A pre-nup is a pre-nuptial agreement between a couple who is about to be married to each other. It sets out, in a legally-binding contract, the duties and liabilities accruing to each party in the event of their marital break-up. An example is the much publicised pre-nup between the American actor Michael Douglas (*Basic Instinct*, *Wall Street*) and the Welsh actress Catherine Zeta-Jones (*Entrapment*, *The Mask of Zorro*). This pre-nuptial agreement, which was designed to safeguard Douglas' estimated US$225 million fortune, will enable Zeta-Jones, who is younger than her husband-to-be by 24 years, to get US$3 million for every year that she is married to him. Although such pre-nuptial agreements makes a mockery of the "till death do we part" ideal of True Love, nevertheless they are very popular among romancing couples in the West, who are very much "in love" with each other, as no doubt Michael Douglas and Catherine Zeta-Jones are (otherwise he would not be divorcing his wife to marry her, while she would not be expecting their first child).[3]

Pre-nups, as a way of organising the relationship between a soon-to-be-married couple, make sense in the illogical land of True Love where one in two new marriages ends in divorce. What is worrying is the advent of the "post-nup" (post-nuptial agreement) as a way of organising the relationship between an *already*-married couple, which sets out the terms of divorce even though the couple are *still* married to each other.[4] Web sites offering legal services have begun advertising post-nups alongside pre-nups. For now, many US courts are wary or ambivalent about post-nups (just as they once fretted over pre-nups), as can be gleaned in the case of the Pacelli couple. 11 years into their marriage, Antonio Pacelli said he would divorce his wife, Francesca Pacelli, unless she agreed to "certain terms regarding their economic relationship". Not wanting to break up her home while their two sons were young, Francesca agreed in 1986 that she would get US$540,000, but no alimony, if they divorced. The couple remained married for eight more years, and then split up. In the acrimonious battle which was fought out in a New Jersey court, the judge ruled the post-nuptial agreement between Antonio and Francesca as fair, but an appeals court overturned the ruling. Post-nuptial agreements, it said, could not be accepted if they were coerced, which was the position of Mrs Pacelli, who told the judge that she had signed "because I didn't want my sons to grow up without a father". Reflecting on this and other cases, a family attorney commented, "If you have a post-nuptial agreement during the course of your marriage, the marriage is doomed … the bond of trust, once broken, is over. Like Shakespeare said, you cannot unring the bell."

The Importance of the Ingroup in Asian Society

In contrast to the strong emphasis on the self in the West, the social group, rather than the individual person, is seen as the basic building block of society in the East. The individual is encouraged to "sacrifice the small me so as to complete the big me", as a popular Chinese saying goes, i.e., the person should put the group's needs before his own personal needs. This social emphasis which is placed on the group vis-à-vis the person is reflected in the influence which the ingroup has over the day-to-day life of the Asian.

An *ingroup* refers to those people who occupy a central position in a person's life, with whom he is willing to cooperate without demanding an equitable return, and for whom separation will lead him to experience discomfort or even pain.[5] An example of such an ingroup is one's family. The more ingroups a person has, the narrower and shallower is the influence of the group over him. The person who lives in a Western society belongs to many different groups, but is generally inclined to maintain his separateness and autonomy from the group. In contrast, the Asian has fewer ingroups, but these groups have a lot of influence on his behaviour.

For example, in Japanese schools, students are grouped into teams called *hans*. Members of each *han* eat and play together, and take turns to perform specific responsibilities, whether it is daily cleaning of the school premises or serving lunch. Competition is based on team, rather than individual, events. Hence the social environment encourages the individual to conform to the group. A student who refuses to do so can be teased by the other members for not fitting into the group, a phenomenon which is known as *ijime* (school bullying).

Other research has highlighted the prominence of the group in Asian society, in comparison with the prominence of the individual in Western society. In a study on group interaction, Wheeler, Reis and Bond asked Chinese university students in Hong Kong to keep a record of their interactions that lasted ten minutes or more, over a period of two weeks.[6] Relative to the standardisation norms developed in the United States for this task, the Chinese have fewer interactions (2.25 versus 6.00) per day, more group interactions (29 percent versus 17 percent), longer interactions (average 61 minutes versus 53 minutes), and fewer interaction partners (Chinese: 15 same sex, 10 different sex; Americans: 22 same sex, 17 different sex). In addition, they found that most interactions among their Chinese respondents occur between the person and the person's group, while most interactions among Westerners occur between two persons. Other studies have found that Asians are more likely to eat in larger groups, while Westerners are more likely to eat in smaller groups; Korean skiers often ski in groups, whereas Americans tend to ski alone or as couples.[7]

Gan-Qing in the Asian Relationship

The Asian sticks with members of his own ingroup, and conforms to their wishes and desires, because of the *gan-qing* which he has developed with them. This term refers to the "human emotion" which endures between two persons through the ups and downs of life. These two persons may be related because they are family members, close friends or business partners. Whatever the basis of the relationship, *gan-qing* typically takes a long period of time to develop, and it evolves in a subtle and imperceptible manner. However, once it has come into being, the parties concerned will look out for the welfare of each other, come what may, to the point of sacrificing oneself for the other person if need be. Westerners, with their culturally-acquired inability to "choose the lighter happiness", will find it strange and perplexing to conduct one's human affairs on this earth in accordance with the dictates of *gan-qing*. But for Asians, it is the social glue that binds them together, through thick and thin. This is depicted in the following boxed article, which looks at *gan-qing* in the world of the Asian pugilist.

Gan-Qing in the World of the Asian Pugilist

Gan-qing runs very deep in Asian society. A movie director in the East has attempted to portray this emotional side of the Asian via a story concerning a Japanese pugilist and his Chinese disciple. The *gan-qing* between teacher and disciple developed accidentally (the Chinese would call it *yuan fen* or fate). The Chinese disciple hailed from a famous pugilistic family with a glorious past. His father, a master pugilist, was in possession of a certain skill which he hoped to pass on to his only son. Unfortunately, the young man had a weak disposition from birth, and so was unable to preserve the family tradition in this particular area. The master pugilist was extremely disappointed in having such a son. He constantly reprimanded him, refusing to take him on as a disciple when the time came. Instead, he made disciples of other young men in the neighbourhood. Not surprisingly, the son grew up to be an unhappy young man.

At this juncture, the story shifted to the Japanese pugilist. He was a master pugilist himself, with one difference: he leapfrogged other master pugilists by stealing their skills. He did this by watching a master pugilist practise his skill, then memorising the steps, and then practising the steps himself. This *modus operandus* was enacted in total secrecy. The master pugilist from Japan heard about the fame of his Chinese counterpart, and decided to steal his skills. So he arrived at his house, posing as a job-seeker. Not knowing that the Japanese was a master pugilist who was going to steal his skills, the Chinese retained his service as an ordinary cleaner in the family compound. This gave the Japanese an opportunity to embark on his *modus operandus*.

While he was stealing the skill of the father, the plight of the son attracted his attention and sympathy. The two struck up a friendship. However, the older Japanese did not reveal his true identity to the younger Chinese. But the Chinese found out the truth, when he caught the Japanese practising his father's skills in secret. Initially, the Japanese wanted to kill the Chinese (dead men tell no tales). However, he could not bring himself to do it, because of the *gan-qing* that had developed between them. Instead, he gave in to the pleading of the young Chinese man to take him on as his disciple. This, of course, had to be done in secret, in order not to expose his real identity. The day came when the Japanese decided to return to his own country. By this time, his Chinese disciple had become an extremely skilful pugilist himself, although no one in the family knew this. In appreciation for what his Japanese teacher had done for him, the Chinese disciple took out a piece of jade carving and gave it to him. This jade carving was to signify their indelible bond as teacher and disciple.

Not long after the Japanese had left, trouble loomed up within the Chinese pugilistic world. A formidable challenger had come to dethrone its head, who was the father of the Chinese disciple. However, he could not fight against the challenger, for he had fallen ill. He instructed his best disciple to stand in for him, but the latter was defeated. It was during this time that his son revealed his prowess as an extremely skilful pugilist by soundly beating the challenger in a straight fight. His fame quickly grew in the community, and his father became extremely proud of him. Before he died, he appointed his son as the new head of the Chinese pugilistic world.

Years passed, and the relationship between China and Japan took a turn for the worse. Japan sent her best fighter to have a duel-to-the-death with the best fighter from China. The new head of the Chinese pugilistic world patriotically stepped forward to serve his country in her hour of need. But when he found out who his opponent was, he became extremely reluctant to engage in this duel. For the fighter from Japan was none other than his former teacher! But the duel-to-the-death had to go on (again, the Chinese would call this fate).

At first, the Chinese disciple could not concentrate on the duel, because of the *gan-qing* which he felt towards his former teacher. It looked like the Chinese was going to lose the fight when the Japanese took out something. It was the piece of jade carving which symbolised their past relationship as teacher and disciple. In an extremely cold and harsh tone of voice, the Japanese fighter told his opponent that he no longer regarded him with any *gan-qing*; he expected the Chinese fighter to show no human emotion to him too. As proof of what he said, he snapped the piece of jade carving in two, and flung it at his opponent's face.

From this point of the duel on, the Chinese fighter blocked out the *gan-qing* which he felt for his teacher. This enabled him to deliver a series of fatal blows on the Japanese, who tumbled onto the floor. As he was falling, something fell out of his shirt. It was another piece of jade carving, similar to the one he had taken out earlier. A closer examination by the Chinese disciple revealed that it was the jade carving which he had given to his teacher many years ago. The hor-

rible truth of this duel-to-the-death came to light: the Chinese disciple had been misled into killing his Japanese teacher. His teacher did
not want to be the one who killed his disciple, because of the *gan-
qing* between them!

Maintaining *Guan-Xi* (Relation) by Giving and Saving *Mian-Zi* (Face)

We have seen from the above story that *gan-qing* is the social glue that
binds Asians together through thick and thin. The deeper the *gan-qing*
between two Asians, the stronger the *guan-xi* (relation) between them,
and the harder will they attempt to maintain this *guan-xi*, so that the *gan-
qing* which "glues" them together will not be "hurt". The Asian maintains his *guan-xi* with his bosom counterpart by giving *mian-zi* (face) to
him in public, or preventing him from losing *mian-zi* in public. An example of giving *mian-zi* is when the Asian praises the work of his friend in
public. An example of preventing the loss of *mian-zi* is when the Asian
refrains from correcting what his friend has said in public (he will do this
correction privately, when no one else is around).

If the Asian fails to give or save the *mian-zi* of his friend in public, he
risks hurting the *gan-qing* between them, which may in turn result in irreparable damage to their *guan-xi*.[8] Under the cultural norm of "mercy
for mercy, and revenge for revenge", the slighted party may seek to make
his adversary "look not good on his own face", so that in the end, both
parties end up with no face. In order to prevent such an interpersonal
calamity from occurring, the system of Asian relations has evolved in
favour of protecting one another's face.[9] Agreeing with this assessment,
McCormack remarked that "saving face might be described as a national
industry … The Chinese proclivity for ready-to-wear excuses, and the
general talent for light fiction of an extemporaneous character, have undoubtedly been fostered by the face-saving habit. The system probably
grew out of a desire to conserve personal dignity on all occasions, and to
follow the usual Chinese practice of handling social situations with vel-
vet gloves … Fear of losing face follows a Chinese more persistently than
his shadow. If he dies in a Western country, his remains must be shipped
back to China, otherwise his ghost will lose face by having to mingle
with haughty foreign ghosts …"[10]

Perception of Conflict in the East and West

This desire to maintain the *guan-xi* with a significant other, and thereby
deepen the *gan-qing* which exists in the relationship, implies that the Asian
is likely to attach a negative valence or feeling to any conflict with a significant other that has the potential to lead to a breaking up of the relationship. He will have the tendency to view such a conflict with a signifi-

cant other in a negative light and attribute destructive properties to it e.g., "conflict in a relationship will cause two persons to split up".[11] The negative perception of conflict in Asian culture is mirrored in its stress on social order and harmony in the wider society, and in fitting in with what the group says and does.

In contrast, in the liberal individualistic society of the West, conflict with a significant other is not regarded as necessarily negative or undesirable. Indeed, it can even be helpful in defining the boundaries of the self, since it brings into sharp relief the person's own desires, preferences and goals in the situation vis-à-vis another person. Because of this, the Westerner has the tendency to regard conflict in a positive light and attribute constructive properties to it e.g., "conflict in a relationship will assist two persons to understand each other better". The positive perception of conflict in this culture is reflected in the social psychological research on groupthink in the West, which looks at the dynamics involved in making faulty group decisions.[12] This line of research indicates that there may very well be beneficial consequences for the group as a whole, if there are minority voices within it that are in conflict with the opinion of the majority. Such dissenting voices, instead of disrupting social order and harmony, stimulate other group members to think about the issue from multiple and divergent perspectives, ultimately enhancing the quality of performance and creativity of the whole group.[13] For more information about the phenomenon of groupthink, see the last chapter of this book. The following boxed article looks at the philosophical assumptions that guide the Asian and Western mind in dealing with a conflict.

A Higher Truth or a Finite Point of View?

We have seen that people in the East and West differ in the way they deal with conflict. This basic difference in conflict resolution can be traced all the way back to the different assumptions the Asian and Western mind make, concerning the possibility of finding out the truth of a certain matter. In the West, there is an inherent faith that when two or more parties put their minds together, a "higher truth" can emerge via their rational and objective analysis of the matter. This optimism in the power of the human mind or reason to do all sorts of things, from unlocking the secrets of the physical universe to resolving impasses in the social and political realm, in the context of a free and open debate between two or more participants, is one of the most significant changes to emerge out of the Enlightenment of the West.[14] No longer do people rely on the authority of popes, kings and princes to decide on a matter. Instead, they are encouraged to make use of their own faculty of the mind to find an objective solution to the problem. This rational habit is deeply ingrained in the Western psyche, reflected in its implicit assumption that in a conflict situation (1) there is an objective and rational solution to the matter (2) which can be arrived at via an objective and rational analysis of the matter and (3) my job is to convince you that the solution which I am proposing is objective and rational, in comparison with the other alternative views which have been put forward. This explains in part why Westerners like to argue with each other, rather than make compromises in which "I win a little and lose a little".

In contrast, the Asian mind is distrustful of human reason, believing that the words of man represent the opinions, affirmations and denials of a particular individual who speaks from his own finite point of view (or as an observant man – ironically from the West, by the name of Benjamin Franklin – once pointed out, in words that remind me of the rational Confucian ministers in my country, "so convenient a thing it is to be a rational creature, since it enables us to find or make a reason for every thing one has a mind to do"). Being thus finite, these opinions, affirmations and denials are necessarily one-sided. Yet most men, not knowing that their opinions are based on finite points of view, invariably consider their own opinions as right and those of others as wrong. When people thus argue each according to his own finite point of view, there is no objective way of deciding the truth of the matter, since in a conflict situation, "although A may be right, B is not wrong either". The Taoist philosopher Chuang Tzu epitomised this position best, when he said to us, in the *Chi Wu Lun*:[15]

> Suppose that you argue with me. If you beat me, instead of I beat you, are you necessarily right and am I necessarily wrong? Or if I beat you, instead of you beat me, am I necessarily right and are you necessarily wrong? Is one of us right and the other wrong? Or are both of us right or both of us wrong? Neither you nor I can know, and others are all the more in the dark. Whom shall we ask to produce the right decision? We may ask someone who agrees with you, but since he already agrees with you, how can he make the decision? We may ask someone who agrees with me, but since he already agrees with me, how can he make the decision? We may ask someone who agrees with both you and me, but since he already agrees with both you and me, how can he make the decision? We may ask someone who disagrees with both you and me, but since he already disagrees with both you and me, how can he make the decision?

To reiterate, in the Asian scheme of things, there is no Holy Grail or Royal Road which will eventually lead one to a "higher truth", as in the West. Instead, where there are human beings, there are always two or more competing versions to an event which has occurred. This notion of a "finite point of view" was fully exploited by the Japanese movie director Akira Kurosawa in his classic film *Rashomon*, in which each of the main characters recalls the same event in a different manner, as well as illustrated in the humorous story of the three Buddhist monks (see story below). As a result of this peculiar way of understanding human nature – and also because of the cultural premium put on face and social order and harmony – two Asians in conflict are often exhorted by a wise elder to speak less. This is because "words left unspoken create room for free advance and retreat", and enable "big things to become small and small things to become nothing". Alternatively, to insist on the rightness of one's point of view, instead of making compromises in which "I win a little and lose a little", may result in a loss of face for both parties, and destroy the social order and harmony between them. This is why "you should not give it your all in a conflict situation, otherwise destiny will prematurely end", because *gan-qing* has been hurt.

The Story of the Three Buddhist Monks

This humorous story of three Buddhist monks is found in *Zen Flesh Zen Bones*, which contains a delectable selection of short but succinct writings on Zen, the Buddhist philosophy of sudden enlightenment.[16] It begins with the opening remark that provided he made and won an argument about Buddhism with those who lived there, any wandering monk could remain in a Zen temple. If he was defeated, he had to move on.

In a temple in the northern part of Japan, two brother monks were dwelling together. The elder one was learned and hardworking, while the younger one was one-eyed and stupid. A wandering monk came and asked for lodging in the temple. In accordance with the custom, he challenged them to a debate about the sublime teachings of Buddha. As the elder monk was tired that day from much studying, he requested that the younger monk take his place, saying to him, "Go and request the dialogue in silence."

A while later, the wandering monk appeared before the elder monk and said, "Your younger brother is a wonderful fellow. He defeated me."

"Relate the dialogue to me," said the elder monk.

"Well," explained the wandering monk, "first I held up one finger, representing Buddha, the enlightened one. So he held up two fingers, signifying Buddha and his teaching. I held up three fingers, representing Buddha, his teaching and his followers, living the harmonious life. Then he shook his clenched fist in my face, indicating that all three come from one realisation. Thus he won and so I have no right to remain here." With this, the wandering monk left.

Shortly after, the younger monk came running in to his brother and asked him, "Where's that fellow?"

"I understand you won the debate," the elder monk replied.

"Won nothing. I'm going to beat him up!"

"Tell me the subject of the debate," said the elder monk.

"Why, the minute he saw me he held up one finger, insulting me by insinuating that I have only one eye. Since he was a stranger I thought that I would be polite to him, so I held up two fingers, congratulating him that he has two eyes. Then the impolite wretch held up three fingers, suggesting that between us we only have three eyes. So I got mad and started to punch him, but he ran out and that ended it!"

Styles of Conflict Management

How a person construes the meaning of an interpersonal conflict will affect the way in which he deals with it. More specifically, a person who believes that conflict will wreck his relationship with a significant other (i.e., he has a negative view of conflict) is more likely to avoid one, and if it can't be avoided, to find ways of ending it quickly, by yielding to the other in the matter, for example. In contrast, a person who believes that conflict is beneficial to the relationship (i.e., he has a positive view of conflict) is more likely to engage in one, and work entirely through the conflict process, instead of short-circuiting it half-way. These contrasting approaches to conflict have been studied by psychologists, who differentiate conflict management styles along two basic dimensions: concern for self versus concern for others.

The first dimension refers to the degree (high or low) to which a person attempts to satisfy his or her own needs and desires. The second dimension refers to the degree (high or low) to which a person attempts to satisfy the needs and desires of the other. Together, both dimensions portray the motivational orientation of a particular individual during an interpersonal conflict. In different combinations, they yield up to a total of five conflict management styles. They are the **obliging** style (low concern for self, high concern for the other), the **dominating** style (high concern for self, low concern for the other), the **avoiding** style (low concern for self and the other), the **compromising** style (average concern for self and the other) and the **integrating** style (high concern for self and the other).[17]

Dealing with Conflict in the East and West

Extraverted-dominant people with an independently-constituted self in the West, who have been imbued with a hedonistic set of personal values, will tend to focus on their own subjective needs and desires in a relationship. Hence, they are likely to be more confrontative in a conflict situation; this is reinforced by the positive view of conflict in this culture. Constrained-submissive people with a relationally-constituted self in the East, who are imbued with a conservative set of personal values that emphasises social harmony and fitting into the group, will tend to focus more on the needs and desires of the other person in the relationship. Hence, they are likely to be less confrontative in a conflict situation; this is reinforced by the negative view of conflict in this culture. Confrontational conflict styles can be seen as a type of individuated behaviour, as it involves differentiating oneself from the social group. Non-confrontational conflict styles can be seen as a type of conforming behaviour, as it involves adapting one's behaviour to harmonise and fit in with the social group.[18]

Empirical research in several countries supports the general postulation that Westerners are more confrontational, while Asians are less confrontational. For example, one study examined preferences for dispute resolution procedures between the Chinese and Americans by asking them to role-play a hypothetical conflict scenario. The Chinese were found to be more likely than the Americans to prefer non-adversarial procedures (negotiation and mediation) over adversarial ones. Such procedures were perceived by the respondents as being more capable of reducing animosity.[19] Other research has examined the conflict patterns of the Japanese. One study found that the Japanese were more likely to avoid conversational topics that they regarded as being a threat to their relationship with another person.[20] Another study found that Japanese students showed a strong tendency to avoid conflict, in contrast to American students. The authors of this study attributed this to the motivation of their Japanese respondents to preserve relational harmony, as well as to their perception of shared responsibility for the conflict.[21]

Ting-Toomey and her colleagues found that American respondents used a higher degree of dominating style in managing a conflict than their Japanese and Korean counterparts, while Chinese and Taiwanese respondents used a higher degree of obliging and avoiding conflict management styles. They also found that self-face concern (concern for one's own face) is more prevalent in the West (America), while other-face concern (concern for the face of the other) is more prevalent in the East (China, Taiwan, Korea, Japan). Finally, they found that the former face orientation was linked with the dominating conflict management style, while the latter face orientation was associated with the avoiding, integrating and compromising conflict styles.[22]

The research of Ting-Toomey and her colleagues highlights the importance of showing and giving face to significant others in the East, which contributes to its social order and harmony. However, the strong emphasis on face in this culture can sometimes lead to a paradoxical phenomenon: the rapid deterioration of relationship between two close individuals.[23] This occurs because each side is not willing to be the first to yield its ground to the other side in a certain matter which implicates both parties, for fear of losing face. But as a wise Chinese man has pointed out, concerning the importance of yielding: "there must be one party who can first admit 'you are right and I am wrong.' If one party is willing to retreat, then they should be able to get along with each other again."[24] Unfortunately, Asian interactants have an excessive concern with preserving their own *mian-zi* before significant others. As a result, in a delicate situation, they may refuse to "lower their head" first, even though they may want to do so deep down inside. This can result in a "storm in a teacup", i.e., a big ado over a trivial matter. In contrast, the system of relations in the West, with its lack of emphasis on *mian-zi*, is less prone to this type of paralysis in a relationship, i.e., Westerners are more ready to offer an apology where it is due, as they are not so concerned with maintaining their own face in the situation.

A wise Chinese lady has described this aspect of the Chinese character as "taking things too seriously", captured in the folk saying, "they won't cry without seeing the coffin". According to her, "Chinese sometimes take things too seriously ... Not until they have destroyed the whole situation and the event becomes very serious will they realise they have done something wrong and regret what they have done. They have made the event too big and cannot find a way to remedy it."[25] Especially problematic is the situation in which one party assumes a higher relational position vis-à-vis the other. In such a situation, this morbid obsession with preserving intact one's *mian-zi* whatever the consequences, may lead the two parties to cease their interaction for a long period of time. This is shown in the story in the following boxed article.

Two Women and a Cucumber

This story, recounted by Chang and Holt (1994), involved a minister's wife, who was accused by her aunt of being a thief. Neither the aunt nor her niece was willing to yield to the other in this matter, for it would mean that she would have to "lower her head" first. As a consequence, they remained separated for more than 30 years – over a cucumber. A 40-year-old female employee is narrating the story:

"She had not talked to her aunt, and had not visited her for more than 30 years. Why? Because when she was a teenager, she went to her aunt's home. Someone stole a cucumber, and her aunt accused her and slapped her face. After she left, she carried her hate from that time on. She no longer spent time with her aunt … in fact, if one party was more mature, then it would not be like that.

"One day while learning about self-awareness, she thought about the incident and went to call her aunt immediately. Her aunt broke down in tears when she received the phone call. She told her aunt, 'Years ago, I did not steal your cucumber.' Her aunt said, 'I know. Because I found out who really stole the cucumber.'

"Now if we think about this, it is very childish. Had her aunt phoned her and said, 'I was too quick to accuse you during the time,' it would have been okay. But her aunt held back and did not want to say. The other side did not want to say either, because she felt that she was hurt. The result is this estrangement for so many years. Orientals are always like that, when they commit an error, they do not want to apologise for it. In fact, you don't even need to be that clear. You probably can just say, 'In fact, I already knew what happened.' You state the event, and she will know that she will not be accused because the truth has come out … the aunt already knew that it was not her niece, but she could not hold down her *mian-zi* to say, 'I already knew it was not you. It was a mistake at that time.' Perhaps inside her heart she did feel guilty. Therefore, when the minister's wife called her, she cried immediately after so many years. You can see that she must feel very guilty. Why do you need to have this guilt for so many years and hurt both of you?"

The Dogmatic Creator

I have talked a lot about the pattern of conflict in the East and West. It is time for me to link it with creativity. There is a close link between culture, conflict and creativity. To understand this link, we need to dwell at length on the nature of the creative act. A *creative act* by definition involves the introduction of novel elements into an established domain, and as such it threatens the conventional manner of doing things. So there will be much resistance faced by the creator. Instead of succumbing to this insidious pressure to conform or toe the line, the creator must be ready to challenge it, by persevering in the face of obstacles. Put in a more succinct and paradoxical manner, the creator is a rather *dogmatic* person, for if he is not dogmatic, i.e., if he does not stubbornly cling on to his ideas, he will not be able to resist the insidious pressure from his community to toe the line by giving up his radical idea or proposal. As Albert Einstein has remarked, "great spirits have always found violent opposition from mediocre minds. The latter cannot understand it when a person does not thoughtlessly submit to hereditary prejudices but honestly and courageously uses his intelligence." An example of such a dogmatic creator is Karl Marx, whose radical ideas of organising society set the whole world on fire. One biographer has painted this vivid description of him: "Marx gave the impression of one who has the right and the power to command respect, whatever his appearance and whatever he did. His manners defied the accepted forms of social intercourse, but were haughty and almost contemptuous. His sharp, metallic voice suited remarkably well the radical verdicts which he was in the habit of pronouncing on men and things. Even at this time he invariably spoke in the form of judgments without appeal, in which was heard the uniform, disagreeably sharp note which dominated everything he said – a note which seemed to express the firm conviction that his destiny was to sway men's minds, to be their law-giver and to lead them in his train."[26]

Nice People Are Not Creative, and Creative People Are Not Nice

This paradoxical notion of the dogmatic creator – which challenges the conventional view of the creator as an innovative individual – leads to another interesting and controversial insight: *nice people are not creative and creative people are not nice.*[27] The reasoning is as follows: "nice" people are agreeable individuals who go along with what the group says, instead of upsetting everyone by doing things their own way. In contrast, creative people are not "nice" because they insist that others should do as they say, no matter how strange their ideas are. The reader who objects to this offensive inference should consider the Faustian bargain of the creative genius, which is elaborated in Howard Gardner's book *Creating Minds*. He should also consider the shabby treatment which Newton and Einstein meted out to their loved ones, which is described in this book. Finally, he should bear in mind that there is a negative side to the dogmatic creator, which is seldom acknowledged, but which is likely to cause a lot of social problems in the community. This negative side consists of an assortment of negative traits, such as being indifferent to common conventions and courtesies, being stubborn and uncooperative, being demanding and assertive, being self-centred and egoistic, being temperamental and moody, and being rebellious and cynical.[28]

Frederick W. Smith and Overnight Delivery: From Utopia to Reality

In support of this paradoxical assertion that the creator is a dogmatic person, Sternberg and Lubart have found that the difference between people who succeed in being creative over long periods of time and those who are but mere flashes in the pan is not in whether they encounter obstacles in their work, but in whether they persevere stubbornly in the face of those obstacles.[29] The flashes in the pan give up the first or second time the going gets tough, whereas the true creators keep a thick skin, bite their teeth and forge ahead, regardless of what other people may say, or of the failures they may encounter. An example of such a dogmatic creator in our modern world is Frederick W. Smith, the founder of Federal Express, the American company which specialises in overnight delivery of parcels to various points of the globe.[30]

The concept of overnight delivery was first mooted in an economics term paper by this Yale undergraduate with a passion for flying. Smith's theoretical delivery company, as explained in his paper, would have a sizable fleet of its own planes and trucks to pick up parcels and deliver them to regional airfields, as well as a central package-rerouting facility located at a major airport near the heart of the country. His trucks would pick up the packages from the customer and carry them to the "spoke" airfields from which the jets could fly them to the centrally located "hub". The packages would be quickly sorted, rerouted and flown out from there to the "spoke" airport nearest the final destination, where ground couriers would finish the deliveries. Flying in the light-traffic hours of the night would help assure the customer of overnight delivery.

Smith's enthusiasm for his theory caused him to work overtime, resulting in a late delivery of his term paper. His economics instructor found the idea to be more utopian than practical: astronomical financing would be required, and the airlines were sure to provide stiff opposition. Federal regulations governing air cargo could stymie the plan. Smith got a C for his term paper, but he did not give up this utopian idea. Instead, putting his money where his mouth was, he invested close to four million dollars he had inherited from his father, and Federal Express was incorporated on June 1, 1971, as an air charter company headquartered at Little Rock.

Smith's company did not exactly get off to a roaring start, in spite of the optimistic forecasts of two consulting firms which he had earlier engaged to make a detailed study of the existing air-freight industry. There was a trickle instead of an avalanche of packages awaiting delivery by Smith's fleet of vans and planes on the first day of business – 18 packages, to be exact. However, this early disappointment was short-lived. Business began to pick up rapidly, as word spread that Federal Express delivered overnight to any point of the globe as promised. The rest, as they say, is history.

A caveat is necessary at this juncture: although there is much truth in the paradoxical assertion that the creator is a dogmatic person – otherwise he will succumb to the insidious pressure to conform – it should be pointed out that not all creators behave like Fred Smith, i.e., they stubbornly promote their idea in the face of strong opposition. A minority with a less combative personality practise a special division of labour, in which they work out their radical idea while leaving it to their friends and supporters to promote it. A prototypical example is Charles Darwin, the scrupulous, mild-mannered and most unlikely originator of the radical theory of evolution via natural selection, who in his youth harboured the ambition of becoming a simple country clergyman, but finally abandoned his Christian faith when he realised – to put it bluntly – that there is no Creator; instead, human beings evolved from the apes.[31] Darwin's reluctant road to fame is described in detail in the following boxed article.

Charles Darwin: The Reluctant Creator

A Martian, in visiting earth for the very first time, will be struck by the great diversity of life on this planet, as well as the web of interdependence between different species. Religious leaders like St Thomas Aquinas had used this fact of life as powerful evidence for a Creator. They reasoned that such an elegant and complex system, with each part perfectly matched to its purpose, which was termed the Great Chain of Beings, could only have arisen by the hands of an almighty God. However, various discoveries had challenged this so-called argument from design.

One was the finding in 1790 by an English land surveyor William Smith while digging a canal that different layers of rock, which represented different time segments of life on Earth (lower layers = earlier era, upper layers = later era), contained different fossils. Another was the finding in 1800 by the French naturalist Georges Cuvier while classifying the then-known fossils, that while many belonged to surviving families of plants and animals, others did not. The third was the finding that the planet Earth was not a few thousand years old, as the Church would have us believe, but millions of years old.[32]

It was the genius of Charles Darwin (1809–1882) that connected these disparate ideas in his theory of evolution via natural selection, which argues that species are not immutable, i.e., fixed for eternity by a Creator. Instead, they undergo changes, too slow to observe, which may, however, over eons of time transform it entirely e.g., apes to human beings. This radical idea alarmed the pious Victorian society of Darwin's day and scandalised the Church, for in one fell stroke, it demolished the argument from design, did away with the Great Chain of Beings, and consigned the notion of Creator to intellectual oblivion.

Darwin stumbled upon the theory of evolution via natural selection very early on in the process. The impetus of this discovery
was his stint as a young and unpaid naturalist on board the *HMS
Beagle*, which sailed off on a voyage around the world in 1831. On
this five-year journey, Darwin collected specimens of every plant and
animal species which he encountered, and began to ask himself questions about how they had evolved. He was particularly intrigued by
the number of variations in the beaks of finches (a type of bird) on
the isolated Galapagos Islands. Some had developed powerful beaks
specialised for cracking hard nuts, while others had developed fine-
pointed beaks suitable for other sources of food. This led Darwin to
propose the theory of evolution via natural selection.

The basic ideas of this theory can be summarised as follows. Individual members of any species compete intensely for survival in a
certain environment. Those members which survive to produce the
next generation embody certain traits, which increase their fitness in
the environment e.g., finches with powerful beaks on an island where
there is an abundance of hard nuts will thrive. These traits are due to
random genetic variations, and they are passed on by heredity. Over
time, each generation will improve adaptively vis-a-vis the preced-
ing generations. In certain cases, this can culminate in the transformation of the original species into one that is new and completely
different e.g., apes to human beings.

According to the investigative journalist Robert Wright, author
of *The Moral Animal: Why We Are The Way We Are*, Darwin saw how
evolution worked two years after the end of his five-year voyage on
the *HMS Beagle*.[33] However, instead of publishing his theory, he bus-
ied himself with other things, like the subclass Cirripedia, known
more commonly as ship barnacles, publishing four thick scientific
volumes on it. All in all, it took him a good 20 years to publicise his
theory of evolution via natural selection. Even then, you could say
that he was a most reluctant creator, who was forced by the circumstances to do it, as the following spate of events would testify.

A young British naturalist by the name of Alfred Wallace had
independently thought out the theory of evolution in 1858, two decades after Darwin had done so. He sent his paper on evolution to
Darwin to solicit his opinion. According to Robert Wright, panic must
have struck Darwin when he read the paper. This was because Wallace
stood poised to snatch the final moment of fame and victory from
Darwin, by preempting him in publishing the theory of evolution.
In a letter, Darwin frantically sought advice on what to do from
Charles Lyell, a good friend who was also an influential member of
the Linnean Society, an elite circle of British scientists (NB: The words

in italics are Wright's interpretations of Darwin's real intention in writing the letter).

> I should be extremely glad now to publish a sketch of my general views in about a dozen pages or so; but I cannot persuade myself that I can do so honourably (*maybe you can persuade me*). Wallace says nothing about publication, and I enclose his letter. But as I had not intended to publish any sketch, can I do so honourably, because Wallace has sent me an outline of his doctrine (*Say Yes! Say Yes!*) ... Do you not think his having sent me this sketch ties my hands? (*Say No! Say No!*) ... I cannot tell whether to publish now would not be base and paltry (*Say Non-Base and Non-Paltry!*).

In a postscript added the next day, Darwin washed his hands of this affair, appointing Lyell as arbitrator: "I have always thought you would make a first-rate Lord Chancellor; and I now appeal to you as a Lord Chancellor." As it turned out, Lyell and Hooker, another influential member of the Linnean Society, decided to treat and publish Darwin's and Wallace's theories as equals. Since Wallace was then in the Malay Archipelago, and the next meeting of the society was imminent, Lyell and Hooker decided to proceed without consulting him. Darwin let them. In Wright's opinion,

> This ranks as one of the most poignant passages in the history of science. Wallace had just been taken to the cleaners. His name, though given equal billing with Darwin's, was now sure to be eclipsed by it ... any lingering doubt about whose name should be attached to the theory would be erased by Darwin's book, which he would now finally produce with due speed. Lest the relative status of the two men escape anyone's attention, Hooker and Lyell, in introducing the papers to the Linnean Society, had noted that while the scientific world is waiting for the appearance of Mr Darwin's complete work, some of the leading results of his labours, as well as those of his able correspondent, should be laid before the public. "Able correspondent" isn't a phrase likely to wind up at the top of a marquee.

Wright went on to speculate that if Wallace had sent his paper to a journal instead of to Darwin, he might be remembered today as the first man to posit the theory of evolution by natural selection, while Darwin's great book *The Origin of Species*, published in 1859 (exactly one year after he received the paper from Wallace) would have been a mere extension and popularisation of another scientist's idea. Whose name the theory would then have carried will forever be an open question. But this is not the end of the saga in Darwin's reluctant road to fame.

As might have been expected, the theory of evolution met with stiff opposition from the Christian Church. Its formulator left it to his good friend and admirer Thomas Huxley, a.k.a. "Darwin's bulldog", to slug it out with the religious leaders of the day. This came about in 1860, one year after the publication of *The Origin of Species*, which was described succinctly as the "book which shook the world". During a debate on the theory of evolution via natural selection, Samuel Wilberforce, a prominent church leader, sarcastically asked on which side of his family Huxley was descended from an ape. Huxley replied, most eloquently for the ages, that he would rather have an ape as an ancestor than a man "possessed of great means and influence and yet who employs these faculties and that influence for the mere purpose of introducing ridicule into a grave scientific discussion". (NB: In the annals of logic, Wilberforce's strategically-phrased question is an example of the notorious genre of argument, utilised frequently by political foes in the East and West, and known by its Latin name of *ad hominem*, i.e., attacking the personality rather than the logic and reasoning of one's intellectual opponent. So Huxley's memorable retort was right on the mark.)

"He's part of the family!"

A Cultural Model of Conflict and Creativity

So far, I have argued that there is a close association between creativity and conflict, i.e., because the idea or proposal which the creator introduces into his community is a radical one, he will face much social resistance. The creator needs to persevere in the face of obstacles, instead of succumbing to this insidious pressure to conform or toe the line. If he does not do so, i.e., if he is not psychologically prepared to make a stance against those opponents of his alternative idea or proposal, he will find it difficult to be creative.[34] The person who succumbs to this insidious pressure to conform is more likely to be found in an Asian society. In this society, the person develops a constrained-submissive personality and possesses an interdependent self-construal. At the same time, he subscribes to a conservative set of personal values and a negative view of conflict. A person with this type of psychological make-up has the tendency to adopt an accommodative stance in any awkward situation that threatens to wreck his relationship with a significant other e.g., he may be obliging to the other person, or avoid the other person to prevent the conflict from intensifying. Although this will enable him to maintain social order and harmony in the relationship, it will also prevent him from behaving in a creative and individuated way. This is shown in the cultural model of conflict and creativity (East) below, which looks at how a Confucian-heritage society socialises its members to behave in a socially-compliant, non-confrontational and uncreative way.

A Cultural Model of Conflict and Creativity (East)

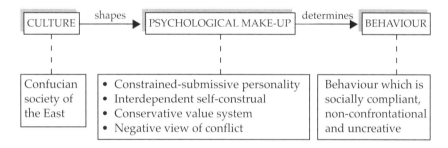

In contrast, the cultural ethos of the West encourages the extraverted person to view himself as a separate entity by differentiating himself from the social group and wider society (i.e., he possesses an independent self-construal). His extraverted and independent nature is matched by a hedonistic set of personal values which emphasises the meeting of subjective needs and desires. In addition, he has a more positive view of conflict. This set of psychological make-up enables him to engage in a confrontational style of behaviour. Although this sort of confrontational and dominant behaviour may adversely affect his relationship with the other party, it will also enable him to behave in a creative and individuated way. This is shown in the cultural model of conflict and creativity (West) on the next page, which looks at how a liberal individualistic society socialises its members to behave in an individuated, confrontational and creative manner.

The Asian Intellectual: Conforming But Courageous

The general reluctance of the Asian to engage in conflict with his community by confronting them with his alternative ideas and proposals, and the zeal with which the Westerner pursues conflict, can be gleaned most clearly in the concept of the intellectual in the East and West.[35] The concept of the intellectual in the Asian tradition can be stated as follows:

A Cultural Model of Conflict and Creativity (West)

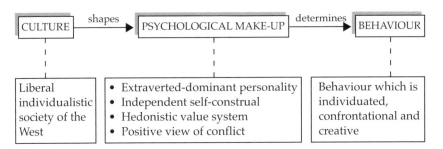

he was an individual who had mastered a particular canon of knowledge, typically of Confucian origin. This mastery was confirmed by passing an examination set by the Imperial Government. Once credentialed, the intellectual could contribute to the canon by modifying it incrementally with interpretations or commentaries. The most famous of these Chinese intellectuals was Chu Hsi (AD 1130–1200), a Sung dynasty scholar-official who virtually reconstituted the Confucian tradition, giving it new meaning, structure and texture, known in the West as Neo-Confucianism, and referred to as *Li-hsueh* or the *Learning of the Principle* in modern China.[36]

However, it was *not* the role of the Confucian scholar to adopt a critical and confrontative stance towards the system which had bred him. Instead, convention, tradition and authority were to be respected, not overturned (e.g., Chu Hsi was enthusiastic in introducing foot-binding in southern Fukien as a means of spreading Chinese culture and teaching the separation of men and women).[37] Rather than tinkering with the system by posing unpleasant questions to those with a vested interest in preserving it, the moral obligation of the Confucian scholar was to take up an official position in the court of the emperor, so as to assist him to maintain law and order in the Celestial Empire. Once in office, the Confucian scholar was obliged to serve as a moral example to those he governed. He was to hold not only himself, but also his colleagues, superiors and even his emperor to the highest standard of conduct, and to criticise them when they failed to uphold these standards. This obligation of the Confucian scholar to "speak out forthrightly and remonstrate without inhibition" might bring extreme misery and hardship to him, but such was the lot of the true Confucian scholar, whose credo could be summed up in the following phrase: "to be the first to worry about the world's problems, and the last to enjoy its happiness".[38]

A good example of the Confucian scholar with moral courage was the Han official Ssu-ma Chien (136–84 BC), who was the Grand Historian to Emperor Han Wu-Ti, who reigned 100 years before Christ was born. Ssu-ma Chien was the author of the mammoth 130-chapter *Historical*

Records, which covered events from the legendary Yellow Emperor down to his own emperor's reign. In spite of his great intellect and achievement, Emperor Han Wu-Ti ordered Ssu-ma Chien to be punished because – unlike the rest of the sycophants in court – he had dared to stand up for Li Ling, a brave cavalry commander who incurred the wrath of the emperor for surrendering to his enemies after a fierce but unsuccessful battle. Li Ling had defeated 30,000 enemy cavalry with only 5,000 Chinese infantry using a new tactic: in front of his line he placed infantry armed with shields and pikes, while behind them were archers with powerful crossbows, some multiple-firing, shooting several bolts at a time. Against this formation, the nomad cavalry charged in vain. But Li Ling was not reinforced, and he had to surrender when his supply of arrows and bolts gave out. The Hun king whom Li Ling fought against was so impressed by his bravery that he treated him with honour, which infuriated Emperor Han Wu-Ti, who ordered the execution of the mother, wife and children of this valiant general. Ssu-ma Chien sprang to his defence in an open and laudatory appeal to the emperor: "He did not die on the field, for he longed to wipe out his defeat and show his gratitude for his emperor's clemency, upon which he dared to count with a clear conscience". Han Wu-Ti, even more furious, ordered that Ssu-ma Chien be arraigned for "attempting to mislead the ruler". He was tried, sentenced and castrated.

Why did Ssu-ma Chien stand out for Li Ling, at the risk of being castrated to become an eunuch, a creature that even Confucius himself had viewed with disgust? "He (Li Ling) had admirable qualities," he explained. "He was not an intimate friend of mine, for he was a soldier and I a civilian. But all I saw of his character pleased me: he was honest in money matters, just to his dependants, respectful to his superiors, devout at the Rites. When I heard him belittled after his defeat, I could not keep silent." With his virility taken from him, Ssu-ma Chien was now a broken man with a degraded body. Nevertheless, he lived on stubbornly to finish the *Historical Records* that alone was breathing life into him, and it later became the standard for the chronology of important events.[39]

Han Yu (AD 768–824) was another Confucian scholar who possessed this type of moral courage. He wrote and presented to the throne a famous memorial protesting against Buddhism at a time when the emperor, besotted by Buddhist superstition, proposed to exhibit in the capital city of Ch'ang-an a celebrated relic, reputed to be a finger-bone of the Buddha himself. For his temerity, Han Yu was banished from the court and sent as a magistrate to the backward and unhealthy district of Guangdong in the southernmost part of the empire. It is said that he administered the district in such strict accordance to Confucian principles that he won the esteem of all the inhabitants.[40] A third fearless remonstrator who made it to the annals of history was Hai Jui (AD 1514–87), who delivered a stringent denunciation of the emperor's Taoist idiosyncrasies at the palace.

The emperor was so enraged with his subject that he ordered the imme-diate capture of Hai Jui, lest he escaped. "Never fear, sire," the eunuch go-between responded. "He has said goodbye to his family, brought his coffin with him, and awaits you at the gate!" Luckily for Hai Jui, the em-peror was so taken aback that he decided to overlook his impertinence.[41]

Another ruler who learned to live with these conscience-awakening scholars was Emperor Han Kao-Tse (206–195 BC), who wrestled the Man-date of Heaven to rule from the incompetent descendents of Shi Huang Ti, the First Emperor of China. Unlike the latter, who was of princely origin, Han Kao-Tse, the inaugurator of the Han dynasty, was an unedu-cated peasant of humble means, and therefore did not have the stomach for the Confucian scholars in his court; he once replied to a tiresome lec-ture from one of their numbers by seizing the man's silk hat and urinat-ing in it.[42] But even he was no match for the wittiness of these Confucian scholars, for when he famously scoffed at one of them, "I won the world on horseback, not by reading books", he got this equally famous and swift retort: "Yes, but can you rule it on horseback?" Han Kao-Tse had to concede that war and peace were two different matters, and so the proto-type of what was to become the Confucian mandarinate of scholar-offi-cials, namely the Chinese intellectual, took shape under his rule.[43]

The Western Intellectual: Shaking the Foundations of the World We Live in

The Western intellectual, unlike his Chinese counterpart, is beholden to no system of thought or institution. On the contrary, he relishes in icono-clastic and impractical ideas which shock the community he lives in (the community, in its turn, often believes that the Western intellectual "lives in an ivory tower", i.e., he is out of touch with reality). Undaunted, he is prepared to "bulldoze" his way through every wall of resistance, in an attempt to impose his radical vision upon his community, i.e., he fits the stereotype of the dogmatic creator who is not nice, and who specialises in innovative pursuits that radically transform the pattern of this world we live in, be it in the realm of astronomy, science, religion, philosophy, poli-tics, biology, psychology or other fields of knowledge.

For example, in astronomy, Nicolaus Copernicus (1473–1543) and Galileo Galilei (1564–1642) engaged in a great struggle with the Christian Church to remove the earth from its perch at the centre of the universe; this clash of the titans of science and religion is recounted in the boxed article at the end of this chapter. In philosophy, Frederick Nietzsche (1844–1900) announced that "we have murdered God" in his prophetic book *Thus Spake Zarathustra* (eventually, Nietzsche was to become insane from his radical thinking, and spend the rest of his life in a mental institution, thus proving his own dictum that "when you look long enough into the abyss, the abyss will look back into you").[44] In politics, Karl Marx (1818–1883) sounded the death-knell of capitalism in his book *The Communist*

Manifesto, which opened with the arresting statement: "a spectre is haunting Europe, the spectre of communism", and ended with the fiery exhortation: "The proletariats have nothing to lose but their chains. They have a world to win. WORKERS OF THE WORLD, UNITE!" (Marx's passionate prose is not surprising, considering this remark of his: "The task of philosophy is not to describe the world, but to change it.")

In biology, Charles Darwin dethroned Man from the head of the biological kingdom, against the protests of the Christian Church, with his theory of evolution via natural selection, which asserted that we evolved from the apes, instead of being descended from Adam and Eve. In psychology, B. F. Skinner (1904–1990) railed against the notion of human freedom and dignity, arguing that we would all be better off living in a scientifically-engineered society. In psychoanalysis, Sigmund Freud (1865–1939) stood the rationality of Man on its head by arguing that we are all influenced by our unconscious wishes and desires. An example is the Oedipus Complex, which asserts that every son harbours an illicit desire to kill his father so that he can have sex with his mother (not surprisingly, this notion of the Oedipus Complex outraged the pious Victorian sensibility of Freud's time, and practically every individual who first heard about it).[45] In physics, Albert Einstein (1879–1955) transformed our thinking about the intricate relationship between space and time and also unlocked the secret power of the atom in his famous equation, $E = MC^2$, which asserted that the energy contained in the atom can be unleashed, and it is equal to the mass of the atom multiplied by the square of the speed of light. This is indeed a lot of firepower, as shown in the atomic explosions at Hiroshima and Nagasaki during World War II, which flattened these Japanese cities completely. This devastating war, which killed over 40 million people in 2,174 days of bloody conflict, inflicted indelible scars in the hearts and minds of those individuals who lived through its horrors.[46] One of them was the existentialist Jean-Paul Sartre (1905–1980), who fought briefly in the French Resistance during the war. In later years – as a result of his war experience – Sartre was to argue that man is not made in the image of God. Instead, he is a useless passion who is condemned to be free in a world where hell is other people. In case the reader thinks that this is an insane idea, it should be pointed out that the Nobel Committee wanted to award Sartre a Nobel Prize for Literature for his radical notion of man; however, Sartre, who had the habit of holding philosophical meetings in cafes located along the River Seine in Paris, rejected it, saying that he did not want to become an institutional icon. In spite of this, Sartre's fame became so widespread that when he died, 50,000 Parisians thronged the streets of Paris to give this philosopher of angst a rousing farewell from this earth.

An erstwhile friend of Sartre who later broke up with him over Marxism was Albert Camus (1913–1960), who chose to remain stoic and defiant, in the face of an absurd and meaningless universe which constantly stabs us from behind with the thought of annihilation. Camus' stoic defiance is forcefully expressed in his essay entitled "The Myth of Sisyphus", which compares the plight of modern man living in an absurd and meaningless universe to the plight of Sisyphus. Sisyphus is the Greek tragi-hero who had been condemned by the gods to ceaselessly roll a rock up to the top of a mountain, whence the stone would fall back under its own weight. The gods had thought with justification that there was no more dreadful punishment for Sisyphus – who stole fire from Heaven to relieve his fellow men on earth from cold and darkness – than futile and hopeless labour. Nevertheless, Camus wrote: "Sisyphus teaches the higher fidelity that negates the gods and raises rocks. He too concludes that all is well. This universe henceforth without a master seems to him neither sterile nor futile. Each atom of that stone, each mineral flake of that night-filled mountain, in itself forms a world. The struggle itself towards the heights is enough to fill a man's heart. One must imagine Sisyphus happy."[47] This philosopher of the Absurd – who was awarded a Nobel Prize for Literature in 1958 – died in an accident while driving a sports car in 1960. He was then only 47 years old. As his one-time friend Sartre remarked, it was a most absurd death.

Chapter Summary

In this chapter, I looked at how Asians and Westerners deal with interpersonal conflict. Westerners adopt a form of relational contractualism which puts themselves first and foremost. In contrast, Asians emphasise the importance of the ingroup in their lives. The Asian style of relationship is governed by *gan-qing* (human emotion), *guan-xi* (relation) and *mian-zi* (face). As such, they have a negative view of conflict. In contrast, Westerners tend to have a less negative view of conflict. The attitude towards conflict influences the conflict style of the Asian and Westerner, with the former being less confrontational and the latter being more so. At this juncture, I made the paradoxical assertion that the creator is a dogmatic person who is not "nice". This is because the radical ideas which he propounds go against the grain of society; he needs to have a stomach for conflict if he is to realise his creative vision. I then introduced my cultural model of conflict and creativity, which asserts that Asians are less creative and confrontational, while Westerners are more creative and confrontational, due to their psychological make-up. As evidence, I compared the conforming but courageous intellectuals in the East to the iconoclastic and status quo-defying intellectuals in the West. The following boxed article provides a historical example of two of these Western intellectuals.

Clash of the Titans: Science versus Religion

The mission of a creator of the highest rank is to provide our world with an alternative vision of reality. However, like the prophet who is not welcomed by those he preaches to, such a creator is more often than not rejected by those with a vested interest in retaining the status quo, reflecting the sentiment of the English poet William Wordsworth in his observation that "the poet is the unacknowledged legislator of the world". The lives and times of Nicolaus Copernicus and Galileo Galilei, two famous Renaissance scientists, as described by Richard Tarnas in his masterly and historical survey of Western philosophy, *The Passion of the Western Mind*, provide us with a glaring example of this Clash of the Titans: Science versus Religion.[48] These two scions of science lived at a time when the Christian Church was at the peak of its ecclesiastical power in the Western world. (NB: In contrast to the Western world, the Asian world has never been religious in this sense of the term, i.e., believing that there is a God who intervened in human history to save us from our sins by sending his Son Jesus Christ to die on the cross of Calvary, and then leaving behind His representative on earth, namely, the Christian Church, to spread His message of peace and salvation before Christ comes back eventually to judge the world. When the rationalist Chinese literati in 16th-century Peking heard about this Gospel or Good News from the famous Italian Jesuit Matteo Ricci, who was also an accomplished man of science, it was Ricci's scholarly knowledge of Renaissance science which they appreciated, and not his communication of God's desire to save this sinful world via his only begotten Son. As one Confucian scholar remarked, "The superiority of the Western teaching lies in their calculations; their inferiority lies in their veneration of a Master of Heaven of a kind to upset men's minds."[49])

The power which the Christian Church held sway over its dominion had enabled it to promote and enforce the medieval view of the universe, which stated that God had made the earth to be the centre of the universe, with the sun and all the other planets revolving around it. This view was exemplified in Ptolemaic cosmology, which postulated a geocentric universe in which the earth was stationary and motionless at the centre of several concentric, rotating spheres, known as epicycles. However, Copernicus, who was trained as an astronomer and mathematician, was perturbed by the failure of Ptolemaic cosmology to account for the apparent retrograde or backward motion of Mars, Jupiter and Saturn. He sought a new solution to this age-old problem of the planets: how to explain the erratic planetary movements by means of a simple, clear and elegant mathematical formula. Copernicus thought that the messy epicycles of Ptolemaic cosmology had produced a "monster", i.e., an inelegant and overburdened conception of the universe which, despite all the complicated ad hoc corrective devices, still failed to account for, or predict, observed planetary positions with reliable accuracy.

At this time, Renaissance Europe urgently needed a better calendar, and the Christian Church, for which the calendar was indispensable in administrative and liturgical matters, undertook its reform. Such reform depended on astronomical precision, and Copernicus, who was a devout Catholic, was asked to advise the papacy on the problem. He informed the Pope that the existing confused state of astronomical science (i.e., Ptolemaic cosmology) precluded any immediate effective reform, and came up with his own creative solution to the matter. This was the heliocentric cosmology, in which the earth (as well as all the other planets in the solar system) rotated daily on its axis and revolved yearly around the sun.

Although this new cosmology fitted the empirical observations much better, it contradicted several passages in the Holy Bible concerning the fixity of the earth. Around this time, the Christian Church – the representative of God on earth which was supposed to bring the message of peace and salvation to mankind – was having a serious internal squabble, with Protestant reformers pitted against the Catholic Church. For example, the Protestant leader Martin Luther, the intrepid reformer from Germany who nailed 95 famous theses to the doors of a Catholic church in Wittenberg in 1517, which lambasted the excesses of papal authority (e.g., the sale of religious indulgences which remitted the sins of the believer), compared the Pope to the Devil. Paying back the compliment, the leading Catholic theologian Sir Thomas More remarked that though Luther talked as if he were "safe in Christ's bosom", in reality "he lies shut up in the Devil's anus" – such was the scatological wit of Reformation polemics.[50]

These Protestant reformers seized upon Copernicus' theory as yet another example of the kind of Hellenistic intellectual arrogance and interpretive sophistry which they most abhorred in Catholic culture. For example, Martin Luther called Copernicus an "upstart astrologer" who foolishly wished to reverse the entire science of astronomy while flagrantly contradicting the Holy Bible. Luther was soon joined by other Protestant reformers like John Calvin, who recommended that stringent measures be taken to suppress this pernicious heresy. Quoting a verse from the Psalms, "the world also is established, that it cannot be moved," Calvin asked, "Who will dare to place the authority of Copernicus above that of the Holy Spirit?"

The Protestant opposition to heliocentric cosmology was so strong that Rheticus, the closest student of Copernicus, had problems publishing his teacher's manuscript, *De Revolutionibus*. He had to move from Poland to Germany before he found a publisher who devised a ploy to publish the manuscript. This involved the insertion of an anonymous preface – without Copernicus' knowledge and therefore permission – stating that the heliocentric theory was merely a convenient computational method and should not be taken seriously as a realistic account of the heavens. So on the last day of his life, in the year 1543, a copy of the published work was finally brought to Copernicus.[51]

The publisher's ploy may have saved the publication and enabled its author to see his work in print before he died. However, Copernicus had indeed been serious about his theory, as a closer reading of the text revealed to Galileo, this other scion of science in this sorry saga of the Christian Church. Galileo had improved the recently-invented telescope and used it to observe the stars in the Milky Way, the craters on the moon and the satellites of Jupiter, as well as the phases of Venus. These empirical observations flatly contradicted the Ptolemaic cosmology. As a result, Galileo switched his support to the heliocentric cosmology, publishing a work on sunspots which predicted victory for the Copernican theory over its Ptolemaic rival.

A Pisan professor, in Galileo's absence, told the Medici (the ruling family of Florence as well as Galileo's employers) that belief in a moving earth was heretical, while a Florentine priest denounced Galileo from the pulpit. In response, Galileo wrote a long and open letter on the irrelevance of biblical passages in scientific arguments, holding that interpretation of the Bible should be adapted to increasing knowledge, and that no scientific position should ever be made an article of Christian faith, for it would be "a terrible detriment for the souls if people found themselves convinced by proof of something that it was made then a sin to believe". Galileo invited the pope and his cardinals to look through his telescope and observe with their own eyes the heavens in their concrete substantiality – fit for empirical investigation, just like the natural phenomena on the earth. However, his offer was declined, for by this time, the Catholic Church – with a renewed sense of the need for doctrinal orthodoxy – felt compelled to take a definite stance against the Copernican hypothesis.

While in an earlier century, more open-minded religious scholars like Thomas Aquinas (who reinterpreted the recently-rediscovered works of the early Greek philosophers, especially Plato and Aristotle, in the light of the Holy Bible, thus providing Christianity with an intellectual foothold) or even the ancient Church Fathers might have considered a metaphorical interpretation of the scriptural passages in question, thereby eliminating the apparent contradiction with science, the emphatic literalism of Luther, Calvin and their followers activated a similar attitude in the Catholic Church. Both sides of the dispute wished to secure an uncompromised solidity with respect to biblical revelation, for it was by now clear to them that Copernicanism posed a fundamental threat to the entire Christian framework of cosmology, theology and morality: the essential dichotomy between the celestial and terrestrial realms, the great cosmological structure of Heaven, Hell and Purgatory, the circling planetary spheres with angelic hosts, God's empyrean throne above all, the moral drama of human life pivotally centred between the spiritual heavens and a corporeal earth – all would be cast into question or destroyed altogether by this new theory. For if the earth truly moved, then no longer could it be the fixed centre of God's creation and His plan of salvation. Nor could man be the central focus of the cosmos.

So in 1616, Copernican books like *De Revolutionibus* were subjected to censorship by religious edict, and the Jesuit cardinal Robert Bellarmine told Galileo that he must no longer hold or defend the concept that the earth moved. Instead, he was advised by the cardinal to treat this subject hypothetically and for scientific purposes only, without taking Copernican concepts as literally true or attempting to reconcile them with the Bible. Taking the hint, Galileo remained silent on the subject for many years, expending his prodigious energy in other directions, but in 1624 he began a book in which he discussed the Ptolemaic and Copernican hypotheses in relation to the physics of tides. In 1630, this book was licensed for printing by Roman Catholic censors at Rome.

The *Dialogue on the Two Chief World Systems* was eventually published in Florence in 1632, but in spite of two official licences, Galileo was summoned to Rome by the Inquisition to stand trial for "grave suspicion of heresy". This charge was based on a report that Galileo had been personally ordered in 1616 by papal authority not to discuss Copernicanism either orally or in writing. Cardinal Bellarmine had died by this time, but Galileo produced a certificate signed by the late cardinal, which stated that he (Galileo) was to be subjected to no further restriction than applied to any Roman Catholic under the 1616 edict. No signed document contradicting this was ever found, but Galileo was nevertheless compelled in 1633 to publicly recant his views on the moving earth (which he duly did on stage, but in an impromptu aside, whispered to posterity that *it moves*), and sentenced to life imprisonment, which was swiftly commuted to permanent house arrest. The *Dialogue on the Two Chief World Systems* was ordered to be burned, and the sentence against Galileo was read publicly in every university. [52]

Unfortunately for the Church, subsequent events proved that in Galileo's forced recantation lay its own defeat, as well as the ultimate victory of Science over Religion. For this decision caused irreparable damage to the intellectual and spiritual integrity of the Christian Church. It would continue to retain much power and loyalty in the succeeding centuries among its followers, whether Catholic or Protestant. However, it could no longer justifiably claim to represent the human aspiration towards full knowledge of the universe, for it had attempted to strangle the scientific spirit.

This effort was not successful: the Inquisition's ban on Galileo's book only caused it to be smuggled to the north, where the vanguard of the Western intellectual quest would thereafter reside. The Church's forced recantation of Galileo and its biblical and unscientific commitment to a stationary earth, as well as its penchant for holding inquisitions which fed its voracious appetite for punitive repression against those who would not submit to its power and authority – by branding them witches, and burning them alive at the stake, creating both Catholic and Protestant martyrs – drastically undercut its status and prestige among the influential intelligentsia.

For example, the French philosopher Voltaire recorded his terrible reproach against the Christian Church in these biting and unsparing words: "… blood should have been shed for so many centuries by men who proclaimed the god of peace. Paganism knew no such fury. It covered the world in darkness, but shed hardly a drop of blood save that of beasts … The spirit of dogma bred the madness of religious wars in the minds of men." Voltaire went on to savour the irony of how Dominican opposition to Chinese ceremonies for reverencing ancestors led to the banning of Christianity in China.[53] Another humanist scholar, Sebastianus Castellio, in reviewing this erstwhile penchant of both Catholics and Protestants to incinerate those people

whose beliefs were different from theirs, provided this damning indictment of the Christian Church: "To burn a heretic is not to defend a doctrine, but to kill a man."[54]

Perhaps with an intellectual and spiritual humility borne of these blunt and brutal criticisms of its bloody and blunderous past, nowadays the Christian Church is more amenable to scientific hypothesising: in 1951, the Catholic Church declared that the Big Bang theory on the beginnings of the universe is consistent with the Holy Bible, while Pope John Paul II – wishing to start the new millennium on the right footing – issued a special apology for the wrongdoings of the Church in the past 1,000 years, which included the mistaken prosecution of Galileo. However, Christian fundamentalists still refuse to accept the Darwinian theory of evolution, in spite of much scientific evidence to support this "single best idea anybody has ever had" – according to the American philosopher Daniel Dennett – which asserts that our ancestors were bipedal and tool-using hominids who lived in the savannas of Africa with all the other wild beasts, and not Adam and Eve who lived in the mythical Garden of Eden with the sly serpent, as the Holy Bible would have us believe.

Notes

1. Etzioni, 1993.
2. Bellah *et al.*, 1985.
3. *The Straits Times*, July 4 & July 12, 2000.
4. *The Straits Times*, June 18, 2000.
5. Triandis, 1995.
6. Wheeler, Reis & Bond, 1989.
7. Triandis, 1995.
8. Chang & Holt, 1994.
9. Westwood, Tang & Kirkbride, 1992; Ting-Toomey, 1988; Lebra, 1984.
10. McCormack, 1924.
11. Ng, 1999.
12. Janis, 1982.
13. Nemeth, 1995.
14. Tarnas, 1991.
15. Fung, 1948; Lin, 1936.
16. Reps & Senzaki, 1985.
17. Rahim & Magner, 1995.
18. Ng, 1999.
19. Leung, 1987.
20. Barnlund, 1975.
21. Ohbuchi & Takahashi, 1994.
22. Ting-Toomey *et al.*, 1991

23. Chang and Holt, 1994.
24. *Ibid.*
25. *Ibid.*
26. Allen, 1969.
27. Ng, 2000b.
28. Davis, 1986.
29. Sternberg & Lubart, 1995.
30. Diebold, 1991.
31. Stewart, 1997.
32. Wright, 1994.
33. *Ibid.*
34. Ng, 1999.
35. Starr, 1997.
36. Tu, 1993.
37. Lin, 1936.
38. Hucker, 1978.

39. Bloodworth, 1967.
40. Smith, 1973.
41. Hucker, 1978.
42. Wills, 1994.
43. Bloodworth, 1967.
44. Stumpf, 1993.
45. Tarnas, 1991.
46. Gilbert, 1989.
47. Camus, 1975.
48. Tarnas, 1991.
49. Gibney, 1992.
50. Rice, 1970.
51. Westman, 1993.
52. Drake, 1993.
53. Boorstin, 1998.
54. Rice, 1970.

── *chapter 8* ──

Can the East Survive the West?

We have seen that the psychological freedom to behave in a creative, task-involved and individuated manner is more likely to be nurtured in the loosely-organised, individualistic and egalitarian society of the West, which places an emphasis on realising one's potential in life. In contrast, the feeling of internal and external coercion is more likely to be nurtured in the tightly-organised, collectivistic and hierarchical society of the East, which places an emphasis on conforming oneself to the social group, as well as on enhancing one's face before significant others in the community. This dichotomy between freedom in the West and control of behaviour in the East is a product of deep cultural, historical and political forces within each society.

The Psychological Freedom to Create in the West

Western society is founded on the ethic of liberal individualism, which emerged out of a long and bloody struggle by the people against arbitrary authority. Having fought so hard to liberate themselves from oppression, Westerners believe that the power of any leader or group in society should be limited by various checks and balances, so as to prevent the individual rights and freedoms of the individual from being encroached upon. For example, the United States is a nation with a rich tradition of moral imperatives, but the most well known is the need to protect the "natural rights" of each individual. This core cultural ideal is rooted directly in the Declaration of Independence and the Bill of Rights, as well as the First Amendment, which protect certain inalienable rights of the individual, including free speech and action, as long as it does not cause any harm to his neighbours. This highlighting of individuals and their rights is objectified and reified in a variety of democratic political institutions, such as the constitutional separation of the power of the executive, legislature and judiciary, which creates a weak government that

155

cannot impose its will on its people. In addition, the media in the West plays a crucial role in this cultural shaping of psychological reality. For example, Hollywood studios are regularly churning out big-budget movies (e.g., *Enemy of the State*) which deal with the moral theme of having to maintain one's guard against any social group or organisation that threatens the freedom of the individual. This moral theme is a reflection of the liberal maxim that the price of freedom is eternal vigilance against tyranny in any form.[1]

The Social Control of Behaviour in the East

In contrast, Asian society is founded on the ethic of Confucianism, which emerged out of the teachings of Confucius, fertilised by ideas from other branches of Chinese philosophy, especially Legalism, an ancient and lethal form of Behaviourism which utilised harsh rules and punishments to control people's behaviour. The Confucian philosophy of government spread from its original source in China to affect the historical development of neighbouring Asian countries, such as Japan and Korea, so that even now in our modern times, with the advent of Western notions of government like democracy and individual rights and freedoms, its influence is still conspicuous in those Asian societies with a Confucian heritage.

Singapore is an example of a modern country which is run in accordance with the Confucian ideology of government, which means to say that its leaders adopt a strict and paternalistic stance towards its people, leading a staff reporter of *The Wall Street Journal*[2] to term it disparagingly as a "nanny state".* In Singapore, the behaviour of its people is strictly regulated via a plethora of laws, rules and regulations which the ruling party, the People's Action Party (PAP), easily passes in Parliament, due to its majority vote (currently it has 83 out of 85 seats in the Singapore Parliament). Some of these laws include the Internal Security Act, under which detention orders without trial for up to two years can be issued, and the Newspaper and Printing Presses Act of 1974, which has been amended several times to give the PAP government a lot of legal clout to deal with "aberrant" publications.[3]

Desire to be free

Besides the tough stance which it adopts towards any politically destabilising forces, Singapore has also earned a dubious reputation all over the world as a "fine" city, i.e., a city where there are hefty fines for minor misdemeanours such as speeding, littering, importing chewing gum for sale, not flushing the toilet after using it, and not topping up the petrol-tank when driving across the Malaysian causeway. This type of

≈≈

* Singaporeans are not the only people in the Asian community who are regarded by these opinionated and insolent commentators from the West as living in a "nanny state". So are the Japanese. In his book *Japan Swings: Politics, Culture and Sex in the New Japan*, Richard McGregor, an Australian journalist, wrote about how "from the moment they leave home to the time they return in the evenings, Japanese people are protected by the inescapable embrace of the Nanny State". Actually, a moment's reflection will reveal to the reader that nanny states are found in the liberal individualistic societies of the West, not the Asian communities in the East. For members who live in these nanny states of the West are an extremely insecure lot. They not only need to be mollycoddled by their expensive therapists, but they also need generous welfare handouts from their government to ease their pain of living in a modern competitive society e.g., if an Australian loses his job, he will receive about A$200 every week from his government to keep him afloat in the turbulent sea of capitalism. In contrast, Asians do not have the habit of running to their therapists (for mollycoddling) or state (for welfare handouts) whenever things go wrong; they can sort out the problem by themselves, with assistance from their family and friends. The self-reliance of these Asians (e.g., Singaporeans and Japanese) puts to shame the insecurity of those Westerners (e.g., Americans and Australians), who live in the nanny states of the West.

≈≈

punitive policy is not without its negative side effects, as shown in the following boxed article, which looks at how the Singapore government uses hefty fines to control the behaviour of its people, making them feel like puppets on a string.

Killing Creativity by Creating the Perfect Society in Singapore

The Singapore government uses hefty fines to control its citizens' behaviour e.g., a fine of S$500 for littering, a fine of S$150 for not flushing the toilet after using it, and so on. In this way, it hopes to preserve the country's image as a "garden city". Unfortunately, like chemotherapy, this policy of controlling behaviour through hefty fines has unintended side effects. An example is the ugly monster of ungracious behaviour, which has rankled the Malaysian authorities, because inconsiderate Singaporeans litter and speed in Johor Bahru, which is separated from the island of Singapore by a one-kilometre causeway. These inconsiderate Singaporeans think that they can speed or litter with no financial qualms, once they are out of their own country.

This raises the moral question of whether the state should make use of punitive measures to elicit civic behaviour from its citizens.

This is because civic behaviour which is elicited in this manner, although having the outward form of graciousness, is in reality insincere, as it is not freely chosen by the person. Instead, being elicited by a punitive threat, it will make itself scarce once this threat is removed.

The use of punitive measures to shape the behaviour of Singaporeans is based on the operant principles of *behaviourism*, of which the most stalwart proponent is Burrhus Frederic Skinner (1904–1990).[4] Skinner was an American psychologist who had an early interest in constructing mechanical devices and in collecting an assortment of animals, which he kept as pets. He was also fascinated with the complex tricks he saw trained animals perform at country fairs. These early interests were destined to play a major role in his work on behaviourism, a special branch in psychology which rejects the notion of free will, as well as of mental states like feeling, thinking and believing, as valid scientific constructs. Instead, this perspective on behaviour regards the person as a puppet which can be manipulated at will by a puppet master to behave in any way he wants it to.

This is achieved via a special technique known as *operant conditioning*. In operant conditioning, the consequences of behaviour are shaped by the experimenter, with the ultimate goal of increasing or decreasing the frequency of a certain response. Behaviour that is reinforced, i.e., followed by rewarding consequences, tends to be repeated. In contrast, behaviour that is not reinforced, i.e., followed by punitive consequences, tends to be extinguished. Complex behaviors can be produced by using this technique of operant conditioning e.g., two pigeons playing a simple game of table tennis by holding tiny bats in their beaks.

Skinner argued that human society can benefit from the scientific principles of behaviourism, and illustrated this in his first novel *Walden Two* (1948). This novel – which explores how science can be used to create the perfect society – is set in a fictional utopian community, where behavioural principles are used to produce happy, productive and cooperative citizens. This book was highly controversial, and met with the ire of many, for it was written during the height of the Cold War, when "Big Brother is Watching You" was still a daily fact of life for the millions of inhabitants of the repressive and totalitarian regime of Stalinist Russia and its satellite states.

Undaunted by his critics, the iconoclastic Skinner went on to write another highly controversial book, *Beyond Freedom and Dignity*, in which he criticised his countrymen's preoccupation with the notion of freedom. Instead, he maintained that free will is a myth, and that our behaviour is always shaped and controlled by others, including parents, teachers, peers, advertising agents, television and radio, Hollywood directors and so on. As for the prospect of human creativity, Skinner stated in a famous paper entitled "A Lecture on 'Having' a Poem" that "a poet is no more responsible for the content or structure of a poem than a chicken is responsible for laying an egg". Instead, each action is seen as a result of the creator's history, and the stimuli and responses that the creator has experienced. In this view, there can be no truly original behaviour or ideas, except as they are an inevitable product of a unique individual's experiences. In other words, Skinner did not believe in creativity.[5]

In addition to dispelling the "myth of creativity", Skinner argued that rather than leaving the control of human behaviour to chance, a society should systematically shape the behaviour of its members for the larger good. This piece of advice has not gone unheeded by the ruling party in Singapore, as it strives to create the "perfect society" based on the Skinnerian paradigm. However, a Skinnerian approach to managing society will prevent the individual from being the master of his own fate. Instead, the individual feels compelled by punitive measures to behave in a certain prescribed way, or else … The end result is a "Skinnerian society" of "pigeon personalities", i.e., a society of people who are motivated to act by prods and punishments. If the ruling party in Singapore wishes to realise its laudable goal of unleashing the creative potential of these pusillanimous and passive people who lack passion and panache, it will need to reconsider not only the encyclopaedic rules and regulations which it has imposed on them. In addition – and even more importantly – it will also need to undergo a fundamental shift in its understanding of human nature, i.e., believing that human beings are not puppets controlled by a puppet master, but individuals with their own autonomous and creative will.

Campaigning for the Thoughts of the People

Singapore is also well known as the city of campaigns, where the government exhorts its citizens to engage in a wide range of behaviour via the national media on an annual basis, from having three or more children if they can afford it and being courteous to people they meet to using Standard English rather than Singlish when they speak (the difference between Standard English and Singlish can be seen in this example: "Would you like some ketchup on your fish balls?" as opposed to "You want sauce on your balls or not huh?"). This heavy reliance on annual campaigns to shape the thoughts of citizens, so that they will think in those ways which are desired by the state, has led Ian Buruma, a liberal critic from the West,[6] to comment that Singaporeans are too afraid to think.*

Freedom to Think in the West

The use of campaigns and state-owned media to shape the thinking of the individual is shunned by many societies in the West, which leave the individual alone to think his or her own thoughts. According to the American Sinologist Professor Munro,[7] this difference in approach towards opinion control in the East and West can be traced back to the contrasting assumptions about the human mind in these two cultures. The assumption behind the Western attitude is that as autonomous agents, people possess a private realm (consciousness, beliefs, thoughts, feelings) that normally does not affect others, and so therefore should remain immune from tampering by external agents. This is expressed in an old English maxim: "The thoughts of man are not tryable; the devil alone knows the thoughts of man." Or to put it more bluntly, what a person thinks in his mind is none of society's business.

Historically it has been one of the major tasks of liberalism to defend this distinction between a man's mind and his actions, and between his intentions and his deeds; otherwise there exists the danger of the individual not being able to defend himself against state action. For example, in *On Liberty*, the English philosopher J. S. Mill wrote: "How much of human life should be assigned to individuality and how much to society? Each will receive its proper share if each has that which more particularly concerns it. To individuality should belong the part of life in which it is chiefly the individual that is interested; to society, the part which chiefly interests society."

In the Hollywood movie *Demolition Man*, this liberal theme of protecting the individual from the encroachment of society is given a futuristic twist. The year is 2032 AD, and the liberal polity has been replaced by a scientifically-engineered and sanitised state which adopts extreme policies, i.e., a "perfect society". For example, it has banned the use of force

~~~~~~

* With this analytical book of mine, I strongly refute Mr Buruma's charge that Singaporeans are too afraid to think. Singaporeans can think for themselves. But whether we think out loud or think in silence is our own business – we don't need an outsider like Mr Buruma to tell us how we should behave. How would Mr Buruma like it if an outsider like myself starts telling the folks back in his country how they should behave? For example, Bill Clinton should not have sex with Monica Lewinsky while he is the President of the United States and a husband of a faithful wife and a father of a teenage daughter who is as old as Ms Lewinsky herself. Or adults in American society shouldn't leave their handguns in places where children can retrieve them, bring them to school, and use them to shoot or kill their classmates.

~~~~~~

by policemen. Instead, policemen are required to be ultra-polite and civil to the criminal they are arresting, by requesting him to *please* put down his weapon before they arrest him. In addition, adults in this ultra-purist state are banned from having sexual intercourse with one another. In return for their abstention from real sex, special helmets which can enable them to experience the "virtual reality" of sex without exposing them to its messiness and diseases (like AIDS) are available for use. The American macho-man Sylvester Stallone 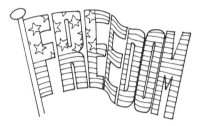 plays the role of a resurrected hero from the sex-obsessed and violent society of the 20th century, who assists the revolutionists in toppling the state and regaining their freedom so that they can, among other things, choose to be assholes if they wanted to!

Control of Thinking in the East

In contrast to this liberal assumption that the autonomous agent should be left alone to his own devices, so long as he does not endanger the lives of others, the assumption behind the Asian attitude is that mental events such as knowing, feeling and believing are usually accompanied by covert "springs of action" or promptings to act, likely to emerge as open conduct. Because such promptings to act may affect others, their existence brings private beliefs and opinions into the public realm, i.e., personal beliefs and opinions are justifiably subject to direction by agents (rulers) representing those who may be affected by these covert springs of action. (If the Western cliché is that it is better for a guilty person to go free than to convict an innocent person, than the Asian cliché may well be that it is better for an innocent person to be convicted if the common welfare is protected, than for a guilty person to be free to inflict further harm on society.) This emphasis on shaping the mind of the individual to protect the rest of the community is reflected in the doctrine of the unity of knowledge and action by Wang Yang Ming, a famous Confucian scholar who lived in China in the 15th century. This doctrine specifically guards against the danger of theoretically isolating the concepts of knowledge and action. Doing so, in Wang's view, will lead people to think only in terms of public, manifest action, and make them unaware of the existence of covert springs of action. As a result, they will not be on their guard against the presence of evil thoughts and intentions, and fail to suppress them before the actual manifestation in conduct occurs. The following passage, which is quoted from Professor Munro in his book, puts this matter succinctly:

> The Teacher said, "You need to understand the basic purpose of my doctrine. In their learning people of today separate knowledge and action into two different things. Therefore when a thought is aroused, although

it is evil, they do not stop it because it has not been translated into action. I advocate the unity of knowledge and action precisely because I want people to understand that *when a thought is aroused, it is already action."*

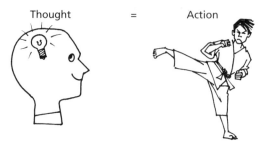

Thought = Action

Asian Insulars versus Western Visitors

The continual hold on power by authoritarian governments like the PAP in Singapore and the Communist Party in China does not augur well for the creativity of their people. My assertion is consistent with the view of Therivel, a keen scholar on creativity. In an insightful article entitled "Long-Term Effects of Power on Creativity", Therivel, using historical examples as proof, argued that authoritarian governments would stifle creativity within the society. He began by making a distinction between *insulars* who live under a *united* form of power (e.g., Singaporeans and Mainland Chinese) and *visitors* who lived under a *divided* form of power (e.g., Americans and Australians). In the insular's society, there is only one domineering power which is not restricted by any major division of power – in other words, there is no possibility of manoeuver for the individual by switching allegiance to another power.[8]

Like Asian insulars, Western visitors who live under a divided power may actually not be any freer in their actions. However, unlike Asian insulars, they live with the knowledge that a major division of power exists within their society and, in case of need, they can switch their allegiance to the alternative power, which will come to their aid to take advantage of the situation (as the saying goes, the enemy of my enemy is my friend). Western visitors know that they can never be too badly harmed, and never be crushed totally, because they can engage in this Machiavellian game of playing one power against another e.g., the vociferous press in the West will always welcome a good fight with the executive arm of the government, unlike the sycophantic press in some Asian societies which will toe the official government line. As a result, Western visitors have faith in themselves as persons in control of important aspects of their lives.

In contrast, Asian insulars living under the united power must show a good face and never exhibit unhappiness, hatred or a desire to revolt. This is because the united power will crush them if they try to do so, and none will come to their rescue, as illustrated in innumerable failed revolts by the peasants in ancient China, who were swiftly and brutally suppressed by the better-armed soldiers in the emperor's army, as well as in the military crushing of the student-led protests in Tiananmen in modern China. Patience, silence, restraint, submission, accommodation, political apathy, hypocrisy and sycophancy, as well as a general channelling of one's nervous energy to materialistic pursuits become habitual modes of behaviour under the united power. To protect themselves, insulars turn to their closest relations (parents, brothers and sisters, spouses), who are expected to help them in case of trouble. The family must be united as the secure haven where each can take off the hated mask of smiling obedience. Once this point is understood, the reader will be able to appreciate a simple yet poignant remark that has been made of the Chinese people: only when they are alone, during the great moments of life, do they throw off the hated yoke of feigned obedience to show themselves as they truly are.[9]

According to Therivel, insulars living under a united form of power will be less creative than visitors living under a divided form of power. This is because their mental scripts tell them how to absorb new information into their conventional mindset, instead of changing their mindset to take in new information. If there are major problems in this process of knowledge acquisition, then it must be due to a lack of fidelity to tradition; in turn, this implies the need to rejuvenate the tradition. This championing of the old by suppressing the new avoids the need for unpalatable accommodations to the new. At the same time, it also eliminates creativity, which requires the destruction of the old to herald in the new. True creativity is extremely difficult to achieve in an insular society because the united power will only bless those works that fit the truth or tradition that has been approved by it. In consequence, anything really new is refused and excommunicated, with no hiding place and little opportunity to move to an independent field free to appreciate and protect it. In the end, the person living in an insular culture is forced to avoid those invisible "out-of-bounds" markers which would raise the ire of the united power* to concentrate on more materialistic pursuits.[10] This type of behaviour is exemplified in the *kiasuism* of ordinary Singaporeans.

≈≈≈

* An example of avoiding these vaguely-defined "out-of-bounds" markers can be seen in the Zunzi Wong incident at the Singapore Art Museum. Wong, a Hong Kong artist, presented a piece of work on Singapore's strict censorship laws. This consisted of a caricature of the Singapore Prime Minister Goh Chok Tong and Senior Minister Lee Kuan Yew, which had Mr Goh as a gardener spraying insecticide labelled "Fines" and Mr Lee patting him on his back. Unfortunately, Singaporeans did not manage to see this piece of creative work, for minutes before the official opening of the exhibition at the museum, Wong's work was taken down, for unknown reasons (*The Straits Times*, July 30, 2000).

≈≈≈

The Long-Term and Negative Impact of United Power on Eminent Creativity

Therivel also argued that the long-term impact of a united power on the creativity (especially eminent creativity) of the insular society will always turn out to be a detrimental one. This is because as power becomes more united, it will gradually destroy the initial diversity of its components, eliminating a channel for eminent creativity. In addition, the united power inadvertently signs its own death knell by developing a proud, cocky and arrogant attitude that chokes off creativity.

An example is the Qing dynasty of China (1644–1911). Throughout the 17th and 18th centuries the Qing emperors were confident that theirs was the greatest civilisation in the world, both in the extent and political influence of their Celestial Empire, and in the measure of its cultural attainments. Education, almost always confined to the Confucian classics, and competitive examinations based on a conventional interpretation of Confucian philosophy, produced a type of mind which was so convinced that the Confucian way of life could not be bettered that it became resistant to change, and closed to all ideas of progress.

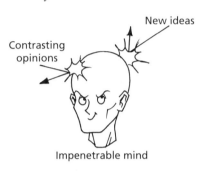

This extreme conservatism in outlook was reflected in the dismissing attitude which the Qing emperor Chien Long adopted towards King George III of England during the closing years of the 18th century. King George III had sent his ambassador to the Qing emperor with some products manufactured in England, as well as a request for formal trading relations to be established between the two empires. In reply, Chien Long issued an imperial edict which stated that "although sending envoys to kowtow and present local products at my court … is a sign of your sincerity, humility and loyalty … it is not right … to request someone to remain … at the capital … Hence we have commanded your tribute envoys to return safely home. You, O King, should simply act in conformity with our wishes by strengthening your loyalty and swearing perpetual obedience so as to ensure that your country may share the blessings of peace."[11]

What King George III failed to obtain from Emperor Chien Long through the peaceful means of dialogue, his successors were to secure forcefully a few decades later from the emperor's descendants, using a new and powerful weapon: fiery cannons mounted on modern steamships which devastated the ancient and weak fortresses along the Chinese coast. Forced by such gunboat diplomacy to accept increasing contact with the representatives of European and American government in the interest of trade, Chinese officialdom slowly began to realise that these Westerners, who were detested and despised as "barbarians", were equally contemptuous of the Chinese government, which they regarded as medieval and obsolete, an anachronism totally out of place in a modern, scientific and technological world.[12]

To many of the more progressive among the leading Confucian officials, the weakness and backwardness of their once proud and mighty country were all too apparent: The Opium War; the Arrow War; the Taiping Rebellion; the sea squabbles with the Japanese over Korea which led to the loss of the Chinese island of Taiwan; the Boxer Rebellion along with the relief of the foreign legation at Peking by the armed forces of nine nations, which forced the imperial family to flee from their palace at the Forbidden City – all these events showed a society which was in a virtual state of collapse. The Chinese response to these attacks from without and revolts from within was various half-baked attempts at reform. In one such attempt, the open-minded but weak-willed emperor Guang-Hsu issued 27 edicts, which were meant to initiate sweeping reforms of the political, educational, economic and military institutions of the empire. Unfortunately, he was thwarted in his attempt by his aunt and real ruler of China, the conservative Empress Dowager Cixi, who put him under house arrest and, in an extremely mean and cruel act, ordered her palace guards to throw his favourite concubine down a well (all this fair maiden had done was to plead with the Dowager to permit her to remain by the side of the emperor whom she loved). Left to languish alone by himself in the Forbidden City, Emperor Guang-Hsu died in 1908. His vicious aunt died soon after. Three years later, the last Qing dynasty was toppled by a Republican rebellion, and the emperors of China lost their Mandate of Heaven to rule – this time for good.

Transforming the Asian Society from Within: The Case of Japan

To prevent history from repeating itself, many Asian countries in the modern world are taking preemptive steps to free up their society and open it to an influx of new ideas from foreign countries, at the same time that they are encouraging their citizens to take charge of their own lives by devolving more power to them. A prime example of this attempt to transform the Asian society from within is the homogenous, tightly-organised and hierarchical nation of Japan. On the first month of the new millennium, a panel of 50 of the nation's top economists, academics, journalists and scientists submitted a report to the then prime minister Mr Keizo Obuchi on the nation's future. These 50 panel members had travelled to China, America, Singapore and South Korea, consulting political and business leaders there as part of their deliberations towards the final report, which they entitled "The Frontier Within: Individual Empowerment and Better Government in the New Millennium".[13]

The panel members described "The Frontier Within" as an extension of the soul-searching in Japan over the last ten years, as it grappled with the political and social fallout following the economic recession in the 1990s. Their opening sentence in "The Frontier Within" says it all: "We share a sense of urgency. We fear that, as things stand, Japan is headed for decline." The panel members went on to list a series of events in the 1990s which they perceived as shattering the Japanese perceptions of themselves as builders of the second-largest economy in the world, after the United States. The most glaring example was the government's response to the 1995 Kobe earthquake, which killed approximately 5,000 Japanese, and exposed the inner workings of the Japanese political and bureaucratic system "like an X-ray", according to Professor Takeshi Sasaki of Tokyo University. At the top was a hapless and powerless prime minister, Tomiichi Murayama, who received less information and at a later time, than US president Bill Clinton in the immediate aftermath of the earthquake, which struck at 5:46 a.m. The first cabinet meeting, at 10 a.m., barely discussed the issue. The Japanese Self-Defence Force (or SDF, as their military is called) was not called in to help until after midday, because of the anti-army stance of the left-wing local governor, whose permission was needed for them to help in a crisis (a local SDF commander was to break down and cry later on, when apologising publicly for the unnecessary loss of life caused by the delay). Numerous offers of foreign help, from Swiss sniffer dogs to foreign doctors and pain-killing drugs were initially rejected by the bureaucracy because they had not passed the necessary red tape.[14]

Even the country's biggest and most notorious *yakuza* gangster group, the Yamaguchi-gumi, headquartered in Kobe, shamed the Japanese authorities by mounting a swift and efficient relief effort. At a cabinet meeting the day after the earthquake, an outspoken female minister, Makitko Tanka, interrupted a flowery report on the situation to suggest that energy food supplements like bananas and cheese be sent to the quake survivors (her male colleagues sneered at her suggestion, with unhelpful remarks such as "Isn't it just like a woman to be thinking only in these terms?" and "What about sending them some rice?"). The public and press reaction to the government's bungling was bitter, as can be seen in this comment by Yasuhiko Shibata of the Yomiuri Shimbun Research Institute: "In the wake of the ... earthquake, it has become clear that Japan is a closed, confused country entering its terminal phase."

To arrest the general deterioration in standards within many aspects of Japanese society, the panel members offered a set of radical recommendations, which covered many areas of Japanese life. These recommendations included the following: an immigration policy to give preferential treatment for foreign students, allowing them to acquire permanent residence status automatically; a requirement for all public institutions to publish in both English and Japanese; a proposal to lower the voting age to 18, as well as to start a national debate on having a direct election of the prime minister; a recommendation to bring in mid-career private-sector individuals into governmental service; and finally, a suggestion to increase the number of lawyers as well as to allow people other than lawyers to provide legal consultations to Japanese citizens. The report ended with the exhortation that every Japanese should be prepared to devote "three generations" towards the realisation of this new Japan. If the Japanese succeed in transforming their society from within, this will not be their first time, as shown in the following boxed article.

Opening up to the West: The Meiji Revolution in Japan

Like China, Japan in the 19th century was ruled by a moribund dynasty that was disintegrating. This was the Tokugawa shogunate, which seized power in 1600 and ruled in the name of the Japanese emperor, i.e., Japanese emperors were allowed to continue their formal reigns at Kyoto, but real power emanated from the shogunate court which was based at Edo (the old name for Tokyo). The Tokugawa shogunate needed an ideology to justify their hold on power; it found this in the doctrines of Neo-Confucianism propounded by Chu Xi, a Chinese philosopher who lived during the Sung dynasty. Chu Xi had taught that the same principle of order bound both the natural world and human political society; hence a strong and harmonious state, organised in a hierarchy of Confucian relationships, was in itself a reflection of Heaven's law, something which should not be transgressed.

Although such a social philosophy fitted a rural society which was recovering from the convulsions of civil war, its conservative nature eventually took the wind out of the Tokugawa shogunate. This can be seen in an unforgettable description of Tokugawa society by a prominent Meiji reformer, Fukuzawa Yukichi:

> The millions of Japanese at that time were closed up inside millions of individual boxes. They were separated from one another by walls with little room to move around. The four-level class structure of warriors, farmers, artisans and tradesmen froze human relationships along prescribed lines ... The walls separating them were as strong as iron and could not be broken by any amount of force. Having no motivation to employ their talents so as to progress forward, people simply retreated into the safety of their own shells. Over the course of many years this routine became second nature to them. Their spirit of initiative was lost.[15]

If the East Asian region of the world had not been so transformed by the aggressive ambitions of mighty nations in the West, the Tokugawa shogunate might have survived. Unfortunately, Japan in the 19th century was faced with the same problem as China: how to deal with the formidable threat from the West. It came most threateningly in the form of a well-armed fleet of six steam-powered ships of a size rarely seen in Japanese waters. The captain who commandered these "menacing black ships", which caused Japanese fishermen to flee frantically towards the safety of the shore "like wild birds at a sudden intruder", was a burly American by the name of Matthew Calbraith Perry.

Perry was the commander-in-chief of the United States Naval Forces of East India, China and the Japan Seas, and Special Ambassador to Japan. He was under strict orders to demand from the highest Japanese authorities the protection of American seamen and property wrecked on their islands or driven into their ports; permission for American vessels to obtain supplies or to refit; and permission to enter one or more of their ports for the purpose of disposing of their cargoes by sale or barter. The strategy Perry was to follow was laid down as clearly as his objectives: if, after having exhausted every argument, the commodore should fail to obtain from the Japanese government any relaxation of their system of exclusion, he would then change his tone.[16]

Like flashes of lightning on the horizon, news of the recent incursions of British and French fleets into China's ports had made its way into Japan. The shock waves of the Opium War – in which the Chinese government attempted to prevent the British from selling opium to its people, but ended up being forced to accept humiliating terms after their defeat by modern steam-powered British warships – convinced many progressive elements in Japanese society that they had some intensive catching up to do if they wished to avoid sharing the same fate as China. This sense of present danger combined with another line of thinking that had also incubated during the Tokugawa reign. This line of thinking was promoted by the 18th-century scholar Motoori Norinaga, and involved delving into the past, in which the ancient idea of a supreme emperor ruling a God-favoured country became attractive once more. It took only a slight leap of the imagination to deduce that the problems afflicting Japan's body politic could be attributed to the shogunate's usurpation of power. Could not these ills be cured – and the foreigners repulsed in the process – by a return to direct imperial rule?[17]

The crisis came to a head in 1867, with demands by leading reformers that the Tokugawa shogunate should abdicate and restore real power to the emperor. A brief civil war led to an Imperial Restoration, which was hailed as the Meiji Revolution (enlightened rule). The main political objective of these Meiji modernisers was to replace the country's ramshackle network of semi-independent clans with a strong centralised state ruled by a divine emperor. This state would be in charge of collecting taxes, enforcing school attendance, running railways and telegraph and postal systems, and imposing standard weights and measures and a uniform currency – all tasks deemed to be essential for national unification.

Inspired by the slogan *fukoku kyohei* (enrich the country, strengthen the army), the Meiji government turned to different countries in the West for different institutions and practices e.g., Britain provided the model for the navy; France provided the model for the army; Germany offered the pattern for the constitution (established in 1889); and America served as a guide in engineering and technology. The traditional samurai class began to diminish in number and stature, while Western-style universities were founded to train a new breed of bureaucrats, diplomats and technical experts. Social customs were subjected to keen scrutiny e.g., mixed bathing in public baths was abolished, and the entire imperial court adopted Western dress. Indeed, cultural life underwent such a profound change that Western admirers of Japan feared that the country's entire heritage of arts and folklore was in jeopardy of being abandoned in favour of a copycat culture of imports and imitations.

However, they need not have feared. Christian missionaries were allowed to preach their faith, but the Japanese did not seem very interested. Even the Western technicians, who were treated with deference, were dismissed at the end of their contracts. For the Japanese were determined not to depend entirely on others. To make this clear, an Imperial Rescript on Education was issued in 1890, which stressed harmony and hierarchy, order, loyalty and benevolence as being the supreme social virtues – ideas based on Confucianism. It was a clear indication of the Japanese will to ensure that modernisation in their country need not mean Westernisation, as well as to follow their own path of *wakon yosai* (Western method, Eastern spirit).

The Japanese succeeded beyond their wildest dreams in their efforts at modernising their country. For by the closing years of the 19th century, Japan was a great power to reckon with, in comparison to the weak nation of China, which was in its death throes. This was ironical, given the fact that for centuries it was the other way round, i.e., it had been the Japanese who had viewed the Chinese with awe, relying on Chinese customs and ideas for constructing their own society. But in 1894, they clashed with their Chinese counterparts over Korea – to determine who should be the "guardian" of this people – and emerged triumphant: the out-of-date Chinese forces were routed by the modern Japanese forces in months, gaining for the victor the island of Taiwan as the spoil of war.

In 1900, Japanese troops joined a multinational team in suppressing the Boxer Rebellion in China. In 1904, the Japanese military took on the mighty Tsarist empire of Russia to settle the fate of Korea. Stalemated on land, the Russians were beaten at sea; the Tsar's Baltic fleet was sunk by the Japanese navy in the Tsushima Straits. The Japanese had done the unthinkable: they had defeated a great Western power by sheer will and effort. By this victory, they sent an unequivocal message to the Western world that Asians were no pushovers; instead people in the East could learn from their counterparts in the West and ultimately beat them at their own game. In my opinion, this is a useful historical lesson to bear in mind for Asians who live in this new millennium.

Maintaining Social Control in the East: The Case of Singapore

When "The Frontier Within" was first published, it attracted its fair share of critics (like all good governmental reports), who charged that if all the recommendations of the panel members were implemented, it would result in an end product which was no longer Japan (one of the critics remarked that the panel members were asking the Japanese not to be Japanese). These critical comments point to an important question which needs to be considered by all those Asian societies which are embarking on a radical course of change. It is this: how can an Asian society preserve its own culture and uniqueness at the same time that it embraces ideas from the West?

An Asian society which has attempted to grapple with this issue is Singapore. Like the late Japanese prime minister Mr Keizo Obuchi, whose concern about the long-term future of Japan propelled him to appoint the 50 panel members to come up with "The Frontier Within", the ruling elite in Singapore has been thinking long and hard of the country's long-term future. The ruling party acknowledges the superiority of the West in nurturing the creativity of its citizens. In addition, it is aware that the amount of social control which it imposes on its own citizens, via a draconian set of laws, rules, regulations and opinion control, has led to many unintended side effects, like a silent and passive majority who gripes about the government in private (in one survey, it was found that nine out of ten Singaporeans who disagree with government policies prefer to remain silent than speak up against them in public; two in three, however, will talk and complain about their unhappiness to their friends and family members[18]). Finally, it is aware of the basic argument by Therivel that an overconcentration of power in the hands of a minority elite can only lead to a stifling of the creative impulse.

However, although the ruling party can see that "under a banyan tree, very little else can grow", it has not run helter-skelter to jump on the Western bandwagon. This is because of what it perceives to be the undesirable social consequences of rampant individualism in the West, which is epitomised by its high divorce rates, its breakdown of the family and its culture of permissive sex and wanton violence. In other words, so long as the "basic instinct" of rampant individualism casts its long and dark shadow over the creative achievements of Western society, Asian political parties like Singapore's PAP are going to act very gingerly when opening the flood-gates of freedom to ignite the creative spark of its citizens. For as Mr Lee Kuan Yew, the father of modern-day Singapore (as well as an essential target of Western liberal critics like the New York columnist William Safire, who has called Lee, among other things, a "tinpot despot" and a "dictator") has said:

I want freedom!

We want law and order!

> Good governance, even today, requires a balance between competing claims by upholding fundamental truths: that there is right and wrong, good and evil. If everyone gets pornography on a satellite dish the size of a saucer, then governments around the world will have to do something about it, or we will destroy our young and with them human civilisation ... The ideas of individual supremacy and the right to free expression, when carried to excess, have not worked. They have made it difficult to keep American society cohesive. Asia can see it is not working. Those who wish for a wholesome society where young girls and old ladies can walk in the streets at night, where the young are not preyed upon by drug peddlers, will not follow the American model.[19]

To forestall a similar erosion in social conduct, the PAP government is still keeping a tight rein on what the Singaporean can do or say, so as to maintain the public mores of society. For instance, although busking is now permitted, there are many rules and regulations in place to control this behaviour. First of all, our would-be busker will need to be a member of an arts group in Singapore. Then he has to put in an application to the National Arts Council for a busking licence, which costs S$30 for three months. He can only perform in a restricted number of venues, and he can only retain part of the money which he has collected from the public to cover the cost of his performance; the rest will have to go back to his arts group, or to a local charity organisation. If the reader thinks that this is a tough set of rules and regulations to follow, he will find that the restriction on performance artists is even more stringent: they are required by law to get a licence from the Public Entertainment Licensing Unit (a police department), submit a synopsis of their performance and put down a security deposit, the amount of which is decided on a case-by-case basis. This set of restrictions was imposed after a homosexual performance artist was convicted in court for snipping his pubic hair in front of a public audience in protest against a police anti-gay action.

Struggling for Psychological Space in Liberty-Scarce Singapore

The close watch and restrictions by the political authority make the artistic community in Singapore feel that there is no space to communicate alternative ideas and visions about what life is all about. As one local playwright has argued, in a conforming, technocratic and materialistic society, with an authoritarian state and a passive people, there is little intellectual, artistic and creative space. There is a need to reduce political domination, to respect and release the artistic and literary sensibilities, so they can add to the "software" of society.[20] In an effort to break the impasse between the individual's desire for freedom in speech and action and the collective need to maintain public law and order, members of the Roundtable, a civic group consisting of private citizens, have suggested that certain places in this highly-regulated city-state be gazetted as "free speech" venues, which individuals and groups can book on a simple, first-come-first-served basis without the need to apply for a police permit. In their letter entitled "The Case for Free-Speech Venues", they argued that this incremental liberalising would benefit the country, as it would give her citizens practice in conducting political debate in a moderate and self-regulated fashion. They pointed out that the government could not monitor and regulate society forever, and in the next phase of Singapore's development, the public would have to be counted on to weigh competing interests and ideas on its own.[21] However, the response from the political authority was predictable, as can be gleaned from the title of their letter, "Free-Speech Venues May Threaten Order". In this letter, they argued that "Singapore is a multi-racial and multi-religious society; race, language and religion remain potentially divisive fault lines which can lead to social unrest and law and order problems if not managed carefully ... We cannot put at risk the racial harmony and sense of public order, peace and safety built up painstakingly over the years. For this reason, we cannot support the setting up of 'free speech' venues."[22]

I myself have written a letter to the local press on how Singapore can have her own Speakers' Corner, albeit with some modifications to suit the realities of living in a multi-racial and multi-religious society (see the following boxed article). I am glad to say that this concerted effort to find a public platform for the Voice of Singapore has borne fruit: recently, the prime minister of Singapore has announced that Singaporeans can have their own Speakers' Corner.[23] But true to its regimented style, the political authority has insisted that Singaporeans must obey the following rules and regulations. Potential speakers will need to register their intention to speak at a police post which is next to the Speakers' Corner; approval will be granted on the spot. Speakers can only display their eloquence from 7 a.m. to 7 p.m. each day. There will be no limit on the number of speakers or the length of speeches. Individual speakers can debate with spectators, although they will not enjoy immunity from Singapore laws e.g., if they make slanderous remarks, they can be sued for defamation. Uniformed police officers will patrol the Speakers' Corner twice a day, but they will adopt a minimalist, hands-off approach. In spite of these innumerable and unnecessary restrictions, this latest development in liberty-scarce Singapore is certainly an encouraging sign for those of us who have been struggling for more psychological space to live as free people in our own society.

Have Speakers' Corner with Modifications

The prime minister has said that Singaporeans are not ready for a Speakers' Corner which would allow people to say what they want freely, without rules.[24] He cited the possible problems that might arise from, say, a speaker who preaches the superiority of his religion over others. Although I agree with him that we must behave with sensitivity in a multi-racial and multi-religious society, I believe ordinary citizens in this maturing democracy are ready for a Speakers' Corner, with some modifications.

I advocate a middle path – in the spirit of "you win some, you lose some". I believe that what the political authorities fear most about free-speech venues is the anarchic tendencies they could unleash – e.g., if racial, religious or political demagogues stoke public sentiment. So I propose that potential speakers should avoid sensitive political, racial or religious issues, if they want to persuade our political leaders to let us try out this experiment. Potential speakers can display their eloquence in non-political topics, with an exotic flavour, guaranteed to arouse the interest of the general audience and invite their spontaneous response.

An example: a would-be speaker could make the non-political assertion that "it is with True Love as it is with ghosts: everybody believes in it, but few people have seen it". To buttress his argument, he can cite the opinions of various individuals, like the English writer and humorist George Bernard Shaw, who once commented that if we wish to read the deeds of love in the papers, we should turn to the homicide column. Or Erica Jong, who remarked, "Men and women. Women and men. It will never work." Or writer and poet Samuel Hoffenstein, who mused, "Breathes there a man with hide so tough, who says that two sexes aren't enough?" Or J. L. Borges, who pointed out, "To fall in love is to create a religion with a fallible God." And finally, the father of psychoanalysis, Sigmund Freud, who defined love as a form of lust, marked by the ordeal of civility, and who reminded us that we are never so vulnerable to pain and suffering as when we love, which perhaps is the reason why those of us who are sensible about love are incapable of it.

I am sure such exotic topics will generate amused and spontaneous participation from the audience, and allow our political leaders to let us indulge in our animated but harmless discussions, and most importantly, enable this fledgling project to take off in this sedate island in the sun. I also suggest that ordinary citizens pool their intellectual resources to develop a code of conduct which all potential speakers should adhere to. It will be appropriate to invite eminent Singaporeans who have a proven track record of service to the nation – such as Professor Tommy Koh and Dr Tan Cheng Bock – to give their suggestions on this code of conduct. At the very least, it should be clear to potential speakers that they must avoid racially or religiously sensitive topics, and refrain from hijacking this experiment for their own narrow political ends. Perhaps our motto should be: "We don't want to start a revolution; we just want to have fun speaking in public."

Potential speakers should indicate in advance the topic they will be speaking on. This information (including time and venue) should be displayed prominently in public, to enable people to decide whether they want to listen to this speaker. Before the speaker begins, he or she should also make a public commitment to the code of conduct which has been developed. The talk should be an occasion for speakers and listeners to engage in light-hearted banter about the topic in question. If anyone tries to politicise the process, responsible members of the audience will have to step in and nip the problem in the bud.

It might be a good idea to have Phua Chu Kang[†] on hand to say "shame-shame" to recalcitrant individuals who insist on killing the goose that lays the golden egg. But because Phua Chu Kang is busy taking English lessons on the advice of our prime minister, this idea is not workable. But the rest are, if we have enough faith in ourselves, and the political authorities would give us all a chance to hear the Voice of Singapore.

[†] Phua Chu Kang is a popular local TV character who speaks in Singlish rather than Standard English. Prime Minister Goh Chok Tong was afraid that Phua Chu Kang would influence Singaporeans (especially students) in the way they speak, which explains why he told the creators of Phua Chu Kang to improve his linguistic ability.

Chapter Summary

In this chapter, I looked at the historical forces which resulted in the social control of behaviour in the East on the one hand, and the psychological freedom to create in the West on the other. I then went on to elaborate on the difference between living as an insular in a society with a united power e.g., Asians like Singaporeans and Mainland Chinese, and living as a visitor in a society with a divided power e.g., Westerners like Americans and Australians. I observed that the long-term impact of a united power on the creativity of its people is a negative one, and will eventually lead to a toppling of the despotic dynasty, whether by a long and slow decline (as in the case of the Qing dynasty of China and the Tokugawa shogunate of Japan) or by a short and quick one (see the following boxed article for a historical example of a short and quick end to a dynasty that was supposed to last 10,000 generations). I then looked at how modern Asian societies like Japan are attempting to transform themselves from within in an attempt to survive in the 21st century. At the same time, I also described how other Asian societies like Singapore are treading the thin line between opening themselves up to the West and maintaining their own cultural uniqueness.

Shi Huang Ti: The Rise and Fall of the First Emperor of China

In the third century BC the land known to its inhabitants as *tian xia* (all under Heaven) – which would become modern China – was a region at war with itself. The seven warring states, which included Chi, Yen, Chao, Han, Wei, Chin and Chu, were ruled by kings and feudal lords, princes and ministers, all competing for power. In the end, it was the state of Chin which emerged triumphant in this all-consuming war. Two men were instrumental in achieving this mother of all victories: Cheng and Li Ssu.

Cheng – the future Shi Huang Ti – was of noble origin, born in 259 BC in the state of Chin. Even as a youth, he was cunning and ambitious. He was described by Cottrell, author of *The Tiger of Chin* as having "the proboscis of a hornet and large all-seeing eyes. His chest is like that of a bird of prey and his voice is like that of a jackal. He is merciless with the heart of a tiger or wolf. When he is in trouble, he finds it easy to humble himself, but when he is enjoying success, he finds it easy to devour human beings."[25]

Li Ssu, on the other hand, was a commoner, born in 280 BC in the state of Chu. But he had one thing going for him: he was a brilliant strategist and planner. This came from his tutelage under the great Confucian philosopher Hsun Tzu, who, unlike his contemporary

Mencius, believed that human nature was essentially wicked. Like his master Hsun Tzu, Li Ssu believed that people were naturally selfish, and so they had to be restrained in the interest of the state and their fellowmen by strict laws and punishments. This was a belief which placed him foremost among a new philosophical school called Legalism. This school of philosophy can be regarded as an ancient and lethal form of behaviourism, in which crimes were punishable by branding, castration, slitting of the nose or tendons, chopping off of toes or feet, or breaking of kneecaps.

Although Li Ssu was a brilliant strategist and planner, he thought the king of Chu unworthy of his attention as a politician, and so he left for the state of Chin in a spirit of *carpe diem* (seize the day): "I have heard that to attain the opportune moment one should not be tardy. Now is the time, when 10,000 chariots are at war, and when the travelling politicians control affairs. At present the king of Chin desires to swallow up the world and rule with the title of emperor. This is the time for the commoners to be busy, and is the golden age of the travelling politicians … Therefore I intend to go westward to the king of Chin."[26]

There he met up with Cheng, and delivered this eloquent and flattering speech: "With Chin's might and its great king's ability, the conquest of the other states would be like sweeping dust from the top of the kitchen stove. Chin's power is sufficient to obliterate the feudal lords, bring to reality the imperial heritage and make the world a single unity. This is the time of 10,000 generations. If now you are negligent and do not press to a finish, the feudal lords will return to strength and combine to form north-to-south alliances against you so that, though you have the ability of the Yellow Emperor, you would be unable to bring them into unity."[27]

Li Ssu won over Cheng, and the two men devised a scheme to bribe those feudal lords who could be won over by gems and money. The rest would be put to the sword. Over the next 17 years, Chin subdued the other six states: Han in 230 BC, Chao in 228 BC, Wei in 225 BC, Chu in 223 BC, Yen in 222 BC and finally Chi in 221 BC. For the first time, China was unified under one imperial dynasty, and King Cheng became Shi Huang Ti, the first emperor of China. However, the newly-installed emperor was concerned that internal enemies as well as the barbarians in the northern borders of his new empire would wrest it from him. This concern was heightened by the numerous attempts which were made on his life after his enthronement as emperor (according to one source, there were at least 15 attempts on his life). As a result, Shi Huang Ti trusted nobody. To divert his subjects from rebellious thoughts, he set about binding his conquests together with an extraordinary series of civil, social and commercial projects. He lined the banks of major rivers, built grand canals and developed a standardised writing system. He also revolutionalised road transport, introducing a programme of road construction to enable food and manpower to be carried to all corners of the empire. In addition, he standardised the cart sizes so that taxes due on goods could be easily assessed; carts could also run in the same ruts, making travel quicker.

Although these projects and practices were constructive and benefited succeeding dynasties, Shi Huang Ti's lasting accomplishment was the Great Wall of China, which he ordered to be built in order to keep out the northern barbarians from invading his unified empire. The Great Wall of China took 12 years to construct, but this construction did not begin from scratch. Hundreds of miles of fortifications had already been built by the warring states. Shi Huang Ti's engineers and workmen strengthened or rebuilt these structures, and constructed many more miles of wall to link them.

When completed, the Great Wall of China was an impressive monument indeed: its total length was 1,400 miles, and stretched from the Yellow Sea in the west to the edge of Tibet in the east. It remains the only man-made object which is visible to American astronauts floating in outer space. The Great Wall consisted of a rampart 20-feet high, linking 40-feet watchtowers spaced equally at the range of an archer's arrow. Each tower was provisioned to withstand a four-month siege. Beacon towers every 11 miles could transmit a message across the empire in 24 hours, and the wall itself was used as a road for transporting troops and provisions. First to be built were the 40-feet watchtowers, constructed on a 40-feet square base. These watchtowers were located where possible at strategic points along the wall, such as hilltops or valley entrances. Between these watchtowers ran the 20-feet-high rampart, to keep out the nomadic invaders from the north.

In every area, the building of the wall posed different problems, which were solved creatively. At its eastern end at Shan Hai Kuan, the wall had to extend into the sea for a short distance, so boats were loaded with huge rocks and sunk to provide a foundation. The central section of the wall was to run through the fertile Ordos region, which was home to the hostile Hsiang-nu tribes. These barbaric tribes had to be driven out first before work could commence. In some regions, the hills over which the wall had to run were so steep that ox-carts and hand-carts could no longer be used to carry the stone.

Instead, men had to carry loads of up to 50 kilograms on their bare backs, or in baskets suspended from a pole. On narrow paths materials were passed along human chains. Rocks that were too heavy for a man to carry would be rolled on logs or manhandled with levers inch by inch up the steep slopes. Some areas that the wall crossed were so precipitous that later generations could not believe that men had carried the building materials; they claimed that goats must have been used.[28]

Work progressed at remorseless speed, and new teams of labourers were constantly being thrown into the frenzy of the construction process. The human cost of building the wall was enormous. From every peasant family of five in the empire, at least two were dragged off to work on the wall, a drain on manpower that made it very difficult for families to run their farms. Convicts sentenced to hard labour on the wall were marched hundreds of miles northward in chains and iron collars; they were dropping from fatigue before they reached the wall. Many of these convicts died on the march. Those who survived the journey were housed in inadequate camps and put to work in blazing sun, driving rain, stinging hailstorms and temperatures that swung from 35°C at the height of summer to −21°C in winter.

Food was desperately scarce. The barren land could not grow sufficient crops, and supplies had to be carried for huge distances by convoys of pack animals, or manhandled in barges up swiftly-flowing rivers, few of which were navigable for any distance. Much of the food was stolen by bandits, lost or eaten during the journey. On one occasion, 182 loads of grain were sent from the Shantung peninsula, but only one reached the wall. Starvation accelerated an already high death rate and led to outbreaks of violence between workers and overseers. Many of those who died while building the wall – from exhaustion or malnutrition – were thrown into the trenches dug out for foundations, or buried inside the wall to act as guardian spirits against the demons of the north who, it was believed, were angered by the building of the enormous fortification. The emperor had heard the prophecy that the wall would not be finished until 10,000 men had been buried in it; even he found this a shocking statistic. Legend has it that he searched out and found a man called Wan – the name means 10,000 in Mandarin – and buried him in the rampart.[29] Modern-day tourists from all over the world treat the Great Wall as a picturesque spot for taking photos to show to the folks back home, but to its builders, it was known as the "Wall of Tears", the "Longest Cemetery of the World" and the "First Gulag in History".

The human expense in building the Great Wall of China, as well as the brutal legalist measures adopted by the emperor and his chief advisor Li Ssu in running the empire, were condemned by the Confucian scholars at court. Some of these scholars went even further, unwisely calling for the downfall of Shi Huang Ti. On hearing of this, Li Ssu told the emperor, "These scholars study the past to criticise the present, burying reality in their empty arguments and rhetoric. They condemn your laws and your orders, and as soon as they hear that a decree has been issued, they debate its merits according to their own school of thought, opposing it secretly in their hearts at court and disputing it openly in the streets. This lowers the prestige of the sovereign. It must be stopped."[30]

Shi Huang Ti, with the counsel of Li Ssu, acted with calculated violence: he ordered 460 of these Confucian scholars to be seized, buried alive and then decapitated. Thousands more were sent to build the Great Wall. Anyone who sympathised with the scholars was punished. Not even the emperor's eldest son, Fu Su, who sided with the Confucians, was spared: on the advice of Li Ssu, he was sent to build the Great Wall. The emperor also set out systematically to destroy the accumulated wisdom of these Confucian scholars. Their scholarly "books" – inscribed wooden strips – were confiscated and burned, although many of the scholars hid them in bricked-up walls at the risk of death. The burning of the books silenced the Confucian scholars; it also ensured that the first emperor who united China would get a bad press from them for perpetuity.

Shi Huang Ti had control over the body and mind of every subject in his empire, but it was not enough for this despotic ruler; he wanted power over death itself. And so he began a search for an elixir of life, which would enable him to live forever. Influenced by Taoist mystics, in 219 BC, Shi Huang Ti sent envoys in search of three mystical mountain islands where immortals were supposed to dwell, in the hope of discovering the magic potions that would enable him to gain immortality. The envoys never returned (some scholars believed that they became the ancestors of the Japanese). Four years later, he ordered a second tour of the empire to hunt for the elixir. Three years after that, he mounted a further search.

Even as Shi Huang Ti persevered in his quest for this elixir of life, he began to prepare for his own death. This came in the form of an enormous tomb which was located at Mount Li in the northern province of Shensi. The mound covering the mausoleum was 300 feet high, and the total circumference of the interior was eight miles. In death, the first emperor of China was to be placed within a central sanctum of palaces and gardens, which was protected by an army of 7,000 terracotta warriors in battle formation. The tomb was filled with priceless objects of gold and silver, and surrounded by subterranean rivers of mercury flowing across an image of the empire under a painted vault of stars. Although Shi Huang Ti had been preparing for his death for some time, still it came rather unexpectedly. In 210 BC, while he was on one of his imperial tours around the eastern part of his empire, ironically to seek the aid of Taoist magicians in securing the elixir of life, Shi Huang Ti suddenly fell ill and died. In all probability, he was killed by an overdose of one of the potions for immortality containing the virulent mercury or phosphorus toxins which he had taken regularly. He was then 49 years old, in the 37th year of his reign, his 12th as emperor.

From his deathbed, Shi Huang Ti had asked his chief eunuch Chao Kao to write a letter to his eldest son, Fu Su, who had been working on the Great Wall. The letter told the young man to accompany his father's funeral cortege to the capital, so implying that he would succeed to the throne. But Li Ssu and Chao Kao, who had together arranged for Fu Su's exile to the Great Wall two years before, wanted to see the throne passed to the younger and more impressionable second son, Hu Hai. They realised that they had to take the emperor's body back to the capital, and that his death should be kept secret as long as possible in order for them to complete their plotting. Afraid that the decomposing body would arouse suspicion, Li Ssu and Chao Kao disguised the smell by burying it in a cart of fish.

Upon reaching the capital at Xianyang, Li Ssu and Chao Kao forged the emperor's signature on a document ordering Fu Su and General Mien Tien, the most powerful ally of Shi Huang Ti, to commit suicide, which they duly did (the scheming duo even provided the swords for the suicide). Li Ssu and Chao Kao took over the government of the empire through the weak Hu Hai. However, Chao Kao was determined to control the empire himself. First, he had Li Ssu executed on trumped-up charges of treason. Then he reduced the weak-minded emperor to a mental wreck before persuading him also to commit suicide.

Unfortunately, when Chao Kao took the imperial seal, he discovered, much to his chagrin, that he had no support. So he quickly installed another of Hu Hai's brothers as emperor. This new emperor, very wisely, had Chao Kao executed, but by then it was too late. The cancerous turmoil in the capital had reached the terminal stage, and the whole empire was falling apart. Rebellions broke out everywhere; one of these rebellions reached the capital itself. After three months of fighting, the rebel forces emerged victorious. They executed the new emperor, and proclaimed a new dynasty by the name of Han in 206 BC. Shi Huang Ti had boasted that his empire would last for 10,000 generations, but in fact it was all over in 15 years.[31]

Tiger of Chin
GAME OVER

Notes

1. McKay, 1994; Markus & Kitayama, 1994.
2. *The Wall Street Journal*, June 2, 1999.
3. Han, Fernandez & Tan, 1998; Hill & Lian, 1995.
4. Wood & Wood, 1996.
5. Skinner, 1972.
6. *The Straits Times*, September 27, 1999.
7. Munro, 1977.
8. Therivel, 1995.
9. quoted in Therivel, 1995.
10. *The Straits Times*, May 26, 1999; Gomez, 1999.
11. Hibbert, 1970.
12. Smith, 1973.
13. *The Straits Times*, February 12, 2000.
14. McGregor, 1996.
15. Gibney, 1992.
16. *Reader's Digest*, 1993.
17. Gibney, 1992.
18. *The Straits Times*, August 15, 2000.
19. Han, Fernandez & Tan, 1998.
20. *The Straits Times*, November 21, 1999.
21. *The Straits Times*, January 20, 1999.
22. *The Straits Times*, January 28, 1999.
23. *The Straits Times*, April 26, 2000.
24. *The Sunday Times*, September 12, 1999.
25. quoted in Guest & George, 1995.
26. *Ibid.*
27. *Ibid.*
28. *Reader's Digest*, 1993.
29. Guest & George, 1995.
30. quoted in Guest & George, 1995.
31. Morton, 1995.

chapter 9

Towards a More Creative Society of Asians

In this book, I have attempted to explain why Asians are less creative than Westerners. As we have seen, the reason has a lot to do with the culture which the individual has been exposed to from young. Culture shapes the psyche of the individual. This in turn gives rise to creative or uncreative behaviour, as the case may be. Creative behaviour is task-oriented and individuated, while uncreative behaviour is ego-oriented and conforming. The liberal individualistic society of the West facilitates the creativity of the Westerner, while the Confucian society of the East inhibits the creativity of the Asian. This causal relationship between culture, psyche and behaviour suggests that Asians are less creative than Westerners *not* by default, but by being exposed to different environmental influences. This implies that Asians can become as creative as Westerners, if not more so, if only a suitable environment can be put in place to facilitate their creativity. In this last chapter, we will look at how this can be done.

Help the Asian Child to Develop a Positive Self-Concept

We have seen that the central focus of the Confucian-heritage society of the East is to raise children who are filial to their parents, and behave in an obedient and respectful manner towards their elders (for a review, see Chapter Two). As a result, Asian caretakers will draw a child's attention to shortcomings, problems or potentially negative features that have to be corrected to meet the expectations or norms common in a social relationship. The  child may in turn develop a habitual attentional bias towards negative self-relevant information. This typically Asian way of raising a child leaves him with the intangible feeling that he is being belittled by his own parents. If we wish to nurture creative children in the family, we need to spend more time in encouraging and complimenting them for doing things right, and spend less time in scolding and punishing them for getting things wrong. By focusing on the positive side of the equation, we will enable the child to develop a positive self-concept. (NB: In making this plea for an enlightened rather than an authoritarian treatment of the child, I am *not* advocating that we should "spare the rod, spoil the child". For I accept that children need to be put in their proper places when they really get out of hand, otherwise we will end up spoiling them. I remember a few spankings which I received from my mother as a child; they were painful, but they contained important lessons about right and wrong which I have not forgotten).

Developing a positive self-concept is crucial for creativity. This is because creativity requires the person to feel confident of himself, i.e., to have faith in his own inner resources as a person. Only then will he be able to attempt to do something that is risky and different from the rest. If a person does not feel confident of himself, i.e., if he does not have faith in his own inner resources as a person, he will not risk venturing into the

Great job!

unknown. Whenever he meets with a novel situation, a little voice inside him will say, "You *can't* do this" or "You must *not* do that." As a result, he will shrink away from the novel situation, and this will reinforce the feeling that he does not amount to anything. In contrast, if a person feels confident of himself, then the little voice inside him will say, "Oh! This is interesting! I wonder how I can do it?" As a result, he will take up the challenge and learn a novel way of doing things. This will reinforce the feeling that he is a person who is capable of mastering something new, if only he will try.

Don't Let the Voice of Judgment Strangle the Creative Spirit of the Asian Child

In *The Creative Spirit*, Goleman and his colleagues have termed the inhibitory voice which discourages us from embarking on creative challenges as the *Voice of Judgment*, or VOJ for short.[1] The VOJ can assume many different forms, depending on the individual person. The voice inside oneself is usually the most daunting, but there is also judgment by others, including cultural judgments such as the rules of proper behaviour which forbid unconventional behaviour. Once it gets hold of us, our VOJ can lead us into a maze of negativity, including the following absurd situation: my VOJ inhibits me from doing something; then it makes me feel depressed about my weakness of will. Next, my VOJ condemns me harshly for being depressed. Then, a friend comes along and chides me for both not following through on my idea and for being depressed!

According to Goleman and his colleagues, in most of us our creative spirit and VOJ continually wage a pitched battle e.g., even before a creative idea reaches conscious awareness, let alone fruition, one's VOJ can cut it down with a fusillade of negative messages like "Who do you think you are?" or "You'll look like a jerk" or "They'll think you're crazy!" A person's VOJ is instilled in childhood, when his parents, teachers and other authority figures try to tell him the right way to behave, peppering their good advice and exhortations with directive words like "Do this!" or "Don't you dare!" or "I'm going to beat you if you don't listen to me!" As a result, the VOJ is internalised in the person, and he carries it with him for the rest of his life, so that when he meets a novel situation which requires him to behave in a different and unconventional manner, he shrinks away from this challenge, instead of confronting it.

Nurture the Autonomy of the Asian Child Instead of Overprotecting Him

To become confident and adventurous, and dare to try out new things, in defiance of their VOJ, Asian children need the space and freedom to explore and manipulate the objects in the sociocultural environment. Successful endeavours in exploring the sociocultural environment will enable them to see the world as a "friendly expanse", rather than as a "horrid empty space". This in turn implies that Asian parents must change their child-rearing mindset: from one which seeks to ensure that no harm should befall their wards, to one which seeks to promote the growing autonomy and independence of their children. The former mindset will lead Asian parents to overprotect their children, and cause them to develop a psychological fear of the unknown, while the latter mindset will lead Asian parents to encourage their children in their independence-striving and creative mastery of the sociocultural environment.

Promote the Asian Family As the "Playground of Life"

In addition, Asian societies need to "fine-tune" the familial aspect of their culture. For example, in Singapore, the government wants to ensure that the family will be the basic building block of society. To realise this goal, it has been promoting a set of family values to Singaporeans. These family values include love, care and concern, mutual respect, filial piety, commitment and responsibility. In its latest blueprint for the nation, entitled "Singapore 21: Together, We Make the Difference", it has continued to emphasise strong and intact families as the foundation of healthy lives and wholesome communities. Besides these five family values, I would suggest an additional and complementary value, which is indicative of the pure delight which suffuses the family as they creatively explore their shared environment together, enabling the child to develop an indomitable spirit of adventure and initiative in the process. It is difficult to pin down this value in actual words, but perhaps an initial idea for this value is "nothing without joy" (from the Italian phrase *niente senza gioia*).

"Nothing without joy" (or some such derivative) emphasises the fact that the Asian family should be more than just a moralistic institution in which proper behaviour is cultivated. In addition, it should serve as the "playground of life", in which the child can grow up to become a confident, mature and responsible adult who maintains the child within that can enable him to be psychologically resilient in the face of adversity. Such a resilient personality can successfully cope with the daunting challenge of being a person in human society – a challenge, I should add – which is compounded by the ever-changing scenes from birth to death, punctuated by grand historical and political forces against which mere beings like us are but insignificant specks of dust in the constantly shifting landscape of human life.

Confucius Is *Not* a Stuffy and Moralistic Old Man

To become these "playgrounds of life", families in the East have a lot to learn from the wholesome, strong, cohesive and creative families in the West, which have been very successful in nurturing children who are confident, adventurous, autonomous, self-determined, creative and infused with *joie de vivre* (to find out more, read *The Seven Habits of Highly Effective Families* by Stephen Covey[2]).

It might be argued that promoting the Asian family as "the playground of life" is alien to the Confucian way of life, which is not concerned with having fun, but with being right. As long as the Confucian bureaucrats are successful in producing a well-ordered framework in which men, women and children can live out their lives, a state wisely and justly administered in which all people are given the opportunity to nourish their living, give decent burial to their dead, and at the end pass into oblivion, mourned only by the closest relatives, who would ask for more? **I would!** More specifically, I would argue that the Confucian way of life places too much emphasis on propriety, i.e., doing what is proper and right, and not enough on creativity, i.e., doing what is different and novel. This extreme emphasis on propriety is a result of the zealous proselytising by the disciples of Confucius, and not by the Master himself. For example, filial piety, which is often stressed by those people with a Confucianist outlook on life, does not occupy a prominent place in the earliest tradition of the *Analects*.[3] It became important only in the Han dynasty onwards, when it was exalted in some Confucian schools as the greatest of all virtues, as for instance in the *Classic of Filial Piety* and in several chapters of the *Book of Rites*. In modern-day Singapore, it is given legal clout with the move to empower the parent to sue his children in court if they refuse to take care of him in his old age. An overemphasis on propriety cannot help but make one think of the comment by a great Jewish teacher: "I prefer a wicked man who knows he is wicked than a righteous man who knows he is righteous."[4]

Indeed, if Confucius were alive today, I believe that he would be amenable to this suggestion of making the family a fun place to live in, of promoting the family as the "playground of life". For as Lau has pointed out, in Confucius' opinion, joy and delight in the Way are not merely confined to the moral side of life.[5] In other words, there is more to life than being moral, prim and proper all the time, or obeying the dictates of the Voice of Judgment. Lau gives this example (*Analects* XI: 26): On a certain occasion, Confucius was sitting with a group of disciples having a conversation. He asked each of them to express his heart's desires. One replied that he wanted to be Minister of War; the second wanted to be Minister of Finance, while the third wanted to be Master of Ceremonies. The fourth disciple, Tseng Tien, was strumming his lute for the group when Confucius requested him to speak. Whereupon Tseng Tien replied, "In late spring, after the spring clothes have been newly made, I should like, together with five or six adults and six or seven boys, to go bathing in the River Yi and enjoy the breeze on the Rain Altar, and then go home chanting poetry." Confucius indicated that on this matter, he was with the simple-minded Tseng Tien, rather than the three lofty-minded disciples who sought the high office of a minister (presumably to save the world). Lau remarked that here was a man who, indeed, appreciated the joys of living, i.e., Confucius is *not* the stuffy and moralistic old man that many people make him out to be.

Playfulness Can Win You a Nobel Prize

I have emphasised the importance of having a playful attitude towards life. This spirit of playfulness will add colour to the drab culture of Confucianism, with its indigestable list of dos and don'ts. In addition, the playful spirit may even win you a Nobel Prize, especially when it is coupled with a tremendous amount of intelligent thinking. The physicist Richard Feynman was one such intelligent but playful Nobel laureate, whose unbridled curiosity about an everyday event led him to a great discovery in science. (Here Confucius has imprinted his words of wisdom for us once again: "The common folks marvel at uncommon things, while the person of genius marvels at the commonplace.") Indeed, playfulness and humour are great antidotes to stultifying habit, a way of stepping outside established categories of thought, and there are significant parallels between the Ha-ha! and the Aha! experience. Feynman himself – no stranger to insight and humour – even called one of his books *Surely You're Joking, Mr Feynman! Adventures of a Curious Character*.[6] The story of how Feynman won his Nobel Prize is described in the following boxed article.

Playing Your Way to a Nobel Prize: The Story of Richard Feynman

Richard Feynman (1918–1988) was one of the brilliant brains behind the Manhattan Project in World War II. The aim of this top-secret project was to beat the Germans and Japanese by building an atomic bomb which could enable the Allied forces, led by the United States, to bring a quick end to the war. Albert Einstein had told President Franklin Roosevelt in 1939 that theoretically speaking, building such a powerful bomb was possible, and most probably, the Germans were trying to do it. Feynman and his team-mates went on to do it first, i.e., they designed and built the atomic bomb from scratch. The awesome power of the atomic bomb was unleashed on Hiroshima and Nagasaki in August 1945, completely flattening the two cities, and bringing the emperor-worshipping and militarised nation of Japan to its knees in an unconditional surrender, without any loss of Allied lives via a prolonged ground battle.

After the war, Feynman went to work as a lecturer in Cornell University. His expertise was in the area of mathematical methods of physics. In *Creators on Creating: Awakening and Cultivating the Imaginative Mind*,[7] Feynman talked about how he would work on preparing his lectures, making up exam problems, and checking that they were sensible ones. He was so exhausted by this process that he would "go to the library a lot and read through *Arabian Nights* and ogle the girls that would go by. But when it came time to do some research, I couldn't get to work. I was a little tired; I was not interested; I couldn't do research!"

During this period, Feynman got a lot of invitations to lecture in various eminent universities. The most eminent of the lot was the Institute for Advanced Study (IAS). Individuals working in this institute – including the legendary Albert Einstein – had been specially selected for their tremendous intellect. They had no classes to instruct, and no teaching obligations whatsoever. Instead, they were left alone unhindered in a lovely house by the woods – Feynman's description of the IAS – to do their research.

Instead of accepting the special professorship which IAS had created for him, Feynman did the preposterous: he turned it down. And his reason? It was such a good deal – better than what Albert Einstein himself had gotten – that it was absurd! He laughed about it as he was shaving, muttering to himself, "What they think of me is so fantastic, it's impossible to live up to it. I have no responsibility to live up to it … these poor bastards can now sit and think clearly all by themselves (in the lovely house by the woods) … but nothing will happen, because there's not enough real activity and challenge." Interestingly enough, Feynman traced one of the root causes of this problem (of nothing happening) to the absence of the picking of the teacher's brain by his students. In his opinion, the questions of students were often the source of new research, as they tended to ask profound questions that he had thought about and then given up on for a while. The students might not be able to see the thing he wanted to answer, or the subtleties he wished to think about, but they reminded him of a problem by asking questions in the neighbourhood of that problem. Because to Feynman teaching students kept life going, he would never accept any position in which somebody had invented a convenient situation for him, where he did not have to teach. That was why he turned down the offer from the IAS.

Feynman reasoned to himself, "It wasn't a failure on my part that the Institute of Advanced Study expected me to be that good; it was impossible. It was clearly a mistake – and the moment I appreciated the possibility that they might be wrong, I realised that it was also true of all the other places, including my own university. I am what I am, and if they expected me to be good and they're offering me some money for it, it's their hard luck." At this juncture, he had another thought: "Physics disgusts me a little bit now, but I used to enjoy doing physics. Why did I enjoy it? I used to *play* with it. I used to do whatever I felt like doing – it didn't have to do with whether it was important for the development of nuclear physics, but whether it was interesting and amusing for me to play with. When I was in high school, I'd see water running out of a faucet growing narrower, and wonder if I could figure out what determines that curve. I found it was rather easy to do. I didn't *have* to do it; it wasn't important for the future of science … that didn't make any difference. I'd invent things and play with things for my own entertainment."

So Feynman developed what he called a "new attitude", which went like this: "I'm burnt out and I'll never accomplish anything, but I've got this nice position at the university teaching classes which I rather enjoy, and I like reading *Arabian Nights* and ogling the pretty girls in the library. So hey, I'm going to *play* with physics, whenever I want to, without worrying about any importance whatsoever." Within a week, Feynman was in the cafeteria and reported that "some guy, fooling around, threw a plate in the air. As the plate went up in the air I saw it wobble, and I noticed the red medallion of Cornell on the plate going around. It was pretty obvious to me that the medallion went around faster than the wobbling."

As Feynman had nothing to do, he started to use complicated mathematical equations to figure out the motion of the rotating plate, and discovered that when the angle was very slight, the medallion rotated twice as fast as the wobble rate. Then he asked himself if there was any fundamental physical reason why it was two to one, and not some other ratio. This set him thinking furiously again, and he succeeded in working out what the motion of the mass particles was, and how all the accelerations balanced to make it come out two to one. Feynman told a colleague, "Hey, Hans! I noticed something interesting. Here the plate goes around so, and the reason it's two to one is ..."

Hans replied, "That's pretty interesting, but what's the importance of it? Why are you doing it?"

"Hah!" Feynman replied with his new-found attitude. "There's no importance whatsoever. I'm just doing it for the fun of it."

Feynman went on to work out the equations of wobbles. This led him to think about how electron orbits started to move in relativity, which led him to a host of other intellectual mind games, like the Dirac equation in electrodynamics, as well as quantum electrodynamics. And according to Feynman, "before I knew it I was *playing* – working, really – with the same old problem that I loved so much, that I had stopped working on when I went to Los Alamos: my thesis-type problems; all those old-fashioned, wonderful things. It was effortless. It was easy to play with these things. It was like uncorking a bottle: everything flowed out effortlessly. I almost tried to resist it! There was no importance to what I was doing, but ultimately there was. The diagrams and the whole business that I got the Nobel Prize for came from that piddling around with the wobbling plate."

Make a Distinction Between Training and Educating Students

Another way of moving towards a more creative society of Asians is to make a distinction between "training" and "educating" students. This is the advice given by Professor Lee Yuan Tseh, a respected Chinese scholar from Taiwan who obtained his PhD from the University of California in Berkeley, won the 1986 Nobel Prize in chemistry, and was subsequently recalled by his country in 1994 to head Academia Sinica, Taiwan's top research institution. In a recent public lecture to a rapt audience of 250 in Singapore, which consisted of educators, researchers and students, as well as concerned parents, entitled "Educating Creative Young Scientists for the 21st Century", Prof Lee observed that Eastern European and Russian students tended to win top prizes in international school contests, but they rarely went on to make scientific breakthroughs (I should add that this is the same situation for East Asian students: see Ng, 2000a). On the other hand, American students did not fare well in these competitions, but many of them later became Nobel Prize winners.[8]

According to Prof Lee, achievements in international competitions are an example of what good training in a regimented education system can produce, while achievements in scientific breakthroughs are the result of being educated in an open, democratic society in which students are encouraged to ask questions and find out answers on their own. Prof Lee asserted that the key to nurturing creativity is to distinguish between training students and educating them to raise new questions and solve problems for the future (this assertion recalls an important maxim of creativity: "genius is the capacity for productive reaction against one's training"). Asian students were not creative because they had been trained to solve problems in order to do well in examinations. However, this had little to do with educating them to solve practical problems in the real world that could lead to a scientific breakthrough. This difference in solving problems (educating versus training) is reinforced by the familial environment in the West and East e.g., in Israel, parents typically ask their children, "What questions did you raise today?" In contrast, Asian parents typically ask their children, "What score did you get?"

How to Become a Creative Student in Six Steps: An Asian Nobel Laureate's View

Prof Lee suggested that Asian students could learn to become creative in six steps.[9] First, Asian students should learn to think independently and question "accepted" answers. Learning from teachers should be secondary to learning on their own. Second, Asian students should learn to ask "good" questions that probe the frontiers of science and stump their teachers. They could find the answers to easy questions on their own. Third, Asian students should learn to view problems from all the different angles, so that they could weigh the pros and cons of every issue. Fourth, Asian students should study a topic thoroughly, as this is the best way to learn about a subject, i.e., don't be performance-oriented; be mastery-oriented instead. Fifth, Asian students should attempt to tackle those "unsolvable problems" (questions or puzzles with no correct answers) so that they would learn to "think deep", i.e., don't be *kiasi* when you solve problems. Finally, the educator in the East should respect his students as "complete persons with the right to express their opinions".

What Sort of Educator Should We Be in the East?

Concerning this last point on the educator in the East, Prof Lee noted that the hierarchical system of education in Asian society does not encourage students to be skeptical, to ask questions and to tell their teachers, "I think you might be wrong." Instead, students feel intimidated by their professors, who seem to know everything. He suggested that university professors should treat students as their equals. Then there would be more dialogue, and they would feel free to ask penetrating questions, which is the hallmark of scientific investigation. He recounted his own experience with his supervisor when he was doing his doctorate at the University of California in Berkeley, "I was baffled that my supervisor answered all my questions with 'How do I know? If I do I would have solved the problem myself.' At first I thought he did not teach me much but I was wrong. He taught me to solve problems for myself." Prof Lee's advice to educators is this: "Don't be afraid to say I don't know, because there are lots of interesting unknowns in science which students should become very curious and want to find out about."

I think educators in the East (including myself) have a lot to learn from our Western counterparts, in this area of relating in an egalitarian manner to our students. My personal experience testifies to this: Educators in the West do not seem to like being addressed by their titles, preferring to be known by their everyday names. I remember when I first stepped into the office of my doctorate supervisor at the Department of Psychology in the University of Queensland, and addressed him as "Dr Griffin". Immediately, his hands shot up in protest, and he told me, "Mark. Please call me Mark." Professing little scientific knowledge in creativity – which was true, for he was an organisational psychologist, not a creativity researcher – Mark went on to assist me to write a PhD thesis on creativity, upon which this book is based. Another educator in the department was a full professor in psychology, but every student in my class called her Cindy. Cindy was to remark later on in reading my term assignment on Advanced Group Dynamics, "I've learned from it, and I'm going to use some ideas which you've suggested in future classes. I hope you don't mind." This display of meekness and humility was amazing considering that Cindy was a full professor of psychology who doubled up as the editor-in-chief of a respected journal in psychology, and as a prolific publisher in the referred journals of psychology, while I had no such claim to title and fame!

My experience in Australia has convinced me that in relating to my students, I should adopt a candid attitude, i.e., although I know some things about the world, there are many other things which I do not know, so my students should treat me as their equal who is a little bit further on the learning curve (which implies they should call me "Kwang", and not "Dr Ng" or "Dr Kwang" or "Sir"). I told my students that they could all catch up and surpass me, if they were willing to put in the requisite effort. It may be argued that such an egalitarian attitude between teacher and student is not appropriate for the Confucian-oriented educational system in the East, in which rank and title are emphasised. However, I think it is right for me to make such a stance. After all, Confucius himself once remarked, concerning the meaning of knowledge, "To say you know when you know, and to say you don't know when you don't know, this is knowledge." Similarly, Mr Lee Kuan Yew, the architect of modern-day Singapore, has remarked, "We've got to try and amend or modify our educational system. Or more important, the mindset. Even though you don't want to question your teacher, you have a question mark against what he has pronounced as inalienable truth and then challenge it quietly and maybe prove him wrong."[10]

How Should We Live in Asian Society?

Besides changing the way we deal with our children at home and our students in school, we will also need to reconsider the way we live in the wider Asian society. The Asian way of living puts a lot of emphasis on the accumulation of materialistic goods, so as to enhance one's social face or *mian-zi* in the community. As a result, the typical Asian behaves in an ego-involved and uncreative manner. This can be seen most clearly in the behaviour of the *kiasu* Singaporean, who queues up overnight just to lay his hands on limited editions of Hello Kitty dolls. The *kiasu* Singaporean is the essential product of a Skinnerian society, in which people and institutions are ranked competitively from top to bottom, and materialistic rewards and punishments serve as a major means of prodding individuals to behave.* Under such circumstances, intelligent individuals with a Machiavellian streak in their character mock any parallel efforts to cultivate core values like integrity and honesty. This fact can be gleaned from the smug comments made by one of the rich and bright but selfish scholars whom we came across in Chapter 6, who had tricked a certain institution in Singapore into giving him a prestigious scholarship to study overseas:

> The uproar that followed our public admission of wanting to break our bonds was incredible … To an extent, the negative reaction from some of the public was expected. But it was out of proportion. Seriously, what do they know about our situation? … They are simply unaware of the plethora of opportunities open to us. They would probably be tempted if so many lucrative offers were made at the same time, with each party aggressively outbidding the other. Yes, we are in demand, but for a reason – because we are worth something. So no, my decision (to break the bond) will not be pegged to the public outcry … it is a myth that a schol-

≈≈≈

* For example, cabinet ministers in Singapore draw an annual salary of more than US$1 million, many times more than their counterparts in America, much to the chagrin of ordinary Singaporeans, who remain unconvinced by the economic argument that ministers should be paid their monetary worth. One of them commented emotionally, "Bill Clinton rules the world while Goh Chok Tong rules a dot! How can they explain that he's paid so much less than our own PM?" (*The Straits Times*, July 6, 2000). Another commented, more rationally, "When market forces are used to justify pay increases in public services, whatever community values we seek to cultivate are eroded easily." (*The Straits Times*, July 21, 2000).

≈≈≈

arship implies a moral obligation. Our scholarship providers did not choose us out of a sense of pity, but by virtue of our merit. Actually the bond borders on exploitation because our value to them is much higher than what they pay us. My seniors, those serving their bonds, complain we are worth so much more … So why take it up in the first place? Well … I do want to work for my sponsors … but only for so long. And we have been told from birth to grab opportunities for progress. I will follow this advice …[11]

Following this advice may work for this cowardly scholar, who spoke to the newspaper reporter "on condition of anonymity", as he did not want to lose his scholarship. However, living in such a Skinnerian society, in which individuals are advised from birth to be competitive and to "grab opportunities for progress", will only frustrate the deeper sense of meaning within the ordinary Singaporean, and create a spiritual void in him.[12] He attempts to fill this spiritual void by acquiring the temporal stuff of this world which everyone else is going after in his society. Unfortunately, acquiring these material goods will not assure him of personal happiness and satisfaction in life.

According to Charles Handy,[13] this is because it does not allow him to satisfy the "deeper hunger", which refers to our human need to understand what life on this earth is about, and to find an answer to the eternal question *why?* For example, why are we born? Why do we die? Is there any truth in the assertion by an ancient Greek philosopher that the best thing in life is not to be born, and the next best thing in life is to die early? Why are some people "good" while other people are "bad"? How can I be sure that what I'm doing is right? What is righteousness? What is justice? What is beauty? Is God like Mickey Mouse? Or is there really a God who created this universe? If there is, why do different people believe in different gods? Why do they kill one another in the name of God? Is God an evil being who is out to make a fool of humankind, as implied by the great English playwright William Shakespeare, when he remarked, "Like flies to wanton boys, are we to the gods, they kill us for their sport." If religion is so divisive, should we believe in God at all? Or should we believe only in ourselves? But if we believe only in ourselves, then wouldn't we become rather selfish? What will become of our society if everyone of us engages in our own selfish pursuits? Will our lives become "nasty, brutish and short" in such a society? Should we allow society to control our actions, so that it will not become a free-for-all? But if we do so, then will we end up being very passive and uncreative, like the *kiasu* Singaporean?

Instead of being concerned with these eternal questions, which characterise the sordid human drama on this lonely planet, and in the process becoming a more self-aware, self-directed and creative individual who lives his life in a meaningful way, the *kiasu* Singaporean escapes from these moral and intellectual dilemmas to indulge in trivial pursuits, like queuing up overnight for Hello Kitty dolls. Like the British who acquired an empire in a fit of absence of mind, his mindless *kiasuism* leads to the rise of the *chindogu* society. *Chindogu* is a Japanese word for all the useless things which a person may be tempted to buy, because others are doing so e.g., a big collection of Swatch watches, designer bags of different shapes and sizes, automated machines which imprint different images on your finger nails and advanced computers which enable you to experience *virtual* rather than *real* reality. This technological penchant for the virtual rather than the real has inspired a wise and poetically-inclined scholar from Hong Kong to pen the following verses:[†]

> *In front of my bed shines the bright moonbeam;*
> *I suspect it's the frost on the floor.*
> *Lifting my head I gaze at the bright moon;*
> *Lowering my head I long for my hometown.*

> *In front of my monitor screen runs some funny images;*
> *I suspect they are virtual realities.*
> *Lifting my head I gaze at these computed creations;*
> *Lowering my head I long for the real things.*

A *chindogu* society may chalk up good economic growth but it will not, on the face of it, provide good enough reasons for working or living. For as Charles Handy has pointed out, if "'buoyant consumer demand' means a world full of junk, it is hard to see why we should want to work so hard for it". In a similar vein, the famous 19th-century economist Adam Smith has remarked, "No patriot or man of feeling could oppose it (growth), but the nature of this growth ... is that it is at once undirected and infinitely self-generating in the endless demand for all the useless things in the world."[14] In a world where millions live in poverty, and where natural resources like the Amazon rainforest and the ozone layer are being depleted rapidly, a *chindogu* society is out of place, a hideous monster created by the Frankenstein of capitalism.

People who are too immersed in the *chindogu* society implicitly assume that so long as they can satisfy those artificial wants which their materialistic society has instilled in them, they will be able to appease the deeper hunger for spiritual meaning. Unfortunately, this is not the case. Money is a necessary but not sufficient condition for happiness. More money will not enable you to live a more meaningful life if you already have enough money to live on. One of the beauties of what little written literature there is by Native American Indians is their clarity on this point.[15]

---

† I would like to express my gratitude to Professor David Y. F. Ho, University of Hong Kong, for granting me the permission to use this poem. The first portion of the poem is Professor Ho's translation of the famous poem by Li Bo. The second is his echo to the first.

For example, the Hopi has a word in their language: *koyaanisqatsi* (this can be roughly pronounced as ko-ya-an-nis-kat-si). This word means "life out of kilter with itself", "crazy life", "life disintegrating", "unbalanced life", and most significantly and indubitably, "a state of life which calls for another way of living". *Koyaanisqatsi* poignantly expresses the current state of imbalance in the lives of many Asians, which comes from living in a tightly-organised, collectivistic and hierarchical society which puts too much emphasis on the acquisition of material goods and the enhancement of one's *mian-zi* before others, and not enough emphasis on living a creative and meaningful life. What these Asians need is to reinvent themselves and their societies, so that they can lead a creative and balanced life that is not out of kilter with itself.

Conflict Is Not Necessarily Bad for the Asian Society

But to enable the Asian to live a creative, meaningful and balanced life, there is one important prerequisite: his society must become more open, and allow him to pose difficult and challenging questions e.g., what type of society should we strive for? Do we want to live in a "perfect" society, like the Singaporeans? At the same time, it must also enable him to communicate his constructive ideas and opinions to the rest of his society. However, in many Asian countries like authoritarian Singapore and Communist China, much restriction is still placed on what the individual can do or say in public, so as to maintain social order and harmony. There is the lingering fear among the political elite in these countries that if they were to create a more open society, i.e., if a diversity of views is permitted to flourish in its midst, then conflict will inevitably be generated, and the hard-won social order and harmony will be destroyed overnight. Although I believe in the importance of social stability and cohesion, I also firmly believe that a certain amount of conflict is good for Asian society.

The argument that conflict can be good for Asian society is seen from a steady stream of scientific research, which indicates that an open society where a diversity of views can flourish will eventually lead to a more creative and intellectually vibrant society, which can make better decisions affecting the lives of its people. For example, the social psychologist Nemeth has reviewed a wide body of studies, and concluded that constructive dissent by a minority group can actively promote the quality of decision-making and performance in the group as a whole.[16] It does this by stimulating all the group members to engage in divergent and flexible thought processes and to search for more information in a relatively unbiased fashion, as well as to consider the matter which is being discussed from multiple perspectives.

Dean Keith Simonton, an American researcher on creativity, has conducted a series of studies on creativity using historical data.[17] His research indicates that the political environment of a society in one generation affects the amount of creativity observed in the next. Consider two aspects of the political environment: political instability and political diversity. *Political instability* is measured by the number of political assassinations, coups d'etat, and contested power claims that occur during a generation. The relationship between this factor in the political environment and creativity for 127 generations of European history is a negative one. In other words, political instability in one generation inhibits creative work in the following generations. *Political diversity*, on the other hand, is measured by the number of independent states that exist during a generation (a 20-year period). 127 generations of European creators (700 BC to AD 1839) were studied. Creative accomplishments across many domains (such as literature, music, visual arts and science) tended to increase as the amount of political diversity in the previous generation increased.

In a similar vein, Smith has noted that it is usual to assume that great advances in the realm of ideas can only take place in times of peace and under stable government, when philosophers, scientists, artists and writers have abundant leisure to pursue undisturbed their creative activities. However, in China as in other countries, this has not proven to be true. Instead, whenever there was diversity in the polity, a great flowering of philosophical thought systems would occur. For example, before its unification by the First Emperor Shi Huang Ti, China saw many contending schools of thought. They included Confucianism, Legalism, Mohism, Taoism, the Yin-Yang School and the School of Names. However, as soon as a dynasty became firmly established there were pressures for conformity to a state-recognised orthodoxy, and a strong discouragement of deviation from the status quo. This eventually resulted in the cultural decline of the country e.g., during the latter half of the Han dynasty.[18]

The Danger Of Groupthink

Permitting a diversity of views to flourish in an Asian society, instead of placing innumerable restrictions on what the individual or group can do or say, has one additional benefit: it can help Asians to avoid the danger of groupthink. *Groupthink* is a mode of thinking that people engage in when they are deeply involved in a cohesive ingroup, when the members' strivings for unanimity override their motivation to realistically appraise alternative courses of action.[19] To put it more simply, during groupthink, individual members try so hard to agree with the group that they make mistakes and commit errors that could easily have been avoided. The social psychologist Irving Janis has described a number of instances of political and military decision-making in America which provide dramatic illustrations of the utmost stupidity shown by groups, in spite of the alleged intelligence of their members. The Bay of Pigs invasion in 1961 is perhaps the best known example. President Kennedy and a small group of advisers had decided to send a relatively small group of Cuban exiles to invade the Cuban coast with the support of the American airforce. Everything went wrong, and within a matter of days the invaders were killed or captured. How, as a group, could President Kennedy and his advisers have been so stupid, as they later admitted themselves? Janis undertook a most careful analysis of all the available documents in the Bay of Pigs fiasco and in other similar blunders e.g., the failure to defend Pearl Harbour from Japanese attack, the escalation of the Vietnam War and the Watergate burglary which culminated in the resignation of President Nixon. He concluded that the decision-makers in these historical blunders became the victims of an extreme form of group polarisation, which he called groupthink.

Groupthink arises when, during the decision-making process, a highly cohesive group of like-minded people becomes so overwhelmed by *consensus seeking* that their *apprehension of reality* is undermined. This process is hastened when certain conditions are fulfilled: when the decision group is highly cohesive, when it is isolated from other sources of information and when its leader clearly favours a particular option. Against the background of these antecedent conditions, the discussion which evolves in the group is likely to be characterised by an *illusion of its own invulnerability*, and by attempts at mutually *rationalising* actions which are in line with the proposed option while at the same time ignoring or discounting inconsistent information. These processes occur at both the intra-individual (*self-censorship*) and inter-individual (*conformity pressures*) level. Even though some members of the group may at one time or another have their private reservations about the proposal being made, they are not likely to express them overtly, as there are *mindguards* who protect the group from information that may shatter its illusion of invulnerability. The ultimate outcome of this vicious cycle of groupthink is a faulty decision which is endorsed by all, but which is far removed from what might be expected if rational and balanced info-seeking and info-providing processes have been operating.

Preventing Groupthink in the Asian Society

In the collective, group-oriented and consensus-minded society of the East, in which there is a narrow and one-sided view of conflict, as well as a cultural tradition of obeisance to authority, be it in the family, school or workplace, it is not impossible for such a phenomenon like groupthink to take root. Scientific research has indicated that Asians can guard themselves against the danger of groupthink in several ways.[20] First and foremost, the Asian leader should be open and consultative, instead of closed and authoritarian. He should also permit a wide spectrum of views to emerge during the group discussion, and encourage each member of the group to voice his personal misgivings of a favoured plan. In addition, the leader should not present such a favoured plan at the outset; instead, his initial task is to describe the problem, not recommend a solution. He should also establish routine procedures in which several independent and smaller groups can work on the same problem. With such a dispersion of energies, it is unlikely that a consensus will develop prematurely. Furthermore, the leader should solicit the opinions of outside experts where possible, to assist in the decision-making process of the group. An additional safeguard will be for him to appoint some members in the group to play the role of the "devil's advocate", whose principal task is to advance unpopular alternatives or to look for loopholes in the favoured plan. Finally, he should hold "second chance" meetings to reexamine the wisdom of the previously accepted decision. This plethora of measures will assist the leader in preventing the phenomenon of groupthink from arising in his group. The following boxed article looks at how President Kennedy used these techniques to neutralise the dangers of groupthink during the Cuban Missile Crisis.

The Cuban Missile Crisis: Saving the World from Nuclear War

The Cuban Missile Crisis took place at the height of the Cold War, when the two reigning superpowers, the United States and the Soviet Union, were trying to establish their hegemony in the world. For 13 days in October 1962, the world swayed on the brink of a nuclear holocaust. The Soviet Union, perhaps at the request of a Cuban government frightened by the misguided Bay of Pigs invasion, was rapidly constructing a missile base in Cuba. To resolve this crisis, President Kennedy once again called on his top advisers to form the Executive Committee of the National Security Council. Though it was somewhat larger than the Bay of Pigs advisory group, many of the same individuals attended its meetings. For five days these men considered the issues, debated possible solutions, and disagreed over strategies. They finally recommended a plan that involved a naval blockade of all Cuban ports. Although the Soviet Union denounced the naval quarantine as piracy, ships believed to be carrying nuclear armaments were successfully directed away from Cuba. Eventually, the Cuban Missile Crisis was resolved, as the Russians agreed to dismantle the launching sites and the Americans promised never to invade Cuba.

As Forsyth has pointed out, the parallels between the Bay of Pigs invasion and the Cuban Missile Crisis are obvious.[21] To a large extent both decisions were formulated by the same people, meeting in the same room, guided by the same leader, and working equally hard under similar time pressures. Both crises occurred in the same area of the world, involved the same foreign powers, and could have led to equally serious consequences. Yet despite these similarities, the Executive Committee worked with admirable precision and effectiveness. This was due to the soul-searching by President Kennedy in the aftermath of the Bay of Pigs fiasco. In the months following this foreign policy setback, he explored and corrected the causes of his group's poor decision. As a result, his new group was prepared to deal with the Cuban Missile Crisis. For a start, no trace of the air of confidence and superiority that permeated the planning sessions of the Bay of Pigs fiasco was in evidence during the Executive Committee meetings. The men knew that they, and their decisions, were imperfect, and that wishful thinking would not improve the situation. President Kennedy repeatedly told the group that there was no room for error, miscalculation, or oversight in their plans, and at every meeting the members openly admitted the tremendous risks and dangers involved in taking coercive steps against the Russians. Each solution was assumed to be flawed, and even when the blockade had been painstakingly arranged, the members developed contingency plans in case it failed. In fact, the group never did reach 100 percent agreement on the decision to turn back Russian ships.

Group members admitted their personal inadequacies and ignorance and willingly consulted experts who were not members of the group. Instead of assuming that the Russians' actions justified any response (including full-scale invasion of Cuba), the committee discussed the ethics of the situation and the proposed solutions. For example, although some members felt that the Russians had left themselves open to any violent response the Americans deemed appropriate, the majority argued that a final cause of action had to be consistent with "America's humanitarian heritage and ideals". A biased perception of the Russian actions was thus successfully nipped in the bud. No norm of conformity was given the slightest opportunity to develop, and each person in the group was able to express doubts and worries openly. Rules of discussion were suspended, agendas were avoided, and new ideas were welcome.

Although pressures to conform surfaced from time to time, group members felt so comfortable in their roles as skeptical critics that they were able to resist the temptation to go along with the consensus. The atmosphere of open inquiry can be credited to changes designed and implemented by President Kennedy. Essentially, he dropped his closed style of leadership to become an open leader as he (1) refused to state his personal beliefs at the beginning of the session, instead waiting until others had let their views be known (2) required a full, unbiased discussion of the pros and cons of each possible course of action (3) convinced his subordinates that he would welcome healthy criticism and condemn "yea-saying" and (4) arranged for the group to meet without him on several occasions. Although some observers interpreted his refusal to rule the meetings with an authoritarian hand as a sign of weakness, the results more than justified President Kennedy's open leadership approach.

In Search of the Soul of Singaporeans

To be fair, the political authority in Asian societies like Singapore is not unaware of the benefits of an open society. This can be seen in the recent decision by the Singaporean government to let the people have their own Speakers' Corner, as well as in its publication of the S21 report. This vision for Singaporeans in the 21st century and beyond, which is based on feedback from thousands of Singaporeans in all walks of life, emphasises what the people and government can do, in order to create a society of active citizens in which every Singaporean matters. For example, the Singapore citizen should "walk the talk", instead of merely criticising the Singapore government in neighbourhood coffee-shops. Similarly, the Singapore government should welcome the suggestions of its citizens, instead of making them feel that their ideas for a better society will only be sucked into a "black hole". As a Singaporean myself, I hope that the vision as spelled out in S21 turns out to be a reality. That is, the government will keep its word and leave its citizens to run their own lives, instead of wanting a controlling stake in everything they do (in one extreme case, Singapore Food Industries, a hyper-competitive government-linked company, which has a paid-up capital of tens of millions of dollars, competed with humble hawkers making their living at roadside foodstalls for a chunk of the barbecued duck-and-rice market in Singapore[22]). In a similar vein, the citizens in this country will make the effort to take up other pursuits in life, besides the pursuit of dollars and cents. The alternative is the scenario which every Singaporean is used to: being shepherded like so many sheep to the bureaucratically-prefabricated templates of everyday life, arguably by the most efficient government in the world. Such a government is not easy to love, because in its obsessive drive to be efficient, it can "squeeze you until your pips squeak". Indeed, many Singaporeans experience their "efficient" government as a sore pain in the butt, and will no doubt identify with the lady in the nursery rhyme below:

> *He keeps a lady in a cage,*
> *Most cruelly all day,*
> *And makes her sing and calls her Miss,*
> *Until she fades away.*

Who Is the True Creator?

In calling for a freer and more open Asian society in which people can live a creative and meaningful life, two caveats are in order. First and foremost, this is not a revolutionary call for a boycott or overthrow of conventional Asian society. This would be a prescription for anarchy. Instead, like Crutchfield, I believe that the true creator is an independently-minded thinker, who is best able to maintain an optimal balance between self-reliance and group identification and to benefit from the favourable contributions of the social group and society while rejecting their unfavourable imperatives and tendencies.[23] Such a true creator escapes the fate of both the extreme conformist and counter-conformist. In the case of the extreme conformist, he is too *oversocialised*, i.e., he follows what the majority says and does unthinkingly. By behaving in this way, he misses out on the chance to become his own person. In the case of the extreme counter-conformist, he is too *undersocialised*, i.e., by rejecting whatever the majority says and does unthinkingly, he misses out on the chance to learn from others. In contrast to them, the true creator is neither too oversocialised nor undersocialised. He is not too oversocialised because he can be independent and take the initiative; he is not too undersocialised because he can tap the resources of the community where appropriate.

Indeed, the true creator is often highly conventional in those ways of social behaviour that facilitate life in the social group, and yet which do not impede his/her own aims as a creator. For example, Einstein in his old age was seen as an internationally-renowned but forgetful genius of science who was kindly, benign and enjoyed the company of children. At the same time, he had one overriding desire, namely, to be left alone when he wanted to be so. One of his biographers described how, in the course of ordinary social interchange, he would "fall silent and stop listening to you. He would rise to his feet without a word, or remain sitting motionless. The effect would be the same. He would be unreachable ... One never got rid of the feeling that his presence among us was only on temporary loan."[24] To put it succinctly, the true creator – in whom creative thinking is at its best – is *someone who can accept society without denying himself*. The journalist, writer and philosopher Albert Camus, who was also the winner of the Nobel Prize for Literature in 1958, was fully conscious of this essential relation of the creator to his larger human society. In his acceptance speech, he wrote:

> And the man who, as often happens, chose the path of art because he was aware of his difference soon learns that he can nourish his art, and his literature, solely by admitting his resemblance to all. The artist fashions himself in the ceaseless oscillation from himself to others, midway between the beauty he cannot do without and the community from which he cannot tear himself. This is why true artists scorn nothing. They force themselves to understand instead of judging. And if they are to take sides in this world, they can do so only with a society in which, according to Nietzsche's profound words, the judge will yield to the creator ...[25]

On Not Blindly Emulating the West

In addition, I am also not implying that Asians should blindly emulate the "free-for-all" societies of the West. The West may be more creative than the East in many ways, but its society is *not* perfect: there are many aspects of its culture which a reasonable and sane person – whether in the East or West – will frown upon. As an example, it is the West which has brought to light the sinister power of the Id via the psychoanalytic genius of Sigmund Freud and his disciples. Even then and ironically, the West seems unable to get over its "honeymoon with human nature".* Instead, in putting so much firepower in the hands of its citizens, it has created a dire situation in which parents and students feel unsafe in schools, even with metal detectors. The tragedy in Columbine High School, in which two teenage American students went on a murderous rampage and killed their teacher and 12 other students before they turned the guns on themselves, has stoked the feeling that American schools are not safe.[26] This feeling was reinforced recently when a seven-year-old boy pulled a loaded gun from his pants (which he had retrieved from his uncle's house) and shot a little girl to death in front of his horrified teacher and classmates at Buell Elementary. An incredulous President Clinton, after hearing about the fatal shooting, said, "Why could the child fire the gun? If we have the technology today to put in child safety locks in these guns, why don't we do it?"[27] I find myself incredulous at Clinton's incredulity, as he is missing the point entirely – why talk about putting safety

≈≈

*   With a few key exceptions, like Joseph Conrad (1857–1924), the Polish-born English novelist with a touch of the mysterious Orient in him, which came from his long sojourn in the Malay Archipelago and on the Congo River as a master mariner. Conrad, who is considered by many literary experts to be among the great modern English prose stylists, wrote such striking novels as *Nostromo* (1904), *The Secret Agent* (1907), *Under Western Eyes* (1911) and *Victory* (1915), which according to the historian Paul Johnson, are actually a series of "despairing political sermons in the guise of fiction". In unison, they present the thesis of the irremediable nature of our human predicament on this earth, i.e., even if we find True Love, believe in God, practise democracy and obey the Mandate of Heaven, it will not make any difference at all, in terms of improving our lot on this lonely planet; in fact, more often than not, it will make things worse. Writing to the English philosopher Bertrand Russell on October 23, 1922 – Russell was then offering "solutions" to *The Problem of China*, his latest book – Conrad insisted, "I have never been able to find in any man's book or any man's talk anything convincing enough to stand up for a moment against my deep-seated sense of fatality governing this man-inhabited world ... The only remedy for Chinamen and for the rest of us is the change of hearts. But looking at the history of the last 2,000 years there is not much reason to expect that thing, even if man has taken to flying ... Man doesn't soar like the eagle; he flies like a beetle." From the perspective of two world wars and current conflicts in our modern world that kill and cripple indiscriminately (giving rise to the wry Stalinist notion that one death is a personal tragedy, while one million deaths are an abstract statistic), I cannot help but concur with Conrad's sombre words.

≈≈

locks in guns to protect children, when the real problem is the easy availability of guns?

Last but not least is the case involving Paladin Press, which is a mail-
order publishing house in America. Paladin Press had published a book
on how to commit murder and get away with it. This book, which has
sold 13,000 copies, is entitled *Hit Man: A Technical Manual for Independent
Contractors*. *Hit Man* provides step-by-step instructions to the reader on
how to sneak into homes, how to use a silencer and how to kill most
effectively – by putting a single bullet between the eyes of the victim.[28] In
1993, it figured in a brutal crime in Maryland: Mrs Mildred Horn, a flight
attendant, was found shot between the eyes in her living room. Nearby
were the bodies of her disabled son and a housekeeper. Police traced the
crimes to her ex-husband Lawrence Horn, a sound engineer living in
Hollywood, who believed that he would inherit an estimated US$2 mil-
lion trust fund if his former wife and son were dead. He had hired a
contract killer by the name of James Perry to commit the crime. When
police searched the home of Perry, they found a copy of *Hit Man*, and the
prosecutors were able to show that he had followed its instruction in 22
specific ways. After Horn and Perry were convicted, the family's lawyer
filed a civil suit against Paladin, charging the publisher with aiding and
abetting the murders. Paladin Press argued in its defence that it published *Hit Man* for fantasy and entertainment, and claimed that the First
Amendment shielded it from liability. However, the Supreme Court in
America rejected this legal defence, forcing Paladin to agree to a multi-
million-dollar settlement over the triple murder. An American law professor commented that the successful lawsuit against Paladin "marks an
important step in combating this country's culture of violence".

The Typical Western Arrogance

What I find highly ironical is that in spite of all these problems in their
own backyard, many hawkish critics in the West still insist on preaching
to the East about various matters e.g., calling Asian leaders "dictators"
and using disparaging terms to describe various Asian societies, such as
Singapore being a "nanny state" filled with citizens who "dare not think".
In my opinion, a good response to this "typical Western arrogance" is to
quote from their sacred scriptures, i.e., the Holy Bible (Matthew 7: 3–5):

> Why do you look at the speck of sawdust in your brother's eye and pay
> no attention to the log in your own eye? How can you say to your brother,
> "Let me take the speck out of your eye", when all the time there is a log in
> your own eye? You **hypocrite**! First take the log out of your own eye, and
> then you will see clearly to remove the speck from your brother's eye.

The Typical Asian Arrogance

In criticising this "typical Western arrogance", I am well aware that there is also such a phenomenon as the "typical Asian arrogance", i.e., there are many conservative critics in the East who are just as guilty of adopting a superior and haughty attitude towards the West. For example, as part of its sustained management of the emotional lives of its people via the national media, the Singapore government continuously exhorts its citizens to refrain from adopting the "decadent" moral values of the West, while preserving its Confucian values. This creates the potential for a sharp rebuke from the other side.

In one incident, a survey by the Political and Economic Risk Consultancy (PERC) identified the Philippines as the most favoured expatriate posting in the region, because of its kaleidoscopic nightlife. Following this report, a Singaporean wrote a letter to the local newspapers, in which he called for the authorities to refrain from loosening regulations governing nightclubs and discos in an attempt to lure foreign talent to work in Singapore. He worried that if Singapore's nightlife were expanded in order to attract expatriates, the Republic would "sacrifice further our already eroding moral values just to accommodate and lure expatriates to work here".[29]

Not surprisingly, many Western expatriates in Singapore who read his letter felt offended. One of them responded with the warning that this type of "Westerner bashing" can thwart the efforts of the Singaporean government to attract foreign talent to its shores. Another replied in a most eloquent and sarcastic manner that she wanted to thank this worried Singaporean for helping her to remember that "we are not perfect, my family and I, but we are people who are unafraid of ideas or practices simply because they differ from our own. We argue and debate, we accept or not, according to our individual differences, and that openness to and debate of different ideas helps make us strong. Our love of one another despite our differences makes us even stronger. Thank you ... for helping me remember this."[30]

Culture Is Nothing to Brag About

In my personal opinion, *culture is nothing to brag about*. As Heelas and Lock have commented, "Our indigenous psychology works to maintain and fulfil what our social world defines as that which we should be. But perhaps this counts against what our basic psychological nature demands of us: in other words, that sociocultural views of the self do not necessarily fulfil the needs of the self as a natural psychological entity."[31] What Heelas and Lock are saying here is that the cultural notion of selfhood which we rely on to be a person in society will not always be good for us, in terms of our psychological health. This is as true in the East as it is in the West.

For example, Western social commentators like Robert Bellah and his colleagues, Amitai Etzioni and Jonathan Sacks, have noted that the Ptolemaic self of liberal individualism puts an undue emphasis on the rights and freedoms of the individual, often at the expense of the significant other and society. A dire consequence of this is the plethora of social problems which plague the minds of policy-makers, welfare workers and concerned altruists, like marriage breakups, single parenthood, the rise of delinquency, a culture of sex and violence and gun-riddled neighbourhoods.

In a similar vein, Asian social commentators like Lu Xun, Lin Yu Tang and Bo Yang have argued that the Galilean self of Confucianism, with its brand of authoritarian moralism, concern for group relations and enhancement of one's *mian-zi* or face, encourages crass materialism and *kiasuism*, stifles the individual from developing his or her potentials, leaves the stranger in an ethical lurch, and leads to a familial nepotism and crony capitalism that increase the coffers of the family at the expense of the state. (Some scholars believe that the twin evils of familial nepotism and crony capitalism were partially responsible for the Asian economic crisis.) Bo Yang in particular, the gadfly on the Chinese body politic, who is constantly urging his Chinese compatriots to know themselves in the Socratic as well as the Buddhist way, has not hesitated to speak out against the less desirable traits of the Chinese via his *zawen*, a brand of satirical essay perfected by Lu Xun in his venomous attack on corrupt Chinese officials in the early 20th century. In one of his *zawen*, Bo Yang introduced the colourful notion of the *soy paste vat* as a metaphor for all the ills of Chinese society, past and present, which is recorded with great wit in his infamous book *The Ugly Chinaman and the Crisis of Chinese Culture*.[32]

East and West, Neither Is Best

To me, it seems rather clear that neither the East nor the West can claim the moral high ground in dealing with each other. Rather than bragging about one's way of life to the other, it might be a more instructive exercise for us to ponder upon the fact that all human beings – including those of us who live in the East and West – are hominid wimps[33] who can trace their ancestry ultimately back to a "protoplasmal primordial atomic globule", as Mary and John Gribbin put it in *Being Human*,[34] a book which takes a look at the person from an evolutionary perspective. Since we all come from slime, there is nothing for us to gloat about.

Two people who grasped this basic truth about human beings were Theodore Roosevelt and William Beebe.[35] Beebe had the habit of visiting Roosevelt from time to time. After an evening's talk in Roosevelt's home at Sagamore Hill, the two men would go out on the lawn and gaze up at the sky and see who could first detect the faint spot of light-mist beyond the lower left-hand corner of the Great Square of Pegasus, and then one or the other would recite, "That is the Spiral Galaxy of Andromeda. It is as large as our Milky Way. It is one of a hundred million galaxies. It is 750,000 light years away. It consists of one hundred billion suns, each larger than our sun." After an interval, Beebe reported that Mr Roosevelt would grin at him and say, "Now, I think we are small enough. Let's go to bed."*

~~~~~~

* Unfortunately, few of us in this world adopt this meek and humble attitude of Roosevelt and Beebe. Instead, we are more inclined to think of ourselves as being different, unique and superior, not only to our own kind, but to every other creature on earth, living or extinct. However, several lines of research indicate that this picture is not valid. First, modern genetic studies have shown that we are almost identical to chimpanzees, our closest relative, who differ from us in a DNA sense by about 1 percent. In fact, we are closer to chimpanzees than they are to the next nearest relative of us both, namely, the gorillas (James Trefil in *Are We Unique?* calculated that in a DNA sense, we are about 70 percent like the humble pumpkin in the supermarket). Second, paleoanthropology, the study of human ancestry via fossil records, indicates that we are an extremely young species, in comparison with the rest of the biological kingdom. A selective look at the whole history of life on earth will underline this assertion. We begin with the formation of the earth some 4,500 million years ago (mya). The "primeval soup" that gave rise to all living organisms (including plants, animals and human beings) can be traced back 3,000–4,000 mya. The dinosaurs, which once ruled the earth, died out at about 65 mya from the atmospheric after-effects of a stray meteorite which hit the earth. By then they had been around for about 160 million years. In comparison to the dinosaurs, we have been around for a mere 100,000 years. Rod Caird, author of *Ape Man: The Story of Human Evolution*, pointed out that if we were to become extinct now, we would seem to future alien paleoanthropologists like "the merest flicker of accidental, momentary development". To give a good idea of how short this flicker is, we can represent the entire span of geological time as a single year, which starts on January 1 and ends on December 31. The formation of the earth will take place on January 1. The "primeval soup" which is the basis of life will appear on February 10. Green plants will colonise the land and jawed fish will evolve in the oceans on October 11. Insects and reptiles will appear around December 4–5. Dinosaurs will become rulers of the earth on December 16, and birds will fly in the sky on December 18. The dinosaurs will disappear on December 26, and they will be replaced by the mammals. One of these mammals which manages to flourish after the death of the dinosaur is the primate, from which our ancestors (*Australopithecus, Homo habilis, Homo erectus*) will evolve. These hominids (human ancestors) will be a common sight on the savannas of East Africa on the mid-morning of December 31. As for us *Homo sapiens*, we only make our appearance at 11:56 p.m., December 31, exactly four minutes before the close of this geologic calendar.

~~~~~~

Chapter Summary

In this final chapter, I looked at various ways in which Asian society can become more creative. First, I argued that Asian parents should assist their children to develop a positive self-concept. This can be achieved by teaching them to choke off the Voice of Judgment (VOJ). Second, I argued that Asian parents should nurture the autonomy of their children, instead of overprotecting them. Third, I argued that the Asian family should be a "playground of life", where children can learn to become resilient adults who maintain a playful attitude towards life. Following this, I made a distinction between training and educating students. I then went on to describe six steps of becoming a more creative Asian student. In addition, I also made some suggestions on how Asian educators could learn from their counterparts in the West in educating students. I turned my attention to the need for Asians to be more concerned about the meaning of existence, rather than the status symbols of society. To achieve this goal, a diversity of views must be permitted to flourish within the society. Although this may lead to some friction, conflict is not necessarily bad for Asian society; in fact, it can even guard Asians against groupthink. Having argued for a more open society where people can speak freely, I added two caveats. First, this is not a revolutionary call for the boycott of conventional society. Second, Asians should not blindly emulate Western society, for it is not perfect. I went on to assert that people in the East and West should refrain from criticising one another's society. Besides, since we come from slime, there is nothing for us to gloat about. Finally, I conclude this book with the following boxed article. I hope that this will be useful to you, the reader, even as you embark on this journey of becoming a more creative self.

Ten Comprehensive Guidelines to Becoming a Creative Asian

In offering these ten comprehensive guidelines to becoming a creative Asian, my guiding philosophy is two-fold: (1) there is much that Asians can learn from their Western counterparts in enhancing their creativity (2) there is much in Asian society which is commendable, and which in my view should be preserved. From this guiding philosophy, a conviction arises: the creative Asian should integrate the best of the East and West, instead of chucking out the East in favour of the West.

Guideline 1: Maintain a flexible discipline in every situation

The strength of the West lies in its flexibility; the strength of the East lies in its discipline. But flexibility in the extreme leads to chaos, while discipline in the extreme leads to a shrivelling up. The creative Asian should maintain a *flexible discipline* in every situation. Flexible discipline helps him not only to be in control of the situation, but also to adapt himself creatively to it.

Guideline 2: Seek peace and harmony within the social group, but don't be afraid to take a moral stance if you have to

Asians have a negative view of conflict, and seek social peace and harmony within their community. Westerners are not afraid of taking a stance against the collective, even if it means conflict and confrontation with it. The creative Asian should strive to preserve social peace and harmony within his community. However, if the situation requires him to take a moral stance against the collective, then he should "bite the bullet in its head", instead of shrinking from conflict and confrontation. Moral integrity is a hallmark of the true creator. It is also the foundation of social life: if one can't even live in good conscience with oneself, how can one live with other people in society?

Guideline 3: Give face to the other, but don't seek to gain face for yourself by the acquisition of material goods

In Asian society, one major way to preserve social harmony is by giving face to the other. This is commendable, as it helps to keep the peace and maintain the relationship. However, in this society, there is also an equally strong emphasis on gaining face for oneself via the acquisition of material goods. This materialistic desire to gain face for oneself can result in a *chindogu* society. It can also lead to envy and jealousy, not to mention a lack of creativity. The creative Asian should give face to the other, but he should not seek to gain face for himself by the acquisition of material goods.

Guideline 4: Infuse yourself with passion; help the poor; be an everyday creator

If the creative Asian doesn't seek to gain face for himself via the acquisition of material goods, then what can he do with his life? How can he occupy his time meaningfully? I have three suggestions. First, he can infuse himself with passion for a certain activity, like the task-involved and creative Westerner. For example, he can try to figure out whether men are really from Mars and women from Venus as an American psychologist has said (I thought they came from Earth!). Or he can challenge the widely-held belief that True Love exists in this world (it doesn't: True Love, like God, is a social construction which creates more problems than it solves). Second, the creative Asian can occupy his time meaningfully by assisting those people who are less fortunate than him. Third, he can strive to be an everyday creator: this will add a lot of zest into his everyday life.

Guideline 5: Be modest, yet believe in yourself

Asians are noted for their modesty, while Westerners are prone to the false uniqueness bias, i.e., to have a high confidence in themselves. While it is good to adopt a modest attitude in life (then one can continue to learn from others, because one does not presume to know everything), it is also good to believe in oneself (then one can undertake challenging tasks that sharpen one's skills). Therefore, the creative Asian should be modest, yet believe in himself. In this way, he remains teachable, while he also gets to function at the edge of his competence (which is a defining trademark of the creator).

Guideline 6: Use reason to prune tradition

The Asian has been brought up to respect tradition, while the Westerner has been brought up to rely on his own powers of reasoning. Tradition enriches our lives e.g., the Chinese New Year is meaningful not because of the red packets which are stuffed with dollar bills, but because of what it symbolises: a time for members of the extended family, who are scattered in the four corners of the earth, to gather together as one united entity. But at the same time, tradition can also cripple the Asian. For example, the ancient Chinese tradition of binding a woman's feet crippled the life of many upper-class Chinese maidens, although it whetted the sexual appetite of the lecherous males in the society (these lecherous males regarded the deformed feet of the crippled maiden as "little lilies" which enabled her to "sway like a tender willow in the gentle breeze"). The creative Asian should learn from his Western counterpart, i.e., he should use his power of reasoning to decide which tradition should be retained and which should be discarded.

Guideline 7: Don't be a pushover!

Sad to say, many elements inside and outside the Asian society prevent the individual Asian from exercising his autonomy or belittle his dignity as a person. For example, the typical Asian is expected to respect his elders, to conform to his ingroup, to obey institutional authorities, to blindly follow rules and regulations, to unthinkingly preserve customs and norms, to heed the Voice of Judgment and to listen to the exhortations of great leaders. And when he does as he is told, other people outside his society make unkind remarks about his behaviour e.g., Asians are too afraid to think, Asians live in a nanny state, and so on. In my opinion, the creative Asian should not be a pushover. Instead, he should assert himself against these internal and external forces that prevent him from exercising his autonomy or belittle his dignity as a person.

Guideline 8: Adopt an experimental attitude by taking calculated risks in life

Research has shown that Westerners tend to adopt an experimental attitude in life, i.e., they try out something new, and they learn from their mistakes. In contrast, Asians have a high uncertainty avoidance, as well as a low tolerance of ambiguity, i.e., in a novel and ill-structured situation in which the operating norms (dos and don'ts) are not clear, the Asian will feel a certain discomfort; he will seek to avoid being in such an ambiguous situation. Instead of behaving in this debilitating manner, the Asian should learn from his Western counterpart, i.e., he should adopt an experimental attitude in life; he should learn to take calculated risks. Only then can he overcome the debilitating fear of the unknown.

Guideline 9: Maintain a playful attitude towards life

There is a famous Western saying: "All work and no play makes Jack a dull boy." I don't know what the equivalent is, or whether there is any equivalent, in the languages of the East. But the empirical research is clear that in order to be a creative Asian, you need to cultivate a playful and humorous attitude towards life, like Richard Feynman, the American scientist who was involved in the Manhattan Project to build the atomic bomb during World War II. You might even find yourself winning a Nobel Prize! And even if you don't, you're in for a good laugh, which is the best medicine in the world (and cost less than what your doctor will charge you)!

Guideline 10: Imagine that you are a butterfly dreaming that you are a human being

Here's one way of maintaining a playful and humorous attitude towards life, but I need to digress a little first, and make the assertion that the Confucian way of life puts a lot of emphasis on social roles, duties and responsibilities. At its worst, it insists that one should maintain social propriety at all times, and keep one's spontaneous emotions in check 24 hours a day, lest these emotions disrupt the smooth functioning of Confuciandom, which is the most dreary of all worlds imaginable, filled with hypocrites and sycophants. The creative Asian should free himself from Confuciandom by adopting the playful and irreverent attitude towards life which the Taoist mind revels and excels in; e.g., like Chuang Tzu, the creative Asian should imagine that he is a butterfly dreaming that he is a human being. Then the humdrum world of Confuciandom may start to look very different indeed.

Notes

1. Goleman, Kaufman & Ray, 1992.
2. Covey, 1997.
3. Smith, 1973.
4. Sacks, 1997.
5. Lau, 1979.
6. Feynman, 1997.
7. Barron, Montuori & Barron, 1997.
8. *The Straits Times,* April 14, 1999.
9. *Ibid.*
10. *The Straits Times,* June 10, 1999.
11. *The Straits Times,* July 19, 2000.
12. Handy, 1998.
13. *The Straits Times,* February 12, 1999.
14. Handy, 1998.
15. Malone & Malone, 1987.
16. Nemeth, 1995.
17. Simonton, 1975 & 1990.
18. Smith, 1973.
19. Janis, 1982.
20. Forsyth, 1990.
21. *Ibid.*
22. *The Straits Times,* June 25, 1999.
23. Crutchfield, 1962.
24. Storr, 1976.
25. Camus, 1958.
26. *The Straits Times,* April 26 & April 27, 1999.
27. *The Straits Times,* March 2, 2000.
28. *The Straits Times,* May 23, 1999.
29. *The Straits Times,* May 10, 1999.
30. *The Straits Times,* May 15, 1999.
31. Heelas & Lock, 1981.
32. Boyang, 1992.
33. Stringer & McKie, 1997.
34. Gribbin & Gribbin, 1995.
35. Wallis, 1965.

Bibliography

Albert, R. S. (1983). Family Positions and the Attainment of Eminence. In R. S. Albert (ed.), *Genius and Eminence: The Social Psychology of Creativity and Achievement*, pp. 141–54. Elmsford, New York: Pergamon.

Allen, J. (ed.) (1969). *One Hundred Great Lives*. Melbourne: Sun Books.

Amabile, T. M. (1996). *Creativity in Context*. USA: Westview Press.

Amabile, T. M. (1990). Within You, Without You: The Social Psychology of Creativity and Beyond. In M. Runco & R. Albert (eds.), *Theories of Creativity*, pp. 61–91. Newbury Park: Sage Publications, Inc.

Ames, C. (1992). Classrooms: Goals, Structures, and Student Motivation. *Journal of Educational Psychology*, 84(3): 261–71.

Ames, C., & Archer, J. (1988). Achievement Goals in the Classroom: Students' Learning Strategies and Motivation Processes. *Journal of Educational Psychology*, 80(3): 260–67.

Arieti, S. (1976). *Creativity: The Magic Synthesis*. New York: Basic Books.

Aronson, E. (1992). *The Social Animal*, 6th edition. New York: Freeman.

Asiaweek, pp. 46–56, May 22, 1998.

Baker, D. R. (1979). *Chinese Family and Kinship*. UK: Macmillan Press Ltd.

Balint, M. (1955). Friendly Expanses – Horrid Empty Spaces. *International Journal of Psychoanalysis*, 36: 225–41.

Barbaranelli, C., Caprara, G. V., & Maslach, C. (1997). Individuation and the Five Factor Model of Personality Traits. *European Journal of Psychological Assessment*, 13(2): 75–84.

Barnlund, D. C. (1975). *Public and Private Self in Japan and the United States*, S. Nishiyama & M. Sano (trans.). Tokyo: Simul Press.

Barron, F. (1969). *Creative Person and Creative Process*. New York: Holt, Rinehart and Winston.

Barron, F., & Harrington, D. M. (1981). Creativity, Intelligence, and Personality. *Annual Review of Psychology*, 32: 439–76.

Barron, F., Montuori, A., & Barron, A. (1997). *Creators on Creating: Awakening and Cultivating the Imaginative Mind*. New York: G.P. Putnam's Sons.

Baumeister, F. R. (1997). The Self and Society: Changes, Problems, and Opportunities. In R. D. Ashmore & L. Jussim (eds.), *Self and Identity: Fundamental Issues*, pp.191–217. Oxford University Press.

Bellah, R. N., Madsen, R., Sullivan, W. M., Swidler, A., & Tipton, S. M. (1985). *Habits of the Heart: Individualism and Commitment in American Life*. New York: Harper & Row.

Berling, J. (1985). Self and Whole in Chuang Tzu. In D. J. Munro (ed.), *Individualism and Holism: Studies in Confucian and Taoist Values*, pp. 101–20. Ann Arbor: Centre for Chinese Studies, The University of Michigan.

Bloodworth, D. (1967). *Chinese Looking Glass*. New York: Farrar, Straus & Giroux.

Bloom, A. (1987). *The Closing of the American Mind*. New York: Simon & Schuster.

Bloom, A. H. (1977). Two Dimensions of Moral Reasoning: Social Principledness and Social Humanism in Cross-Cultural Perspective. *Journal of Social Psychology*, 101: 29–44.

Bloom, B. S. (1985). Generalisations about Talent Development. In B. S. Bloom (ed.), *Developing Talent in Young People*, pp. 507–49. New York: Ballantine Books.

Blumenthal, E. P. (1976). *Models in Chinese Moral Education: Perspectives from Children's Books*. University Microfilms Nos. 77–7876.

Boey, K. W. (1976). *Rigidity and Cognitive Complexity: An Empirical Investigation in the Interpersonal, Physical and Numeric Domains Under Task-Oriented and Ego-Oriented Conditions*. PhD thesis, University of Hong Kong.

Bond, M. H., Wan, K. C., Leung, K., & Giacalone, R. A. (1985). How Are Responses to Verbal Insult Related to Cultural Collectivism and Power Distance? *Journal of Cross-Cultural Psychology*, 16(1): 111–27.

Bond, R., & Smith, P. B. (1996). Culture and Conformity: A Meta-Analysis of Studies Using Asch's (1952b, 1956) Line Judgement Task. *Psychological Bulletin*, 119(1): 111–37.

Boorstin, D. J. (1998). *The Seekers: The Story of Man's Continuing Quest to Understand His World*. New York: Random House.

Bornstein, R. F. (1992). The Dependent Personality: Developmental, Social and Clinical Perspectives. *Psychological Bulletin*, 112(1): 3–23.

Bo Yang (1992). *The Ugly Chinaman and the Crisis of Chinese Culture*, D. J. Cohn & J. Qing (trans. and eds.). Sydney: Allen & Unwin.

Branden, N. (1980). *The Psychology of Romantic Love*. New York: Bantam Books.

Branson, R. (1998). *Losing My Virginity: The Autobiography*. London: Virgin Publishing.

Brewer, M. B. (1991). The Social Self: On Being the Same and Different at the Same Time. *Personality and Social Psychological Bulletin*, 17(5): 475–82.

Brown, K. A. (1988). *Inventors at Work: Interviews with 16 Notable American Inventors*. Redmond, Washington: Microsoft Press.

Butler, R. (1987). Task-Involving and Ego-Involving Properties of Evaluation: Effects of Different Feedback Conditions on Motivational Perceptions, Interest and Performance. *Journal of Educational Psychology*, 79: 474–82.

Caird, R., & Foley, R. (1994). *Ape Man: The Story of Human Evolution*. New York: Macmillan.

Camus, A. (1958). Camus at Stockholm: The Acceptance of the Nobel Prize. *Atlantic Monthly*.

Camus, A. (1975). *The Myth of Sisyphus and Other Essays*, J. O. Brien (trans.). Harmondsworth: Penguin Books.

Chan, D. (1994). *Kiasuism* and the Withering Away of Singaporean Creativity. In D. Cunha (ed.), *Debating Singapore: Reflective Essays*, pp. 71–5. Singapore: Institute of Southeast Asian Studies.

Chan, K. S., Gelfand, M. J., Triandis, H. C, & Tzeng, O. (1996). Tightness-Looseness Revisited: Some Preliminary Analyses in Japan and the United States. *International Journal of Psycholoy*, 31(1): 1–12.

Chang, H., & Holt, G. R. (1994). A Chinese Perspective on Face as Inter-Relational Concern. In S. Ting-Toomey (ed.), *The Challenge of Facework: Cross-Cultural and Interpersonal Issues*, pp. 95–133. Albany, New York: State University of New York Press.

Covey, S. R. (1997). *The Seven Habits of Highly Effective Families*. New York: Golden Books.

Crutchfield, R. S. (1962). Conformity and Creative Thinking. In H. E. Gruber, G. Terrell & M. Wertheimer (eds.), *Contemporary Approaches to Creative Thinking: A Symposium Held at the University of Colorado*, pp.120–40. New York: Prentice Hall, Inc.

Csikszentmihalyi, M., & Getzels, J. W. (1971). Discovery-Oriented Behaviour and the Originality of Creative Products: A Study with Artists. *Journal of Personality and Social Psychology*, 19: 47–52.

Csikszentmihalyi, M. (1996). *Creativity: Flow and the Psychology of Discovery and Invention*. New York: HarperCollins Publishers.

D'Andrade, R. G. (1984). Cultural Meaning Systems. In R. A. Shweder & R. A. LeVine (eds.), *Culture Theory: Essays on Mind, Self and Emotion*, pp. 88–122. New York: Cambridge University Press.

Davis, G. A. (1986). *Creativity Is Forever*. Iowa: Kendall/Hunt Pub. Co.

Deci, E. L., & Ryan, R. M. (1985). The General Causality Orientation Scale: Self-Determination in Personality. *Journal of Research in Personality*, 19: 109–34.

Deci, E. L., & Ryan, R. M. (1987). The Support of Autonomy and the Control of Behaviour. *Journal of Personality and Social Psychology*, 53: 1024–37.

Deci, E. L. & Ryan, R. M. (1995). Human Autonomy: The Basis for True Self-Esteem. In M. H. Kernis (ed.), *Efficacy, Agency and Self-Esteem*, pp. 31–49. New York: Plenum Press.

Deci, E. L., Vallerand, R. J., Pelletier, L. G., & Ryan, R. M. (1991). Motivation and Education: The Self-Determination Perspective. *Educational Psychologist*, 26(3 & 4): 325–46.

Devan, J. (1994). Comparing the Singaporean Undergraduate with the American. In D. Cunha (ed.), *Debating Singapore: Reflective Essays*, pp. 65–70. Singapore: Institute of Southeast Asian Studies.

Diebold, J. (1991). *The Innovators: The Discoveries, Inventions and Breakthroughs of Our Time*. New York: Truman Talley Books/Plume.

Doi, L. T. (1973). *The Anatomy of Dependence*. Tokyo: Kodansha.

Dollinger, S. J., Leong, T. L, & Ulicni, S. K. (1996). On Traits and Values: With Special Reference to Openness to Experience. *Journal of Research in Personality*, 30: 23–41.

Drake, S. (1993). *Galileo*. Microsoft Corporation: Microsoft (R) Encarta.

Dunn, J., Zhang, X., & Ripple, R. (1988). A Study of Chinese and American Performance on Divergent Thinking Tasks. *New Horizons*, 29: 7–20.

Dweck, C. S. (1986). Motivational Processes Affecting Learning. *American Psychologist*, 41(10): 1040–48.

Dweck, C. S., & Leggett, E. L (1988). A Social-Cognitive Approach to Motivation and Personality. *Psychological Review*, 95: 256–73.

Dworkins, R. (1978). *Taking Rights Seriously*. Cambridge, MA: Harvard University Press.

Emerson, R. W. (1841). *Essays*. Boston: J. Munroe.

Ericsson, K. A., & Charness, N. (1994). Expert Performance: Its Structure and Acquisition. *American Psychologist*, 49(8): 725–47.

Ericsson, K. A., Krampe R., & Tesch-Romer, C. (1993). The Role of Deliberate Practice in the Acquisition of Expert Performance. *Psychological Review*, 100: 363–406.

Esler, A. (1997). *The Western World: A Narrative History*. New Jersey : Prentice Hall, Inc.

Etzioni, A. (1993). *The Spirit of Community*. USA: Crown Publishers Inc.

Feather, N. T. (1992). Values, Valences, Expectations and Actions. *Journal of Social Issues*, 48: 109–24.

Feynman, R. P. (1997). *"Surely You're Joking, Mr. Feynman!": Adventures of a Curious Character*. New York: W.W. Norton.

Forsyth, D. R. (1990). *Group Dynamics*, 2nd edition. California: Brooks/Cole Publishing Company.

Frankl, V. E. (1984). *Man's Search for Meaning*, revised edition. New York: Pocket Books.

Fromm, E. (1976). *To Have or To Be?* Bantam Book.

Fung, Yu-Lan. (1948). *A Short History of Chinese Philosophy*. New York: The Macmillan Company.

Gardner, H. (1993). *Creating Minds: An Anatomy of Creativity Seen Through the Lives of Freud, Einstein, Picasso, Stravinsky, Eliot, Graham and Gandhi*. New York: Basic Books.

Gibney, F. (1992). *The Pacific Century: America and Asia in a Changing World*. New York: Macmillan Publishing Company.

Gilbert, M. (1989). *Second World War*, revised edition. London: Fontana Paperbacks.

Glover, J. A., Ronning, R. R., & Reynolds, C. R. (eds.) (1989). *Handbook of Creativity: Perspectives on Individual Differences*. New York: Plenum Press.

Goh, .C. T. (1997). Shaping Our Future: Thinking Schools, Learning Nation. Opening speech at the 7th International Conference on Thinking, Singapore.

Goleman, D., Kaufman, P., & Ray, M. (1992). *The Creative Spirit*. New York: Plume.

Gomez, J. (1999). *Self-Censorship: Singapore's Shame*. Singapore: Think Centre.

Gribbin, J., & Gribbin, M. (1995). *Being Human: Putting People in an Evolutionary Perspective*. London: Phoenix.

Guest, R., & George, A. S. (1995). *History's Turning Points*. UK: Boxtree Limited.

Han, F. K., Fernandez, W., & Tan, S. (1998). *Lee Kuan Yew: The Man and His Ideas*. Singapore: Times Edition Pte Ltd, The Straits Times Press.

Handy, C. (1998). *The Hungry Spirit: Beyond Capitalism – A Quest for Purpose in the Modern World*. London: Arrow Books Limited.

Harrington, D. M., Block, J. H., & Block, J. (1987). Testing Aspects of Carl Rogers's Theory of Creative Environments: Child-Rearing Antecedents of Creative Potential in Young Adolescents. *Journal of Personality and Social Psychology*, 52: 851–56.

Hayes, J. R. (1989). Cognitive Processes in Creativity. In J. A. Glover, R. R. Ronning, & C. R. Reynolds (eds.), *Handbook of Creativity*, pp. 135–46. New York: Plenum Press.

Heelas, P., and Lock, A. (1981). (ed.). *Indigenous Psychologies: The Anthropology of the Self*. New York: Academic Press.

Helmreich, R. L., Spence, J. T., Beane, W. E., Lucker, G. W., & Matthews, K. A. (1980). Making It in Academic Psychology: Demographic and Personality Correlates of Attainment. *Journal of Personality and Social Psychology*, 39: 896–908.

Hibbert, C. (1970). *The Dragon Wakes: China and the West, 1795–911*. New York: Harper & Row.

Hill, M., & Lian, K. F. (1995). *The Politics of Nation Building and Citizenship in Singapore*. London: Routledge.

Ho, D. Y. F. (1981). Traditional Patterns of Socialisation in Chinese Society. *Acta Psychologica Taiwanica*, 23(2): 81–95.

Ho, D. Y. F. (1994). Filial Piety, Authoritarian Moralism and Cognitive Conservatism in Chinese Societies. *Genetic, Social and General Psychology Monographs,* 120: 349–65.

Ho, D. Y. F., Chan, S. F., & Peng, S. Q. (2000). An Investigative Research in Teaching and Learning in Chinese Societies. Manuscript submitted for publication.

Hofstede, G. (1980). *Culture's Consequences: International Differences in Work-Related Values.* Beverly Hills, California: Sage.

Hsu, F. L. K. (1955). *Americans and Chinese.* London: Cresset Press Ltd.

Hsu, F. L. K. (1985). The Self in Cross-Cultural Perspective. In A. J. Marsella, G. DeVos, & F. L. K. Hsu (eds.), *Culture and Self: Asian and Western Perspectives,* pp. 24–55). New York: Tavistock Publications.

Hu, H. C. (1944). The Chinese Concept of "Face". *American Anthropologist,* 46: 45–64.

Hucker, C. O. (1978). *China to 1850: A Short History.* California: Stanford University Press.

Hui, C. H., & Villareal, M. J. (1989). Individualism-Collectivism and Psychological Needs: Their Relationships in Two Cultures. *Journal of Cross-Cultural Psychology,* 20(3): 310–23.

Hwang, K. (1989). Human Emotion and *Mian-zi*: The Chinese Power Game. In K. S. Yang (ed.), *The Psychology of the Chinese.* Taipei: Kui-Kuan Books, Inc. [In Chinese]

Janis, I. L. (1982). *Groupthink: Psychological Studies of Policy Decisions and Fiascoes.* Boston: Houghton Mifflin.

Jaquish, G. A., & Ripple, R. E. (1984–85). A Life-Span Development Cross-Cultural Study of Divergent Thinking Abilities. *International Journal of Aging and Human Development,* 20(1): 1–11.

Johnson, P. (1992). *Modern Times: The World from the Twenties to the Nineties.* Revised Edition. USA: HarperPerennial.

Kasser, T., & Ryan, R. M. (1996). Further Examining the American Dream: Differential Correlates of Intrinsic and Extrinsic Goals. *Personality and Social Psychological Bulletin,* 22(3): 1996.

Kennedy, P. (1988). *The Rise and Fall of the Great Powers: Economic Change and Military Conflict from 1500 to 2000.* London: Fontana Press.

Kim, U. (1995). *Individualism and Collectivism: A Psychological, Cultural and Ecological Analysis.* Denmark: NIAS Publications.

Kingston, M. H. (1977). *The Woman Warrior: Memoirs of a Girlhood Among Ghosts.* London: Picador.

Kitayama, S., Markus, H. R., & Lieberman, C. (1995). The Collective Construction of Self-Esteem: Implications for Culture, Self and Emotion. In J. Russell, J. Fernandez-Dols, T. Manstead, & J. Wellenkamp (eds.), *Everyday Conceptions of Emotion: An Introduction to the Psychology, Anthropology and Linguistics of Emotion,* pp. 523–50). Dordrecht, The Netherlands: Kluwer Academic Publishers.

Kitayama, S., Markus, H. R., Matsumoto, H., & Norasakkunkit, V. (1997). Individual and Collective Processes of Self-Esteem Management: Self-Enhancement in the United States and Self-Depreciation in Japan. *Journal of Personality and Social Psychology,* 72(6): 1245–67.

Koestner, R., & Zuckerman, M. (1994). Causality Orientations, Failure and Achievement. *Journal of Personality,* 62(3): 321–46.

Lasch, C. (1979). *The Culture of Narcissism: American Life in an Age of Diminishing Expectations.* New York: Norton.

Lau, D. C. (1979). *Confucius: The Analects*. Harmondsworth: Penguin Books Ltd.

Lawson, S. (1996). Politics and Cultural Myths: Democracy Asian Style versus the West. *The Asia-Pacific Magazine*, pp. 38–41.

Lebra, T. S. (1976). *Japanese Patterns of Behaviour*. Honolulu: University of Hawaii Press.

Lebra, T. S. (1984). Nonconfrontational Strategies for Management of Interpersonal Conflicts. In E. S. Krauss, T. P. Rohlen, & P.G. Stenhoff (eds.), *Conflict in Japan*, pp. 41–60. Honolulu: University of Hawaii Press.

Lepper, M. R., Greene, D., & Nisbett, R. (1973). Undermining Children's Intrinsic Interest with Extrinsic Rewards: A Test of the "Overjustification" Hypothesis. *Journal of Personality and Social Psychology*, 28: 129–37.

Leung, K. (1987). Some Determinants of Reactions to Procedural Models for Conflict Resolution: A Cross-National Study. *Journal of Personality and Social Psychology*, 53(5): 898–908.

LeVine, R. A., & White, M. I. (1986). *Human Condition: The Cultural Basis of Educational Developments*. New York: Routledge & Kegan Paul.

Levy, H. S. (1970). *Chinese Footbinding: The History of a Curious Erotic Custom*. London: Spearman.

Liu, I. (1986). Chinese Cognition. In M. H. Bond (ed.), *The Psychology of the Chinese People*, pp. 73–105. New York: Oxford University Press.

Liu, T. Y., & Hsu, M. (1974). Measuring Creative Thinking in Taiwan by the Torrence Test. *Testing and Guidance*, 2: 108–9.

Lin, Y. T. (1936). *My Country, My People*. England: Windmill Press.

Low, L. (1998). *The Political Economy of a City-State: Government-Made Singapore*. Singapore: Oxford University Press.

Lubart, T. I. (1990). Creativity and Cross-Cultural Variation. *International Journal of Psychology*, 25: 39–59.

MacKinnon, D. W. (1978). *In Search of Human Effectiveness*. Buffalo, New York: Creative Education Foundation.

Malone, T. P., & Malone, P. T. (1987). *The Art of Intimacy*. New York: Prentice Hall Press.

March, R. M. (1996). *Reading the Japanese Mind: The Realities Behind Their Thoughts and Actions*. Tokyo: Kodansha International.

Markus, H. R, & Kitayama, S. (1991). Culture and the Self: Implications for Cognition, Emotion, and Motivation. *Psychological Review*, 98: 224–53.

Markus, H. R., & Kitayama, S. (1994). A Collective Fear of the Collective: Implications for Selves and Theories of Selves. *Personality and Social Psychology Bulletin*, 20(5): 568–79.

Markus, H. R., Kitayama, S., & Heiman, R. J. (1996). Culture and Basic Psychological Principles. In E. T. Higgins, & A. W. Kruglansik (eds.), *Social Psychology: Handbook of Basic Principles*, pp. 857–914. New York: The Guilford Press.

Marsh, E. W., & Kirkland, D. (1998). *James Cameron's Titanic*. London: Boxtree.

McAdams, D. P. (1992). The Five-Factor Model in Personality: A Critical Appraisal. *Journal of Personality*, 60(2): 329–61.

McCormack, E. (1924). *Audacious Angles on China*. New York: Appleton.

McCrae, R. R. (1987). Creativity, Divergent Thinking and Openness to Experience. *Personality and Social Psychology*, 52(6): 1258–65.

McCrae, R. R. (1993-1994). Openness to Experience as a Basic Dimension of Personality. *Imagination, Cognition and Personality*, 13(1): 39–55.

McCrae, R. R. (1994). Openness to Experience: Expanding the Boundaries of Factor V. *European Journal of Personality*, 8: 251–72.

McCrae, R. R. (1996). Social Consequences of Experiential Openness. *Psychological Bulletin*, 120(3): 323–37.

McCrae, R. R., & Costa, P. T. (1995). Trait Explanations in Personality Psychology. *European Journal of Personality*, 9: 231–52.

McCrae, R. R., & Costa, P. T. (1996). Toward a New Generation of Personality Theories: Theoretical Contexts for the Five-Factor Model. In J. S. Wiggins (ed.), *The Five-Factor Model of Personality: Theoretical Perspectives*. New York: The Guilford Press.

McCrae, R. R., & Costa, P. T. (1997). Personality Trait Structure as a Human Universal. *American Psychologist*, 52(5): 509–16.

McCrae, R. R., Costa, P. T., & Yik, M. S. (1997). Universal Aspects of Chinese Personality Structure. In M. H. Bond (ed.), *The Handbook of Chinese Psychology*. Hong Kong: Oxford University Press.

McCrae, R. R., & John, O. P. (1992). An Introduction to the Five-Factor Model and Its Applications. *Journal of Personality*, 60: 175–215.

McGraw, K. O., & McCullers, J. C. (1979). Evidence of a Detrimental Effect of Extrinsic Incentives on Breaking a Mental Set. *Journal of Experimental Social Psychology*, 15: 285–94.

McGregor, R. (1996). *Japan Swings: Politics, Culture and Sex in the New Japan*. Singapore: Reed Academic Publishing Asia.

McKay, D. (1994). *Politics and Power in the USA*. USA: Penguin Books.

Mente, de B. L. (1995). *NTC's Dictionary of Japan's Cultural Code Words*. USA: National Textbook Company.

Morris, P. (1996). Asia's Four Little Tigers: A Comparison of the Role of Education in Their Development. *Comparative Education*, 32(1): 95–109.

Morris, P., & Sweeting, A. (1995). *Education and Development in East Asia*. New York: Garland Press.

Morton, W. S. (1995). *China: Its History and Culture*. USA: McGraw-Hill.

Mumford, M. D., & Gustafson, S. B. (1988). Creativity Syndrome: Integration, Application, and Innovation. *Psychological Bulletin*, 103: 27–43.

Mumford, M. D., Mobley, M. I., Reiter-Palmon, R., Uhlman, C. E., & Doares, L. M. (1991). Process Analytic Models of Creative Capacities. *Creativity Research Journal*, 4(2): 91–122.

Munro, D. J. (1977). *The Concept of Man in Contemporary China*. Ann Arbor: University of Michigan Press.

Nakane, C. (1973). *Japanese Society*. UK: Penguin Books Ltd.

Nemeth, C. J. (1995). Dissent as Driving Cognition, Attitudes and Judgements. *Social Cognition*, 13(3): 273–91.

Ng, A. K. (1999). An Empirical Comparison of the Intentional Worlds of the Asian and Westerner. PhD thesis, University of Queensland.

Ng, A. K. (2000a). A Sherlock Holmes Mystery: Why Do East Asian Students Perform Better Than Their Anglo-Saxon Counterparts in International Maths and Science Olympiads, Yet Feel Unconfident in Themselves and Fail to Go on to Win Nobel Prizes? Manuscript submitted for publication.

Ng, A. K. (2000b). Why Nice People Are Not Creative and Creative People Are Not Nice: A Cultural Model of Conflict and Creativity. Manuscript in preparation.

Nicholls, J. G. (1984). Achievement Motivation: Conceptions of Ability, Subjective Experience, Task Choice, and Performance. *Psychological Review*, 91: 328–46.

Nicholls, J. G., Cheung, P C., Lauer, J., & Patashnick, M. (1989). Individual Differences in Academic Motivation: Perceived Ability, Goals, Beliefs, and Values. *Learning and Individual Differences*, 1(1): 63–84.

Nirmala, M. (1999). Courtesy: More Than a Smile. Singapore: The Singapore Courtesy Council.

O'Malley, R., & Thompson, D. (1977). *Rhyme and Reason: An Anthology.* UK: Hart-Davis Educational.

Ohbuchi, K. I., & Takahashi, Y. (1994). Cultural Style of Conflict Management in Japanese and Americans: Passivity, Covertness, and Effectiveness of Strategies. *Journal of Applied Social Psychology*, 24: 1345–66.

On, L. W. (1996). The Cultural Context for Chinese Learners: Conceptions of Learning in the Confucian Tradition. In D. A. Watkins & J. B. Biggs (eds.), *The Chinese Learner: Cultural, Psychological, and Contextual Influences*, pp. 25–41. Hong Kong: Comparative Education Research Centre.

Pan, L. (1990). *Sons of the Yellow Emperor: The Story of the Overseas Chinese.* London: Secker & Warburg.

Patterson, O. (1991). *Freedom.* New York: Basic Books.

Pelto, P.J. (1968). The Difference Between "Tight" and "Loose" Societies. *Transactions*, pp. 37–40.

Peng, S. S., & Wright, D. (1994). Explanation of Academic Achievement of Asian American Students. *Journal of Educational Research*, 87: 346–52.

Pepper, F. S. (ed.) (1984). *Handbook of 20th Century Quotations.* London: Sphere Study Aids.

Perkins, R. M. (1993). Personality Variables and Implications for Critical Thinking. *College Student Journal*, 27(1): 106–11.

Pusey, A. W. (1977). A Comparative Study on Achievement Motivation Between Chinese and Americans. Master's thesis, Bucknell University.

Quah, M. L., & Ho, W. K. (eds.) (1998). *Thinking Processes: Going Beyond the Surface Curriculum.* Singapore: Prentice Hall.

Rahim, M. A., & Magner, N. R. (1995). Confirmatory Factor Analysis of the Styles of Handling Interpersonal Conflict: First-Order Factor Model and Its Invariance Across Groups. *Journal of Applied Psychology*, 80(1): 122–32.

Reader's Digest (1993). When, Where, Why and How It Happened: History's Most Dramatic Events, and How They Changed the World. The Reader's Digest Association Limited.

Reeve, J., & Deci, E. L. (1996). Elements of the Competitive Situation That Affects Intrinsic Motivation. *Personality and Social Psychology Bulletin*, 22(1): 24–33.

Reps, P. & Senzaki, N. (1985). *Zen Flesh, Zen Bones: A Collection of Zen and Pre-Zen Writings.* Boston, Tokyo: Charles E. Tuttle Co., Inc.

Richard, R. (1990). Everyday Creativity, Eminent Creativity and Health. *Creativity Research Journal*, 3(4): 300–26.

Rice, E. F. (1970). *The Foundations of Early Modern Europe: 1460–1559.* UK: W. W. Norton & Company, Inc.

Ripple, R. (1989). Ordinary Creativity. *Contemporary Educational Psychology*, 14: 189–202.

Roberts, J. M. (1987). *The Penguin History of the World.* Penguin Books.

Roden, G., & Hewison, K. (1996). A "Clash of Cultures" or the Convergence of Political Ideology? In R. Robinson (ed.), *Pathways to Asia: The Politics of Engagement*, pp. 29–55. Australia: Allen & Unwin.

Rohlen, T. P. (1989). Order in Japanese Society: Attachment, Authority and Routine. *Journal of Japanese Studies*, 15: 5–40.

Rossman, J. (1931). *The Psychology of the Inventor: A Study of the Patentee*. Washington: The Inventor's Publishing Company.

Rowen, H. S. (1998). The Political and Social Foundations of the Rise of East Asia: An Overview. In H. S. Rowen (ed.), *Behind East Asian Growth: The Political and Social Foundations of Prosperity*, pp. 1–38. London: Routledge.

Runco, M. A. (ed.). (1994). *Problem-Finding, Problem-Solving and Creativity*. Norwood, New Jersey: Ablex.

Russell, B. (1979). *History of Western Philosophy*. George Allen & Unwin (Publishers) Ltd.

Ryan, R. M., Connell, J. P., & Grolnick, W. S. (1992). When Achievement Is Not Intrinsically Motivated: A Theory of Internalisation and Self-Regulation in School. In A. K. Boggiano, & T. S. Pittman (eds.) *Achievement and Motivation: A Social-Developmental Perspective*, pp. 167–88. Cambridge: Cambridge University Press.

Sacks, J. (1997). *The Politics of Hope*. London: Jonathan Cape.

Sakaiya, T. (1993). *What is Japan?*, 1st English language edition, S. Karpa (trans.). New York: Kodansha America, Inc.

Schlessinger, B. S., & Schlessinger, J. H. (1996). *The Who's Who of Nobel Prize Winners: 1901–1995*. Arizona: Oryx Press

Schwartz, S. H. (1992). Universals in the Content and Structure of Values: Theoretical Advances and Empirical Tests in 20 Countries. *Journal of Experimental Social Psychology*, 28: 1–65.

Schwartz, S. H. (1994). Beyond Individualism and Collectivism: New Cultural Dimensions of Values. In U. Kim, H. C. Triandis, C. Kagitcibasi, S. C. Choi, & G. Yoon (eds.), *Individualism and Collectivism: Theory, Method and Applications*, pp. 85–122. USA: SAGE Publications, Inc.

Schwartz, S. H. (1996). Value Priorities and Behaviour: Applying a Theory of Integrated Value Systems. In C. Seligman, J. M. Olson, & M. P. Zanna (eds.), *The Psychology of Values: The Ontario Symposium*, 8: 1–24. New Jersey: Lawrence Erlbaum Associates.

Schwartz, S. H., & Bilsky, W. (1990). Toward a Theory of the Universal Content and Structure of Values: Extensions and Cross-Cultural Replications. *Journal of Personality and Social Psychology*, 58: 878–91.

Sheldon, K. M. (1995). Creativity and Self-Determination in Personality. *Creativity Research Journal*, 8(1): 25–36.

Shoji, K. (1995). Current Problems in Japanese Middle School Education. In K. Ishido & D. Myers (eds.), *Japanese Society Today*, pp. 77–80. Australia: Central Queensland University Press.

Simmons, J. (1996). *The Giant Book of Scientists: The 100 Greatest Minds of All Time*. USA: Carol Publishing Group.

Simonton, D. K. (1975). Sociocultural Context of Individual Creativity: A Transhistorical Time-Series Analysis. *Journal of Personality and Social Psychology*, 32: 1119–33.

Simonton, D. K. (1990). Political Pathology and Societal Creativity. *Creativity Research Journal*, 3(2): 85–99.

Skinner, B. F. (1971). *Beyond Freedom and Dignity*. New York: Knopf.

Skinner, B. F. (1972). *Cumulative Record: A Selection of Papers*, 3rd edition. Englewood Cliffs, New Jersey: Prentice Hall.

Skinner, B. F. (1976). *Walden Two*. New York: Macmillan.

Smith, D. H. (1973). *Confucius*. UK: Maurice Temple Smith Ltd.

Starr, J. B. (1997). *Understanding China: A Guide to China's Economy, History and Political Structure*. New York: Hill and Wang.

Sternberg, R. J., & Lubart, T. I. (1995). *Defying the Crowd: Cultivating Creativity in a Culture of Conformity*. New York: The Free Press.

Stevenson, H. W., & Lee, S. (1990). Context of Achievement. *Monographs of the Society for Research in Child Development*, serial no. 221, vol. 55, nos. 1–2.

Stevenson, H. W. (1998). Human Capital: How the East Excel. In H. S. Rowen (ed.), *Behind East Asian Growth: The Political and Social Foundations of Prosperity*, pp. 147–64. London: Routledge.

Stewart, R. (1997). *Ideas That Shaped Our World: Understanding the Great Concepts Then and Now*. London: Marshall Publishing.

Stringer, C., & McKie, R. (1997). *African Exodus: The Origins of Modern Humanity*. New York: Henry Holt and Company.

Stromberg, R. N. (1996). *Democracy: A Short, Analytical History*. New York: M. E. Sharpe.

Storr, A. (1976). *The Dynamics of Creation*. Harmondsworth: Penguin.

Stumpf, S E. (1993). *Socrates to Sartre: A History of Philosophy*. USA: McGraw-Hill.

Sullivan, M. (1979). Values Through Art. In R. Terrill (ed.), *The China Difference: A Portrait of Life Today Inside the Country of One Billion*, pp. 305–25. USA: Harper & Row.

Tan, A. (1989). *The Joy Luck Club*. New York: Ivy Books.

Tang, N. M. (1992). Some Psychoanalytic Implications of Chinese Philosophy and Child-Rearing Practices. *Psychoanalytic Study of the Child*, 47: 371–89.

Tarnas, R. (1991). *The Passion of the Western Mind: Understanding the Ideas That Have Shaped Our World View*. New York: Harmony Books.

Temple, R. (1986). *The Genius of China: 3,000 Years of Science, Discovery and Invention*. New York: Simon & Schuster.

Therivel, W. (1993). The Challenged Personality as a Precondition for Sustained Creativity. *Creativity Research Journal*, 6(4): 413–24.

Therivel, W. (1995). Long-Term Effect of Power on Creativity. *Creativity Research Journal*, 8(2): 173–92.

Therivel, W. (1999). Why Mozart and Not Salieri. *Creativity Research Journal*, 12(1): 67–76.

The National Productivity Board of Singapore (1992). *Productivity Concepts and Their Applications*. Singapore: The National Productivity Board.

The Economist, Those Educated Asians, p. 33, September 21, 1996.

The Straits Times, Swotting It Out in Hotel – Over the New Year, p. 10, January 4, 1999.

The Straits Times, Take a Walk Among the Fishes, p. 51, January 9, 1999.

The Straits Times, The Case for Free-Speech Venues, p. 40, January 20, 1999.

The Straits Times, Free Speech Venues May Threaten Order, p. 40, January 28, 1999.

The Straits Times, If I Am Rich, Why Am I Blue?, p. 3, February 4, 1999.

The Straits Times, The Importance of Being True to Oneself, p. 49, February 12, 1999.

The Straits Times, Bad Times, But Gambling Continues, p. 2, April 4, 1999.

The Straits Times, The US$100,000,000,000 Man, p. 6, April 10, 1999.

The Straits Times, Tell Teacher, I Think You May Be Wrong, p. 38, April 14, 1999.

The Straits Times, Encouraging Asians to Ask Questions, p. 39, April 14, 1999.

The Straits Times, Clinton Urges End to Culture of Violence, p. 13, April 26, 1999.

The Straits Times, 100,000 Mourn Victims of School Shooting, p. 11, April 27, 1999.

The Straits Times, Volunteerism Not Part of Singapore's Culture, p. 53, May 7, 1999.

The Straits Times, Don't Relax Rules to Attract Expats, May 10, 1999.

The Straits Times, Political Groups on Campus? Why Not? May 12, 1999.

The Straits Times, Offensive to Say Expats Hold Inferior Values, p. 64, May 15, 1999.

The Straits Times, Book Publisher to Pay for Murders by Reader, p. 5, May 23, 1999.

The Straits Times, Public Debate and OB Markers, p. 40, May 26, 1999.

The Straits Times, Why Singapore Fared Better Than Other Asian Nations, p. 38, June 10, 1999.

The Straits Times, Can Singaporeans Shake Off Their Passivity?, p. 62, June 12, 1999.

The Straits Times, Tuition May Hurt Grades, p. 3, June 15, 1999.

The Straits Times, Entrepreneurial Levels Vary Widely Among Countries, p. 50, June 23, 1999.

The Straits Times, Taking Singapore Inc. to a New Peak, p. 74, June 25, 1999.

The Straits Times, Einstein: Confused in Love and Sometimes, in Physics, p. 59, September 3, 1999.

The Straits Times, A Callous Way with Women, p. 59, September 3, 1999.

The Straits Times, Singapore Not Ready for Speakers' Corner, p. 33, September 12, 1999.

The Straits Times, Have Speakers' Corner with Modification, p. 42, September 14, 1999.

The Straits Times, Are Singaporeans Too Afraid to Think?, p. 34, September 27, 1999.

The Straits Times, Singaporeans' Behaviour Called Into Question, p. 45, October 2, 1999.

The Straits Times, Give the Arts Free Rein to Bloom, p. 41, November 21, 1999.

The Straits Times, That's Sir Virgin, If You Don't Mind, p. 78, January 1, 2000.

The Straits Times, Long Queues for Cutie Kitty Collectibles, p. 3, January 7, 2000.

The Straits Times, Scratching Cars Is a Singaporean Ill, p. 35, January 12, 2000.

The Straits Times, Kitty Mania: Craze Spits at the Spirit of Singapore 21, p. 56, January 22, 2000.

The Straits Times, Feline Frenzy, p. 1, January 28, 2000.

The Straits Times, 6 Held as Hello Kitty Queues Turn Ugly, p. 3, January 28, 2000.

The Straits Times, Japan: A Third Opening?, p. 48, February 12, 2000.

The Straits Times, She Was Shot Dead by Her Six-Year-Old Classmate, p. 14, March 2, 2000.

The Straits Times, Speakers' Corner at Hong Lim Park from August, p.1, April 26, 2000.

The Straits Times, Of Asian Descent, They Are US' First Teamers, p. 7, May 13, 2000.

The Straits Times, Exam Papers of Top Primary Schools Going for $60, June 10, 2000.

The Straits Times, Troubling New Trend in US: Post-Nuptial Agreements, p. 7, June 18, 2000.

The Straits Times, What If We Split, Darling?, p. 3, July 4, 2000.

The Straits Times, Pay Rise for Ministers: Too Much, Too Early, p. 34, July 6, 2000.

The Straits Times, Huge Payout for Zeta-Jones, p. 12, July 12, 2000.

The Straits Times, Rethink, or Quit Scholarship Now, p. 2, July 12, 2000.

The Straits Times, Why It's Not a Sin: Such Bonds Border on Exploitation, p. 46, July 19, 2000.

The Straits Times, Don't Let Market Forces Overrun Society, p. 69, July 21, 2000.

The Straits Times, Return of the Native Wit, p. 49, July 30, 2000.

The Straits Times, The Bare Facts About British Streakers, August 9, 2000.

The Straits Times, The Silent Majority, p. 35, August 15, 2000.

The Sunday Times, Singapore Not Ready for Speakers' Corner, p. 33, September 12, 1999.

The Wall Street Journal, Creative Spark: Stern Singapore Hopes Relaxing Some Rules Is Good for Business, p. A1, June 2, 1999.

Ting-Toomey, S. (1988). Intercultural Conflict Styles: A Face-Negotiation Theory. In Y. Kim & W. Gudykunst (eds.), *Theories in Intercultural Communications*, pp. 213–35. Newbury Parks, California: Sage.

Ting-Toomey, S., Gao, G., Trubisky, P., Yang, Z., Kim, H. S., Lin, S., & Nishida, T. (1991). Culture, Face Maintenance, and Styles of Handling Interpersonal Conflict: A Study in Five Cultures. *The International Journal of Conflict Management*, 2: 275–96.

Trefil, J. (1997). *Are We Unique? A Scientist Explores the Unparalleled Intelligence of the Human Mind*. New York: John Wiley & Sons.

Triandis, H. C. (1995). *Individualism and Collectivism*. USA: Westview Press, Inc.

Tu, W. M. (1985). Selfhood and Otherness in Confucian Thought. In A. J. Marsella, G. DeVos, & F. L. K. Hsu (eds.), *Culture and Self: Asian and Western Perspectives*, pp. 231–51. London: Tavistock Publications.

Tu, W. M. (1993). Confucianism. In A. Sharma (ed.), *Our Religions*, pp.139–228. San Francisco: HarperCollins Publishers.

Vincent, A. (1995). *Modern Political Ideologies*, 2nd edition. USA: Blackwell Publishers Ltd.

Wallis, C. L. (1965). *The Treasure Chest: A Heritage Album Containing 1064 Familiar and Inspirational Quotations, Poems, Sentiments and Prayers from Great Minds of 2,500 Years*. San Francisco: Harper & Row.

Weisz, J. R., Rothbaum, F. M., & Blackburn, T. C. (1984). Standing Out and Standing In: The Psychology of Control in America and Japan. *American Psychologist*, 39: 955–69.

Westfall, R. S. (1993). Isaac Newton. Microsoft Corporation: Microsoft (R) Encarta.

Westman, R. S. (1993). Nicholaus Copernicus. Microsoft Corporation: Microsoft (R) Encarta.

Westwood, R. I., Tang, S. F. Y., & Kirkbride, P. S. (1992). Chinese Conflict Behaviour: Cultural Antecedents and Behavioural Consequences. *Organisation Development Journal*, 10(2): 287–301.

Wheeler, L., Reis, H. T., & Bond, M. H. (1989). Collectivism–Individualism in Everyday Life: The Middle Kingdom and the Melting Pot. *Journal of Personality and Social Psychology*, 57: 79–86.

Whitney, K., Sagrestano, L. M., & Maslach, C. (1994). Establishing the Social Impact of Individuation. *Journal of Personality and Social Psychology*, 66(6): 1140–53.

Wills, E.J. (1994). *Mountain of Fame: Portraits in Chinese History*. New Jersey: Princeton University Press.

Wilson, J. Q. (1993). *The Moral Sense*. New York: Free Press.

Wood, S. E., & Wood, E. G. (1996). *The World of Psychology*, 2nd edition. USA: Allyn & Bacon.

Wright, R. (1994). *The Moral Animal: Why We Are the Way We Are*. UK: Abacus.

Wu, K. M. (1982). *Chuang Tzu: World Philosopher At Play*. New York: Scholars Press.

Yamada, K. (1991). Creativity in Japan. *Leadership and Organisation Development Journal*, 12(6): 11–4.

Yang, K. S. (1986). Chinese Personality and Its Change. In M. H. Bond (ed.), *The Psychology of the Chinese People*, pp. 106–70. Hong Kong: Oxford University Press.

Yik, S. M, & Bond, M. H. (1993). Exploring the Dimensions of Chinese Person Perception with Indigenous and Imported Constructs: Creating a Culturally Balanced Scale. *International Journal of Psychology*, 28(1): 75–95.

Yoshimura, N., & Anderson, P. (1997). *Inside the Kaisha: Demystifying Japanese Business Behavior*. Boston: Harvard Business School Press.

Yu, E. S. H. (1974). *Achievement Motive, Familism, and "Hsiao": A Replication of McClelland-Winterbottom Studies*. PhD thesis, University of Notre Dame.

Yu, A. B., & Yang, K. S. (1994). The Nature of Achievement Motivation in Collectivist Societies. In U. Kim, H. C. Triandis, C. Kagitcibasi, S. C. Choi, and G. Yoon (eds.), *Individualism and Collectivism: Theory, Method and Applications*, pp. 239–50. USA: SAGE Publications, Inc.

Zechmeister, E. B., & Johnson, J. E. (1992). *Critical Thinking: A Functional Approach*. Belmont, California: Wadsworth, Inc.

Zeng, K. M. (1999). *Dragon Gate: Competitive Examinations and Their Consequences*. London: Cassell.

Zuckerman, H. (1977). *Scientific Elite: Nobel Laureates in the United States*. New York: Free Press.

Index